UNDERSTANDING
BASEBALL

UNDERSTANDING BASEBALL

A Textbook

Trey Strecker,
Steven P. Gietschier,
Mitchell Nathanson,
John A. Fortunato *and*
David George Surdam

McFarland & Company, Inc., Publishers
Jefferson, North Carolina

RECENT WORKS ALSO OF INTEREST AND FROM McFARLAND

Sports Sponsorship: Principles and Practices, John A. Fortunato (2013)

The Ball Game Biz: An Introduction to the Economics of Professional Team Sports, David George Surdam (2010)

The Great Match and *Our Base Ball Club: Two Novels from the Early Days of Base Ball,* Anonymous and Noah Brooks. Edited by Trey Strecker and Geri Strecker (2010)

The Fall of the 1977 Phillies: How a Baseball Team's Collapse Sank a City's Spirit, Mitchell Nathanson (2008)

The Collected Baseball Stories, Charles Van Loan. Compiled by Trey Strecker (2004)

LIBRARY OF CONGRESS CATALOG ONLINE DATA

Strecker, Trey, 1966–
    Understanding baseball : a textbook / Trey Strecker, Steven P. Gietschier, Mitchell Nathanson, John A. Fortunato and David George Surdam.
        p.   cm.
    Includes bibliographical references and index.

    ISBN 978-0-7864-7631-2 (softcover : acid free paper) ∞
    ISBN 978-1-4766-1889-0 (ebook)

    1. Baseball.   2. Baseball—History.   I. Title.

GV862.5 2015
796.357—dc23   2014028506

BRITISH LIBRARY CATALOGUING DATA ARE AVAILABLE

Front cover image of baseball on grass © iStock/Thinkstock

Printed in the United States of America

McFarland & Company, Inc., Publishers
    Box 611, Jefferson, North Carolina 28640
    www.mcfarlandpub.com

Table of Contents

Introduction

TREY STRECKER

Understanding Baseball: A Textbook is intended to serve as a multidisciplinary—even interdisciplinary—introduction to the academic study of baseball, baseball history, and baseball culture in American life. The book takes this multidisciplinary approach because the scholarly study of baseball seldom, if ever, falls neatly within the boundaries of a single academic discipline. For example, to understand an event like the 1919 Black Sox scandal, in which eight Chicago White Sox players conspired with gamblers to deliberately lose the World Series, students might read historical media coverage of the World Series, the exposure of the scandal, and the ensuing trial. They might read biographies of key figures such as Joe Jackson, Buck Weaver, Charles Comiskey, or Kenesaw Mountain Landis, or study the intersection of baseball and gambling throughout the deadball era (1901–1919). They might examine how the organizational structure of the baseball business changed in the wake of the scandal or how narratives of the scandal (and the lifetime banishment of the eight Black Sox players) have evolved in novels, films, and popular media of the last century.

The study of baseball history and culture reveals the national game as a contested field where debates about sport, character, work and play, the country and the city, labor, race, and a host of other issues circulate. While the Black Sox scandal is a salient event in baseball history, many moments from baseball history resonate in this way. Understanding baseball, then, calls for careful consideration of several different perspectives and what each contributes.

This textbook is not meant to provide a comprehensive or exhaustive treatment of its subject. Rather, it is our hope that the book will suggest different routes to studying, researching, appreciating, and contributing to ongoing conversations about baseball, its history, and its culture.

1

The book is organized so readers may read the entire volume from beginning to end, or they may choose to sample from specific sections as their interests lead them. Each chapter introduces a specific disciplinary approach to baseball and covers some representative questions scholars from that academic field might consider. Readers will notice that several significant events—the 1876 founding of the National League, the Black Sox scandal, and the integration of Major League Baseball, among others—recur in different chapters, each time viewed through a different disciplinary lens.

Not all disciplines are included in this textbook. The current volume includes chapters on baseball history, economics, media, law, and fiction. To keep a manageable focus, these chapters tend to focus on Major League Baseball. We hope that future editions of the book will include more on women and baseball, the Negro Leagues, the minor leagues, and the international game, as well as additional disciplinary perspectives (such as sociology, philosophy, political science, gender studies, anthropology, art, and film).

There are many excellent histories of baseball, as well as excellent textbooks on sports economics, sports media, sports law, and sports fiction. Students (and instructors) can sometimes find themselves overwhelmed by the vast number of sources available in print and online. Intended as a readable textbook for undergraduates (and perhaps advanced high school students) and their instructors, this volume can be used either as a course's central text or as a supplemental text in conjunction with other readings. In both cases, this book is designed to offer insights and inroads into baseball history as an enjoyable and rewarding academic subject and one worthy of careful scholarly attention.

The citation style in *Understanding Baseball* varies from chapter to chapter. In keeping with the book's multidisciplinary approach, rather than impose one discipline's documentation style on the entire volume, each chapter uses the citation format appropriate to its subject.

1

History

STEVEN P. GIETSCHIER

For most of the twentieth century, people interested in baseball accepted as true the story that West Point cadet Abner Doubleday had invented the game himself and shown it to his friends during the summer of 1839 in the village of Cooperstown, New York. At mid-century, the Doubleday tale remained alive in popular imagination, but a few students of the game had come to prefer the alternative version of its origins first advanced by sportswriter Henry Chadwick in 1860, that baseball derived from an English game called rounders and had been imported into the United States. More recently, well after scholars had thoroughly discredited the Doubleday myth, new research not only refuted Chadwick's rounders thesis, but also uncovered intriguing evidence about how baseball might actually have begun.

The Doubleday story proved attractive and durable because the game's adherents, who had been calling baseball America's national pastime since 1856, insisted that their favorite sport had to have American origins. To many, baseball had become more than a game. It was a fundamental component of America's national culture. But no one person invented baseball, not Abner Doubleday or anyone else. Broadly speaking, baseball is a stick-and-ball game that evolved from simpler folk games that go back in time as far as ancient Egypt and perhaps farther. Some stick-and-ball games use curved sticks to move a ball along the ground. Others, including baseball, employ straight sticks to propel a ball through the air. Certain stick-and-ball games played in England and in Europe serve as forerunners to baseball, and exactly how the modern game developed from these folk games is a subject historians and other scholars continue to explore.

By the middle of the eighteenth century, boys and girls and perhaps adults, too, were playing a game called "base-ball" in England and maybe elsewhere, sometimes using a bat and sometimes striking the ball with the hand. The word "base-ball" appears in print at least as early as 1744. In that year, John Newbury, an Englishman, published *A Little Pretty Pocket-Book, Intended for the Instruction and Amusement of Little Master Tommy and Pretty Miss Polly*. This ninety-five-page book, considered the first publication devoted to entertainment for children, described thirty-two games and activities, including "base-ball." A woodcut illustration shows three players, apparently adults, each standing next to a substantial post. None of the three holds a bat, but one is preparing to toss a ball underhand while another is ready to hit it with his hand. The poem accompanying this scene describes the game:

> The Ball once struck off,
> Away flies the Boy
> To the next destin'd Post,
> And then Home with Joy.

In 1796, Johann Gutsmuths, a German physical educator, published a description of *Ball mit Freystaten (oder das englische Base-ball)*, which translates as "ball with free station (or English base-ball)." In this game, clearly a precursor to baseball, the pitcher stood only five or six steps from the batter, and the stations (or bases) were no more than ten or fifteen feet apart. The batter used a bat about two feet long and had three tries to hit the ball, pitched underhand. After doing so, he or she ran counterclockwise from base to base; the number of bases depended upon the number of players. Fielders put out batters by catching the ball on the fly, throwing the ball to the proper base, or touching or hitting the runner with the ball. Each team got one out before being retired. European settlers in North America brought this game or variations on it with them. In the New World, playing base-ball did not remain solely a children's activity. By the time of the American Revolution, men were playing it in significant numbers and were adapting the rules to suit their abilities.

Playing base-ball was not universally accepted as proper recreation. Some people considered the game a nuisance or a waste of time. Some cities and towns passed ordinances restricting or outlawing it, and those who desired to keep the Sabbath as a day of rest sought to prohibit ball playing on Sundays as a matter of religious principle. Nevertheless, by the 1820s, enough young American men were playing baseball that the game had become a common form of recreation in many villages and cities. The "base-ball fraternity," the group of those attracted to the game as players and spectators, was especially robust in New York and Brooklyn, then separate cities, and on a number of college campuses. There were no uniform rules for this informal play, and even the name of the game varied from one place to another, sometimes "base-ball" or "town-ball" or "round-ball" or just "playing ball." Historians have not uncovered enough evidence to document the exact path of baseball's evolution, but what is clear is that early versions of baseball, most of them quite casual, were being played in many locations, especially in the northeastern part of the United States, throughout the first several decades of the nineteenth century.

Although the Doubleday legend did not satisfactorily explain how baseball spread from Cooperstown to places like New York, early historians believed that the first game between two organized clubs occurred at the Elysian Fields, a privately owned resort in Hoboken, New Jersey, on June 19, 1846. This match saw the New York Base Ball Club defeat the Knickerbocker Base Ball Club by the lopsided score of 23–1. Later research has uncovered prior games and social clubs predating these two, organized by groups of men for the purpose of playing ball, at first as an amusement and source of exercise among themselves, but eventually against members of other clubs. In 1823, for example, a New York newspaper, the *National Advocate*, published a report that "a company of active young men" described as "an organized association" would be playing baseball on the following Saturday afternoon and that spectators were invited. Forming a club to play baseball proved especially attractive to prosperous members of the middle class, who were sometimes at liberty to leave work in mid-afternoon to engage in recreation.

The Knickerbocker Base Ball Club—the word comes from Washington Irving's fictional character, Diedrich Knickerbocker, in his satire, *A History of New York*—was long identified as the first club organized to play baseball. Historians now recognize several older clubs, including the Eagles, Gothams, Magnolias, Olympics, and Washingtons, as well as the New York Club, but the Knickerbockers are still acknowledged for fixing a firm roster of members, establishing regular days for play, and writing a formal set of club rules, fourteen covering playing the game and six concerning administrative matters. Members of the Knickerbockers were thoroughly middle class with professional or white-collar jobs. In addition to playing ball, the club, which at one time had more than two hundred members, sponsored suppers, formal balls, and other events to promote health and recreation.

At one time, Alexander Joy Cartwright, Jr., a bank teller turned bookseller, a volunteer firefighter, and a charter member of the Knickerbockers, received credit for formulating the club's rules. Indeed, the National Baseball Hall of Fame inducted Cartwright in 1938 for writing these rules, lauding him on his plaque for three significant innovations: "Set bases 90 feet apart, established 9 innings as game, and 9 players as team." Later research revealed that Cartwright does not deserve such recognition. Evidence strongly suggests that a group of Knickerbockers, not one individual, codified their rules and that when the club played its version of baseball on a diamond-shaped field, the distance between the bases and the number of innings varied from game to game, while the number of players per side could be as few as seven or as many as eleven. Still, the club's decision to write down its playing rules was a valuable contribution. So, too, was its introduction of two improvements on how the game was played: establishing foul territory and outlawing the painful technique of "soaking" or "plugging," i.e., putting a batter or runner out by hitting him with a thrown ball.

A fair number of early baseball players also played cricket, but over a short period of time, the older game gave way to the newer. In the 1850s, the number of baseball clubs exploded as urban workers sought recreational respite in an increasingly industrial society. A Brooklyn newspaper, *Porter's Spirit of the Times*, reported in 1856 that baseball was being played on every empty lot in and around New York, and the next year, a song called "The Baseball Fever" complained in jest that merchants had to close their stores because "their hands are all out playing." Some new clubs followed the Knickerbockers' lead and organized social activities besides baseball. Others, often drawing young men from a specific neighborhood or a particular occupation, concentrated solely on playing the game. At first, members of each club played mostly among themselves, organizing only a few matches against other clubs each year, but soon inter-club competition became more popular, and the need arose for common rules. In January 1857, fourteen clubs playing some variety of baseball in and around New York sent representatives to a convention. Using the Knickerbockers' code as a template, the assembled delegates agreed to a uniform set of playing rules while making three major changes: fixing the distance between bases at ninety feet, setting the pitching distance at fifteen yards, and declaring the winner of a game to be the club scoring the most runs after nine innings instead of the one scoring twenty-one runs (or aces) first. These rules, modified many times, remain the basis for the modern game of baseball.

The consensus reached at the 1857 convention represented the triumph of the "New York game" over several other varieties of ball, but one, the "Massachusetts game," sometimes called "round-ball," persisted in New England. The Massachusetts game featured teams of ten to fourteen players, a slightly smaller ball than the New York game, and a field with no foul territory. The batter (or "striker") stood midway on one side of a sixty-foot square, each corner of which was a base. The rules allowed "soaking" and required overhand throwing instead of underhand pitching. Innings concluded after just one out, but since it took a hundred runs to win a match, play often carried over to a second day. In 1857, Edward Saltzman, a member of the New York club called the Gothams, moved to Boston and organized the Tri-Mountain Club to play the New York game. After this club demonstrated the New York rules on Boston Common in 1858, spectators slowly began to express a preference for the quicker New York version, although the Massachusetts game persisted into the 1860s.

New York's standing as the nation's largest city gave the game as played by the 1857 rules a certain prominence. So, too, did stories and editorials about baseball published in New York's many newspapers. Henry Chadwick, who had emigrated from England to Brooklyn in 1837, became the game's most enthusiastic journalistic advocate. He wrote newspaper stories that reviewed individual matches, popularized clubs and players, and helped explain the nuances of the game to spectators, who were sometimes called cranks—from the German "krank" meaning "sick"—or fans—perhaps a corruption of "fanatics." Chadwick devised the set of symbols—including the arcane "K" to denote a strikeout—to describe each play of a match, and he adapted the cricket box score to baseball, creating a concise table to summarize an entire game. He also began to use statistics to measure players' performances, at first simply counting outs, runs, and hits, but soon introducing the concept of averages. In 1860, Chadwick began editing the first baseball annual, *Beadle's Dime Base Ball Player*, and he used this publication to promote and refine the game. At various times in his long career, he campaigned for the infield fly rule, against allowing games to end in a tie, and against gambling.

In March 1858, twenty-two clubs from the New York area held a second convention. They amended the playing rules slightly and organized the game's first administrative authority, the National Association of Base Ball Players (NABBP). Delegates to the convention drafted a constitution and by-laws under which other clubs could seek membership. To join the association, an applicant club had to have at least eighteen members and be approved by a two-thirds vote. Dues were set at five dollars per year. In this way, the association grew quickly to become a national organization with clubs across the country, some of whom formed state and regional associations. The NABBP also attempted to govern the eligibility and conduct of individual players. Each had to be a member of an association club for thirty days before being allowed to play in a game against another association club. No player was allowed to bet on the outcome of a game, and none could receive compensation for playing. The association was thus an organization of amateur ball players, formed at a time when the game they played for fun was already beginning to change.

Later in 1858, clubs in Brooklyn challenged clubs in New York to a three-game series matching the best players from each city against one another. The teams arranged to play at a neutral site, the Fashion Race Course, a racetrack on Long Island that had a new stone grandstand. Fans flocked to these all-star games in large numbers, despite an admission charge of fifty cents, making these the first games people paid to watch. The New Yorkers won the first game, 22–18; the Brooklyn team came back to win the second game, 29–8; and the New Yorkers rebounded to take the third game, 29–18. Clubs from the New York metropolitan area also competed each year for the "whip pennant," a symbol of supremacy won by Brooklyn clubs every year until 1867, when the Unions of Morrisania in the Bronx were victorious. Baseball was becoming a very popular game, and the steady growth of the NABBP reflected the spread of the game before and after the Civil War. The NABBP's tenth convention in 1866 attracted delegates from more than two hundred clubs, mostly from the northeastern United States but also from as far away from New York as Maryland, Ohio, Kentucky, Tennessee, Missouri, Kansas, and Oregon.

The very popularity of the amateur game sowed the seeds of change. Intra-club matches played for recreational and social purposes were still prominent, but clubs began to schedule more matches against one another. In 1862, William Cammeyer, a Brooklyn department store owner who also operated an ice skating pond, decided to drain the pond, level the ground to create a smooth playing field, and erect a fence around the outside. His intention was to stage baseball games and to charge admission. He built a wooden grandstand seating 1,500, constructed a clubhouse, and opened an adjacent saloon for fans. On May 15, the Union Grounds made its heralded debut as a baseball park. Cammeyer flew the American flag and the pennants of the competing teams, and a band played "The Star Spangled Banner" before the match began. Other entrepreneurs followed suit. The "enclosure movement," as it was called, offered clubs the chance to play matches before crowds of paying fans and tempted them to bargain for a slice of the gate receipts. Some clubs fielded more than one team, but they sent their best players or "first nines" to compete against other clubs. Soon, clubs stressed winning over fraternity, and they began to recruit new members because they could play the game well.

Innovations such as competing for championships, selling tickets to spectators, and seeking players based on ability helped transform baseball from amateur game to professional sport. In a quest to play better, clubs began to practice, and club members started specializing in one defensive position. Pitchers began to chafe at the rules that confined them and started challenging batters. The 1857 rules required pitchers to deliver or "pitch" the ball underhand, with a locked wrist, so that batters could put it into play easily and fielders could display their prowess. Teenager Jim Creighton, playing for the Niagara Club of New York, is generally credited with developing a low, swift delivery that became known as "speed pitching." Technically violating the rules, Creighton taught himself to snap his wrist as he brought his right arm around, propelling the ball with both speed and accuracy. Creighton's delivery was illegal, but when Henry Chadwick commended him for his "head work," the change was irrevocable. Matches became faster and more interesting, attracting more fans. Moreover, Creighton's skill as both a pitcher and a batter made him baseball's first star attraction. In 1859, he joined the Brooklyn Excelsiors, probably becoming the sport's first paid player, and he led them to many victories by wide margins. When batters adjusted to the velocity of his deliveries, he learned how to change speeds and regained the upper hand. In 1862, Creighton, only twenty-one, suffered a severe injury, rupturing his bladder while running the bases after hitting a home run. He died several days later of internal hemorrhaging.

The quest for playing excellence led inevitably to professionalism. Creighton may have been the first paid player, but he was not alone for long. Some clubs lured skilled players with financial gifts. Others offered players salaries for jobs they did not have to perform. George Wright, a star shortstop, left the Gothams in 1867 for the Washington Nationals. Their roster listed him as a clerk for the federal government, but his office address was really a public park. Many clubs began playing regularly for gate receipts that could be redistributed to one or more players. The NABBP, still committed to amateurism, proved unable to stifle any of these developments. Nor could it deal effectively with a practice called "revolving," players making agreements to play with one club only to jump elsewhere for a better offer. The advent of professionalism and the heightened sense of competition also introduced gambling into baseball. At first, fans (and players, too) were content merely to wager on the outcome of games, but within a short period of time, gamblers attempted to ensure their success by bribing players to fix games. Throwing games became known as "hippodroming," and both players and entire clubs took part. In one notorious incident, the NABBP disciplined three players for fixing a game in 1865, but all three eventually secured their reinstatement. The Troy (NY) Haymakers, a club controlled by gamblers and political boss and former boxer John Morrissey, were infamous for not playing on the square. Baseball had become a tough, physical game, marked by rough tactics, skirting the rules, and attacks on umpires. The sense of fair play that had defined the amateur game had fast disappeared.

In 1869, Cincinnati businessmen who wanted their city to have a winning baseball club announced that they would field a team composed entirely of paid players. The roster of the Red Stockings included George Wright at shortstop and his older brother Harry as centerfielder and manager. Starters earned between $600 and $1,200 for the season, and the club carried three substitutes as well. The Red Stockings were a superb team. They played the first six weeks of the season at home before going on tour, first to the East Coast and then west as far as California. Except for one controversial tie against the Haymakers, the Cincinnati club finished the season undefeated, winning nearly sixty games by an average score of 40–10. The following year, the Red Stockings won another twenty-seven games before losing to the Brooklyn Atlantics, who scored three runs in the bottom of the eleventh inning to win, 8–7. A crowd of perhaps twenty thousand paid fifty cents apiece to watch this game, but the Red Stockings were not a business success. Their expenses were high, and their revenues tumbled after they lost several more games. The club disbanded after the 1870 season when the owners decided that making a profit was no longer probable. Nevertheless, the appeal of the amateur game faded.

As the number of amateur clubs dwindled, professional players gained more influence over how the sport would be organized. In March 1871, representatives from ten clubs met in a New York saloon to form a new organization, the National Association of Professional Base Ball Players (NAPBBP), generally recognized by later historians as professional baseball's first league. Each of the founding clubs agreed to play a best three-of-five series against every other club, a commitment of between twenty-seven and forty-five league games each, but enforcing this agreement proved difficult. Like the NABBP, the National Association, as it was called, was run by players without a strong central administration, and it endured some of the same difficulties as its predecessor. Players often engaged in rowdy conduct and sometimes came to games drunk. Revolving and hippodroming continued unabated, and gambling was a continuing problem. Most particularly, the National Association suffered from rickety finances and a lack of competitive balance. One club, the Boston Red Stockings, won four consecutive pennants and proved so dominant that some poor teams refused to complete their seasons, citing insufficient funds or an unwillingness to travel for meaningless games. This inequality destabilized the association and led to its demise after the 1875 season.

The Boston club was called the Red Stockings because its roster featured Harry and George Wright and two other star players from the disbanded Cincinnati Red Stockings, plus two excellent players from the Forest City club of Rockford, Illinois, pitcher Albert Spalding and second baseman Ross Barnes. In 1871, the National Association's inaugural season, former Cincinnatian Cal McVey batted .431 for Boston, and Barnes hit .401, while Spalding, only twenty years old, won nineteen games, more than any other pitcher. In a pennant race marred by disputes over forfeited games, Boston finished second to the Philadelphia Athletics, a powerful club led by third baseman Levi Meyerle. He was a horrendous fielder, but he led all players with a .492 batting average and a .700 slugging percentage. The next four seasons went Boston's way. Barnes and Spalding were the National Association's outstanding batter and pitcher, respectively, and their club compiled a cumulative record of 205–50, winning each pennant with relative ease. Twenty-three different clubs played in the National Association, referred to henceforth as the Association.

Only Boston, Philadelphia, and the New York Mutuals played all five seasons, while thirteen clubs survived for a single season or less. In 1875, thirteen clubs began play, but only seven finished their schedules as the Red Stockings won their fourth straight pennant by 18.5 games.

By the end of the 1875 season, some stockholders in National Association clubs were convinced that professional baseball could be a profitable business if a league were run properly. William Hulbert, a major stockholder in the Chicago White Stockings, spearheaded an insurgency. Midway through the 1875 season, he had covertly signed Spalding, Barnes, McVey, and catcher Deacon White to play for Chicago in 1876. In February, he gathered representatives of several clubs in a New York hotel ostensibly to discuss reforming the Association, but in reality to create a new league. Hulbert faced censure for stealing Boston's players, but his proposal aimed at much more than avoiding discipline. His plan was to establish the National League of Professional Baseball Clubs, an organization to be directed by owners, not players, with clubs limited to cities with populations over 75,000. Hulbert wanted to install competent, well-financed leadership while curbing the rough play and abuses that had tarnished the Association. He argued successfully that the National League should prohibit selling beer and whiskey in its ballparks, outlaw games on Sundays, and forbid cursing and drunkenness. He believed that a league run on sound business principles could keep players' salaries in check and generate substantial profits for club owners. Moreover, he asserted that clean, honest baseball, devoid of the crooked play and gambling that had crippled the Association, would appeal to respectable Victorian sensibilities embodied in a middle-class clientele willing to pay fifty cents for a ticket, instead of the Association's twenty-five cents. The National League began play in 1876 with eight teams, and Hulbert's White Stockings, the club later known as the Cubs, won the first pennant. When the New York and Philadelphia clubs, mired near the bottom of the standings, refused to make their final western road trips, Hulbert expelled them, demonstrating his commitment to a league run much differently than its predecessor.

As baseball evolved from amateur to professional sport, its governing bodies tinkered with the playing rules annually, not only to meet the changing needs of the game on the field but also to maximize the sport's entertainment value. These modifications were often complicated and subtle, but the goal was always to hone the competitive relationship between the team at bat and the team in the field. Rules-makers sought a balance between offense and defense that would produce exciting games with just enough scoring to attract large numbers of spectators. Even after the founding of the National League—and continuing to the present—the rules committee made changes, some major and some minor, nearly every off-season to adjust for the next year's play.

In the nineteenth century, the playing field itself underwent significant alterations. The infield, i.e., the area circumscribed by the three bases and home plate, has always been called a diamond, but in reality it is a square with one base located at each of its four corners. Under the 1857 rules, first base, second base, and third base were canvas bags, 12 inches square and painted white, and they were centered upon the corners of the diamond. In 1877, the bases became 15 inch squares, and in 1887, first base and third base were moved inside the foul lines, putting them entirely in fair territory. Home base and the pitcher's point, as they were originally called, were circular iron plates painted white. Home base became a square in 1868, and in 1877, it, too, was moved completely into fair territory. Then, in 1900, the four-sided home base became the familiar five-sided home plate. The pitcher's point, originally located 45 feet from home base, was further defined by a straight line extending 2 yards to each side. In time, the line became a box, and by 1881, the pitcher's box was a 6-foot square with its front line 50 feet from home base. In 1887, the depth of the box was reduced to 5½ feet, and the pitcher was required to begin his delivery with 1 foot on the back line, 55 feet, 6 inches, from home base. In 1893, the rules committee eliminated the box entirely, replacing it with a rectangular rubber plate moved back an additional 5 feet, i.e., 60 feet, 6 inches, from home base.

The desire to maintain equilibrium between offense and defense also led to changes to the rules on balls and strikes. The 1857 rules gave the batter three strikes, but umpires were not allowed to call balls. The batter was supposed to ask for a pitch in a specific location and swing when the pitcher delivered the ball as requested. Pitchers soon began to tempt batters with pitches deliberately wide of the mark, and batters retaliated by not swinging at all, sometimes for minutes on end. In 1863, the rules empowered the umpire to warn a pitcher for failing to deliver hittable pitches and to call the next unsatisfactory pitch a ball. If the pitcher persisted, the umpire could call two more balls, after which the batter would be awarded first base. In 1875, every third unsatisfactory pitch had to be called a ball, so that a batter would walk, in effect, on nine balls. Over the next few years, the number of balls allowed shrank several times until, in 1889, the rules settled on four balls becoming a walk.

In an effort to restrain Creighton and other pitchers who followed him, the rules changed in 1863, requiring the pitcher to have both feet on the ground when delivering the ball. Enforcement proved difficult. Since many games ended prematurely when a team left the field in protest, the rule had to be relaxed. In 1872, pitchers were allowed to use a bent-arm delivery and to release the ball sidearm from as high as the hip. Pitchers continued to push the limits, and when catchers began to wear protective equipment (masks in the 1870s and chest protectors in the early 1880s), throwing overhand, as opposed to pitching underhand, became practical. The rules legalized pitching from shoulder height in 1883 and modern, overhand pitching in 1885. Alterations to the strike zone came concurrent with these changes. In 1871, the rules required a batter to call either for a high pitch or a low pitch, creating, in effect, two strike zones. In 1885, having batters call for pitches was eliminated, and the unified strike zone stretched from the shoulders to the knees. Subsequent adjustments to both the top of the zone and the bottom have been frequent, often as the result of disputes over proper enforcement of the rule.

The National League, henceforth called the League, struggled in its initial years to fulfill Hulbert's vision. Every club committed to play a set schedule, and each respected the others' territorial rights by not playing games in any other League city against non–League clubs. Hulbert also clamped down on revolving by prohibiting any club from signing a player under contract to another League club. Still, financial stability and economic success came slowly. Of the six clubs that completed the 1876 season, only Chicago made money. Cincinnati required new ownership during the 1877 season to stay afloat, and after that season, Hartford, Louisville, and St. Louis dropped out, to be replaced by Indianapolis, Milwaukee, and Providence. The year 1879 was no better. Indianapolis and Milwaukee left, and four new cities joined for 1880: Buffalo, Cleveland, Syracuse, and Troy. Overall, twenty-one cities hosted National League clubs from 1876 through 1899. Only in 1900, after a chaotic decade, did the familiar eight-team league emerge, with clubs in Boston, Brooklyn, Chicago, Cincinnati, New York, Philadelphia, Pittsburgh, and St. Louis. This arrangement proved stable and lasted through 1952.

Hulbert's dual role as president of the National League and the White Stockings caused some difficulties, especially since his club won three pennants in the League's first six years, but he showed no reluctance to deal with controversy. Besides expelling two clubs in 1876, he acted decisively in 1877 to uphold the Louisville club's expulsion of four players for throwing games, and he was persistent in searching for entrepreneurs with sufficient capital to undertake club ownership. In addition, when some clubs suggested that the League's fifty-cent ticket price was too high, or that Sunday baseball should be allowed, or that the sale of alcoholic beverages in League ballparks should be permitted, he adamantly stuck to his principles. Hulbert died just before the start of the 1882 season, but his intransigence on these points had already brewed a rebellion. The Cincinnati club, trying to attract fans from the city's large German population, not only rented its ballpark to other clubs on Sundays but also sold beer at all games played there. Hulbert marshaled enough votes to expel the club after the 1881 season, but the enthusiasm for mixing beer with baseball could not be denied, not just in Cincinnati but in other cities as well.

Fairly quickly after the National League's birth, club owners came to believe that the path to sustainable profitability was blocked by excessive player salaries. In 1878, League officials announced their intention not to pay higher salaries than revenues justified, and in 1879, Hulbert declared that salaries must be reduced if baseball was "to be conserved in its best state." Soon, owners realized that the clubs themselves were driving salaries up by competing for each other's players. The solution, an idea introduced perhaps by Boston owner Arthur Soden, was to eliminate competition for the best players by allowing each club to "reserve" the services of a certain number of players from one season to the next. Each owner agreed, quite simply, not to negotiate with any player reserved by any other League club. At first, clubs reserved only five players each, and some players so designated considered it an honor, an indication of their value; but George Wright, who was reserved by the Providence club against his will, chose to retire rather than play for the salary Providence offered. Players who felt restrained by being reserved could seek employment with non–League clubs, but over time, this escape route narrowed. The number of players that clubs reserved grew in 1883 to eleven, in 1886 to twelve, and in 1887 to fourteen, a club's entire roster at that time. Clubs also began writing the reserve clause, as it came to be called, into player contracts and interpreting it to mean that a player could be reserved year after year, i.e., forever, without his consent.

There were no other leagues in existence in 1876, so the National League did not initially define itself as a "major league" in the modern sense. Still, it was an exclusive organization that bred resentment. Some non–League clubs chose not to pursue League membership, but others did and were rebuffed. About sixty clubs were playing professional baseball independently, but Hulbert's plan was to limit the League to just eight, the optimal number, he said, for a fair schedule with reasonable travel expenses. As the League's promise of profitability slowly materialized, some outsiders complained that the National League was a monopoly. The best players tended to gravitate to League clubs, especially those that were well run, and the League as a whole showed no reluctance to sign players already under contract to non–League clubs. Hulbert and his colleagues did develop a plan to establish a group of subsidiary clubs under the League's aegis, but hardly any clubs accepted this deal. Seventeen non–League clubs formed the International Association of Professional Base Ball Players, a quasi-league, in 1877, but this rival grouping proved to be a loose organization that gave the National League little to fear. After that season, the League created the "League Alliance," trying to formalize its relationship with outside clubs, but few took advantage of an arrangement that imposed more restrictions than the benefits it offered.

Some non–League club owners, dissatisfied that their cities could not gain admission to the National League, took action. In 1881, a group led probably by newspaperman O.P. Caylor of Cincinnati established a new league, calling it the American Association. It began play in 1882 with teams in six cities (Baltimore, Cincinnati, Louisville, Philadelphia, Pittsburgh, and St. Louis), all of them excluded from the League. The Association adopted a different ball as its "official baseball," used a slightly different rule book, employed a permanent umpiring staff, and targeted the working class as its fan base. It set the price of a ticket at twenty-five cents, allowed Sunday games, and eschewed Victorian values by permitting teams to sell beer in their ballparks. Perhaps not surprisingly, the Association's first season was a financial success. All six clubs made money, and together they attracted more paying customers than the League's eight clubs. The overall quality of playing talent in the Association did not approach its competitor, but the upstart organization did cause the League to take notice.

The relationship between the National League and the American Association varied from cooperative in some instances to contentious in others. At first, Association clubs declined to sign players reserved or expelled by League clubs, and teams from both organizations played spring exhibition games against one another. Before long, though, two players under contract to Association clubs jumped to the League, and unbridled competition for players ensued. The Association also embargoed its clubs from playing any more games against League clubs, but the threat of expulsion did not dissuade the reincarnated Cincinnati Red Stockings, Association champions in 1882, from playing a two-game post-season series against the Chicago White Stockings, League champions for the fourth time.

In 1883 three representatives from the League, including new president Abraham Mills, met with three representatives from the Association to smooth out their differences. They agreed to respect each other's lists of reserved players and to end the ban on inter-league play. They also signed the Tripartite Pact, a peace accord that linked them as partners with a less ambitious regional league called the Northwestern League. This treaty gave all three leagues certain territorial rights, but it established the National League and the American Association as major leagues with the Northwestern League assuming a subsidiary or "minor league" role. As other minor leagues came into existence and signed onto this arrangement, the Tripartite Pact became known as the National Agreement, the contractual foundation for the hierarchical structure that became known as Organized Baseball.

In 1884, the National League and the American Association worked together to oppose the emergence of a third major league, the Union Association, that lasted only one tumultuous season. In other ways, the peace expected from the National Agreement remained uneasy. Clubs in each organization continued to sign players already under contract to the other, and in 1885, the National League added a Union Association club, the St. Louis Maroons, to compete directly with the American Association's Browns. Over the next five seasons, the National League lured four American Association teams to its ranks: Pittsburgh in 1886, Cleveland in 1889, and Brooklyn and Cincinnati in 1890. Still, there was some effort to cooperate. After the 1884 season, the League allowed its champion to begin playing the Association champion in a post-season competition that, starting in 1885, was called the "World Championship Series."

Although the American Association lasted only ten seasons, its clubs produced a number of outstanding players, some of whom were good enough to be inducted to the National Baseball Hall of Fame, a private, not-for-profit organization that began electing former players in 1936. The Association's first star was Pete Browning, an outfielder who played for Louisville. Browning was an alcoholic, and he suffered from mastoiditis, an infection of the bone behind the ear that affected his hearing, but he won two Association batting titles and came within a point of a third. Bid McPhee, another star, is generally regarded as the best second baseman of the nineteenth century. He played eighteen seasons in Cincinnati, eight in the Association followed by ten in the League. Not much of a hitter, although he led the Association in triples in 1887, McPhee was a superb fielder and was one of the first second basemen to position himself considerably away from the base. Pitcher Tony Mullane was a stylish showman on the mound, renowned for his dark, wavy hair and his waxed mustache. He won thirty or more games five seasons in a row and was fully capable of pitching with either hand.

Owners in both the National League and the American Association adhered to a "gentleman's agreement" that excluded black players from club rosters even though determining whether a player was "white" or "black" could sometimes be tricky. Recent research has suggested that William White, a pinch-hitter for the League's Providence Grays in 1879, may have been an African American. Moses Fleetwood Walker, a catcher who played for the Association's Toledo Blue Stockings in 1884, was black and was long identified as the first African American to play major league baseball. Walker hit only .263 in forty-two games, but he was a fine defensive catcher, and in July, his brother, Welday, an outfielder, joined him on the Toledo club and played five games. Fleet Walker faced Jim Crow discrimination in many cities. In Louisville he sat out a game when a player on the home team refused to play against him. In Richmond the Blue Stockings manager held him out of an exhibition game after receiving a letter threatening Walker's life. When the Chicago White Stockings came to Toledo for an exhibition game, Chicago's star player and manager, Cap Anson, nearly pulled his team off the field rather than play against a black player. Toledo left the Association after one season. Neither Walker brother played in the majors again, nor did any other African American until 1947.

Three different clubs won the first three American Association pennants, but in 1885, the St. Louis Browns won the first of four consecutive flags. They were a superior team featuring excellent hitting, pitching, and fielding. Their manager was Charlie Comiskey, a feisty, young, and innovative first baseman, and their best player was left fielder Tip O'Neill, who batted .435 in 1887 and helped his team score 1,131 runs in 138 games. The Browns' owner was a flamboyant saloon and grocery store owner named Christian Von der Ahe. A German immigrant who spoke heavily accented English and called himself "Der Boss President," Von der Ahe barely understood baseball as a game but saw it as grand entertainment. He built a racetrack around his ballpark and brought in a Wild West show and other promotions to attract fans. He was also more than glad when spectators visited his nearby saloon before, during, and after Browns games. After winning their first pennant, the Browns scheduled a 12-game series against the White Stockings, but it ended in dispute after 7 games, 1 of which ended in a tie and another in a forfeit. St. Louis defeated Chicago, 4 games to 2, after the 1886 season and then lost consecutive post-season series to the Detroit Wolverines and the New York Giants.

Total attendance at American Association games topped one million in six of its ten seasons. National League attendance generally lagged behind, but in 1887, League clubs drew 1.4 million fans to the association's 1.3 million. The following season, the League's Giants became the first club to draw more than 300,000, and in 1889, the Association's Brooklyn Bridegrooms surpassed that by attracting 353,690. Baseball was a hit. Both leagues were playing 140-game schedules, and some clubs were clearing $100,000 a year in profits. Rules changes had made the game lively and enjoyable to watch, and the public responded. Daily newspapers printed game accounts, statistics, and feature stories on prominent players, and two sportswriters hoped they could find a national audience for weekly sporting newspapers focused on baseball. Francis Richter founded *Sporting Life* in Philadelphia in 1883, and Alfred Spink countered with *The Sporting News*, published in St. Louis starting in 1886. After that season, pitcher-turned-owner Albert Spalding shocked the baseball world by selling the contract of King Kelly, the star player on his White Stockings, to Boston for an unprecedented $10,000. In June 1888, the *San Francisco Examiner* published a poem called "Casey at the Bat," and after the season, Spalding took an all-star team on a world tour to demonstrate the American game to all who cared to see it. At a dinner celebrating the return of the entourage to New York in the spring, Mark Twain, one of the evening's guest speakers, called baseball "the very symbol, the outward and visible expression of the drive, and push, and rush and struggle of the raging, tearing, booming nineteenth century!"

Despite this exuberance, some players harbored a growing sense of dissatisfaction that a larger portion of the sport's prosperity was not coming their way. If it was true that clubs' revenues were rising, players argued, their salaries were not keeping pace. Clubs, in fact, had attempted to impose a $2,000 ceiling on player salaries in 1885. In response, several players expanded on an idea to form a benevolent association for sick and needy players. Led by Giants captain Monte Ward, unusual because he was a college graduate, they established the Brotherhood of Professional Base Ball Players, a trade union dedicated to safeguarding players' interests, individually and collectively. Ward spoke out vigorously against salary limits, the reserve clause, blacklisting, and other perceived economic ills. In 1887, the Brotherhood sought to be recognized as the players' agent for collective bargaining. Club owners, acting like other business and industrial leaders throughout America's Gilded Age economy, refused.

While Ward was out of the country on Spalding's tour, John Brush, owner of the League's Indianapolis club, proposed a rigid salary classification plan designed both to control labor costs and to solve disciplinary problems. Brush's system divided all players into five classifications based on their "habits, earnestness, and special qualifications" while fixing salaries at $1,500 for a Class E player up to $2,500 for a player in Class A. Abraham Mills, no longer League president, called Brush's idea "technically illegal" and declared that any club manager that "can't handle salary with the powerful reserve rule at his command ought to have a wet nurse." Some thought Brush's idea unworkable because clubs would more than likely pay some players additional salary surreptitiously, but it passed anyway. Members of the Brotherhood considered a strike, especially after negotiations with the League to repeal the plan stalled, but Ward acted on a more ambitious thought. In November 1889 he announced that the Brotherhood had located enough backers to organize its own league.

The Players National League of Base Ball Clubs competed directly with the National League while more or less ignoring the American Association. It placed clubs in seven League cities (Boston, Brooklyn, Chicago, Cleveland, New York, Philadelphia, and Pittsburgh) and put an eighth club in Buffalo. Defying the capitalist ethos of the time, the upstart league operated as a cooperative. Players and owners shared administrative control. A governing senate composed of two representatives from each club—one chosen by the players and one by the "contributors," as the backers were called—served as the league's tribunal. Similarly, an eight-man board, four elected by the players and four by the contributors, ran each club. The league abandoned the reserve clause and the Brush classification plan in favor of a complicated scheme to divide revenues equitably. Each player who joined the new league signed, at his 1889 salary, either a three-year contract or a one-year deal with a two-year option. Bidding to attract fans, the Brotherhood attacked the League directly in a publication it called a manifesto: "There was a time when the League stood for integrity and fair dealing; today it stands for dollars and cents.... Players have been bought, sold or exchanged, as though they were sheep, instead of American citizens." But the Players League mimicked its competitor by refusing to sign black players and alienated working class fans by forbidding Sunday baseball and banning the sale of alcoholic beverages at games.

The new league recruited most of its players for the 1890 season from the National League, but it was the American Association that suffered most. Two Association clubs, Brooklyn and Cincinnati, moved to the League before the season began. Another two, the Kansas City Blues and the Baltimore Orioles, left the Association and became minor league clubs. Replacement Association clubs in Rochester, Syracuse, and Toledo, plus a new club in Brooklyn, proved weak on and off the field. The Brooklyn Gladiators, in fact, lasted only until August 25. The Association's commitment to Sunday baseball also proved disruptive. An invigorated Sabbatarian movement, committed to prohibiting recreation such as baseball on Sundays, staged frequent protests at Association ballparks. A total of 124 players appeared in at least ten Players League games. Of these, 81 came from the League, 28 from the Association, and the rest from minor league clubs. Winning the pennant were the Boston Reds, a club that featured several former League stars. The Players League led its rivals in attendance, but the entire season was marred by prolonged wrangling in court after court as the new league argued the legality of the reserve clause and clubs contested their rights to players whose contract status was uncertain. Baseball appeared to be a chaotic enterprise, and all three leagues paid a severe economic price for irritating their fans. The Players League lost an estimated $340,000, and in January 1891, after just one season of play, it stood ready to capitulate.

Discussions to bring peace among the three leagues began soon after the owner of the Cincinnati club, after only one year in the National League, sold out to a group of Players League owners. Other National League owners, including Spalding, knew they were in trouble, but in the end it was Ward and the Brotherhood that lost out. Early hope for an equitable consolidation collapsed when several Players League owners put their personal interests above those of their league and their player partners. In January 1891, after Ward and other players were denied seats at the negotiating table, the Players League officially dissolved, and the Brotherhood collapsed. Players League clubs in Brooklyn, New York, and Pittsburgh combined with their National League rivals, and Spalding's White Stockings bought the contracts of the players in the Players League Chicago club. The Association dropped three weak clubs and reorganized its Philadelphia club, while picking up the Players League's

Boston club and adding two more. This restructuring did the Association little good. Its owners continued to squabble with the League, causing lucrative inter-league spring exhibitions and the post-season championship series to be canceled. The League outdrew the Association in 1891, and after the season, the Association, financially weakened top to bottom, sought a truce.

The Association hoped for a consolidation of two leagues into one, but it got a merger in name only. Four Association clubs (Baltimore, Louisville, St. Louis, and Washington) joined the eight League clubs to form the National League and American Association of Professional Base Ball Clubs. This new organization bought out the remaining Association clubs and gave in on several old points of contention, allowing Sunday games and the sale of alcohol and permitting some tickets to be sold for twenty-five cents. More importantly, this twelve-team league was an overt monopoly whose owners tended to act as captains of industry or magnates controlling a trust, even to the point of buying stakes in one another's clubs. This practice, termed syndicate baseball, called into question the honesty of the competition on the field, as owners often shuffled players from one club to another. A dozen teams also proved to be too many. Each season a fair number of clubs fell out of the pennant race early, destroying fan interest as the schedule ground to its conclusion. The league tried a couple of gimmicks to spike enthusiasm, but neither worked. In 1892, clubs played a split season with Boston winning the first half and Cleveland winning the second half before Boston won a playoff for the overall championship. From 1894 through 1897, the second-place club took on the first-place club in a post-season competition for the Temple Cup, but these series were marred by a decided lack of fan interest. After the 1899 season, owners recognized the folly of their grandiose endeavor. They eliminated four clubs (Baltimore, Cleveland, Louisville, and Washington) and reverted to an eight-team league.

In the 1890s, the sporting press still sometimes identified clubs by the cities in which they played ("the Brooklyns" or "the Clevelands," for example), but more often, they began calling clubs by nicknames, some of which stayed stable for decades while others changed more than once. Thus, the best two teams in this decade were called the Boston Beaneaters and the Baltimore Orioles. The Boston club, today's Atlanta Braves, is the only one that has played major league baseball every season from 1871 to the present. The team began as the Red Stockings in the National Association and was known at various times as the Red Caps, the Doves, the Rustlers, the Braves, and the Bees before reverting to the Braves in 1941. This same club moved to Milwaukee in 1953 and to Atlanta in 1966. After winning four pennants in the National Association's five years, the Boston club won its first three National League pennants in 1877, 1878, and 1883. After the 1889 season, the club replaced manager Jim

Hart with Frank Selee, the first National League manager without experience as a major league player. Selee drilled his players in the fundamentals, and he was particularly fond of the stolen base and the hit-and-run. He was also a superb judge of playing talent. He signed pitcher Kid Nichols and second baseman Bobby Lowe, but defections of other key players to the Boston club in the Players League condemned the Beaneaters to fifth place in 1890. Thereafter, Selee's team won three straight pennants starting in 1891 and two more in 1897 and 1898. Nichols developed into a Hall of Fame pitcher who won thirty or more games seven times, and he was complemented by three other Hall of Fame inductees, third baseman Jimmy Collins and outfielders Hugh Duffy and Tommy McCarthy, dubbed the Heavenly Twins for their spectacular play and firm friendship. Duffy was a tremendous batter. He hit .440 in 1894, the record for the highest single-season batting average ever, and after he retired, he enjoyed a long career as manager, coach, scout, and hitting instructor; one of his star pupils was the young Ted Williams.

The Orioles, National League pennant winners in 1894, 1895, and 1896 and second-place finishers the next two years, were a completely different kind of ball club. Led by manager Ned Hanlon, Baltimore played a scrappy, aggressive style that became known as "inside baseball." Like Selee, Hanlon schooled his team to execute the fundamentals well. He instructed outfielders to hit the cutoff man with their throws and had pitchers cover first on ground balls hit to the first baseman's right. The Orioles bunted, stole bases, and took the extra base at every opportunity. If their offense had a motto, it was outfielder Wee Willie Keeler's simple mantra, "Keep your eye clear and hit 'em where they ain't." Shying away from no tactic that might bring them a victory, Baltimore tailored its playing field to fit its game. The club's groundskeepers manicured the base paths to keep bunts in fair territory and hardened the dirt in front of home plate so that "Baltimore chops," balls deliberately hit right into the ground, would bounce high in the air and allow batters to reach first base safely. More scurrilously, the Orioles skirted the rules whenever they could, hiding extra balls in the long outfield grass, obstructing opposing base runners, and cutting the distance between first base and third by making the turn well inside second base whenever the umpire could not see them. Baltimore's players filed their spikes to use against opponents, and they rarely forsook a chance to press their case, however outlandish, with an umpire.

Baltimore was the team against which many rooted, so when the Beaneaters dethroned the three-time champions in 1897 and 1898, fans throughout the twelve-team league rejoiced. Still, the Orioles were a powerful team led by a quartet of baseball immortals, Keeler, third baseman John McGraw, catcher Wilbert Robinson, and outfielder Hughie Jennings. After winning the 1894 pennant, Baltimore declined to take the first Temple Cup series seriously, dropping four straight games to the Giants. The next season, Jennings, McGraw, Keeler, and outfielder Joe Kelley all hit better than .365, but the Orioles lost the Temple Cup series again, this time to the Cleveland Spiders. Baltimore came back to defeat Cleveland in 1896 and won the cup again in 1897 after finishing second to Boston. The Orioles may have been the most aggressive team in the league, but baseball in the 1890s was a rough-and-tumble game played by ambitious men who gave no quarter. The sportsmanship that had governed how the game was played in its amateur days had little effect. All teams played a rowdy style, including fighting, indecent language, abuse of the rules, and wrangling with umpires. In 1898, owners put in place the Purification Plan, to curb some of this behavior, but clubs regularly undercut umpires' authority by paying fines levied against players.

The 1890s also brought to a close a period of frequent rules adjustments, the result of which could be called the advent of the modern game of baseball. Besides setting the pitching distance at 60 feet, 6 inches, from home base, rules-makers adopted the infield fly rule in 1893, reducing the chance that an infielder could turn a pop fly into a double play by trickery, and introduced the balk rule in 1899. Teams used engineers to lay out their diamonds precisely, and some began painting part of the center field fence a dark color to help batters see the pitched ball. The new pitching distance handicapped pitchers for a while. The league's composite batting average rose from .245 in 1892 to .280 in 1893 and .309 in 1894 (when four players besides Duffy hit better than .400), and pitchers were forced to adjust. This took several seasons. Pitchers learned to pace themselves to throw the longer distance, and catchers began to offer hand signals to call for one of an array of pitches with names that are no longer used, including "inshoot," "outcurve," "jump ball," and "drop." The leading pitchers in the 1890s regularly threw over 400 innings per season, completed most of the games they started, and compiled won-lost records that are fairly incomprehensible today. Over the eight seasons starting in 1892, Nichols led all pitchers with 239 wins, while Cy Young, so named because his specialty was "cyclone" or fastball pitching, averaged 394 innings pitched and was well on his way to 511 career wins, the most ever. Batting averages fell off after 1894, but batters skilled enough to do so could attempt to wear pitchers out by fouling off good pitches interminably. Foul balls not caught on the fly did not count as strikes (but not the third strike) until 1901.

Late in 1893, a Cincinnati newspaperman named Ban Johnson accepted an invitation to become president of the Western League, a dormant minor league whose clubs had been located in small Midwestern cities. Elected president, secretary, and treasurer, Johnson sought to resurrect his league by moving weak clubs to bigger cities and overseeing every club's operation closely. Running a successful minor league was not easy. Major league clubs not only had the right to draft minor league players, that is, to acquire their contracts for fixed sums below market value, but also to "farm" them, that is, to place them on any minor league that would accept them. Johnson objected to the National League more than once about these destabilizing tactics, but to no avail. He was ambitious, too, and he found his opening when National League owners, having decided that a twelve-club league was unworkable, cut back to eight after the 1899 season. Johnson changed the name of the Western League to the American League, and he moved his Grand Rapids (MI) club to Cleveland and his St. Paul (MN) club to Chicago. A year later, after claiming major status for his league, he pulled out of the National Agreement so that he would not have to respect the reserve clause, began to sign National League players, shifted two clubs into abandoned League cities (Baltimore and Washington) and moved two more, as direct challenges, into Boston and Philadelphia.

National League owners frequently fought among themselves and rarely spoke with one voice, but Johnson, in the words of *The Sporting News*, was a "benevolent autocrat" who ruled the American League with an iron hand. He held a financial stake in some of his clubs and exerted control over all of them. He determined who their owners would be, where they would play, and, in some cases, which players they would employ. In addition, since Johnson did not countenance the National League's rowdy style of play, he recruited a staff of competent umpires whose authority to discipline outrageous behavior he supported without question. Fans responded favorably. In 1901, the newer league outdrew the older in two of the three cities in which they competed head-to-head, and in 1902, American League attendance exceeded National League attendance by more than a half million. Johnson's quest to sign National League players at first involved only those who had not signed contracts for the upcoming season, but the situation got messy quickly as each league raided the other's rosters indiscriminately. Clubs waged war in the press and in the courts, and players' salaries, now that there was bidding for their services, rose accordingly. Fearful that Johnson was about to move his Baltimore club to New York after the 1902 season to compete directly in the nation's largest market, the National League sought a truce, offering the American League equal standing as a second major league. The Orioles became the New York Highlanders (later the Yankees), the two leagues sorted out the disputed player contracts, and they signed a treaty that led to a new national agreement. Overall administrative control was given to a three-man National Commission composed of the presidents of the two major leagues and, as chair, a third person elected by the other two.

Both leagues played the 1903 season without incident, but certain resentments remained. Thus, near the end of the season, Barney Dreyfuss, owner of the Pittsburgh Pirates, who were about to win the National League pennant, wrote to Henry Killilea, whose Boston club was about to win the American League pennant, and suggested that their two clubs play a best-of-nine postseason series as a sign of interleague peace. Killilea agreed, and Johnson gave his consent. Pittsburgh pitcher Deacon Phillippe won three of the first four games in the series, but Boston recovered to win four straight and capture the championship. This was the birth of the modern World Series (originally the World's Series) although this first time it was a private deal between two club owners and not an agreement between leagues. In 1904, the Giants won the National League pennant, but their manager, John McGraw, bore a grudge against Johnson, and he refused to play the American League champion Philadelphia Athletics. The public outcry against this snub was so great that New York owner John Brush subsequently proposed that the World Series become an annual affair, a best-of-seven competition governed by a code called the Brush Rules. Both leagues agreed. In 1905, the Giants and the Athletics won their respective pennants again, and New York won a remarkable World Series, four games to one. Each game was a shutout with Giants pitcher Christy Mathewson winning three.

Concurrent with the peace negotiated between the National League and the American League, the minor leagues, acting together, signed a pact with the majors called the Major-Minor League Agreement. Individual minor leagues had been party to the National Agreement since 1883, but these relationships often turned unsatisfactory. Seeking an improved bargaining position, seven minor leagues met in 1902 to establish the National Association of Professional Baseball Leagues. They signed a ten-year agreement that embraced both the reserve clause and the player draft among themselves, set in place salary limits and club territorial limits, and empowered a board to arbitrate disputes. In allying itself with the majors a year later, the National Association forsook independence for stability and accepted a position subordinate to the majors. The Major-Minor Agreement reaffirmed the right of major league clubs to draft players from the minors. It also divided all minor leagues into a hierarchy with four levels (classes A, B, C, and D) based primarily on the population of each league's city. This classification system, although altered significantly several times, is still in effect.

The years between 1903 and 1914, when World War I began in Europe, were a period of peace and prosperity for major league baseball. Attendance grew nearly every season, and the sport received increased coverage in newspapers, magazines, and books. In 1908, composer Albert von Tilzer and lyricist Jack Norworth, neither of whom had ever seen a baseball game, wrote a hit song, "Take Me Out to the Ball Game," that has endured as an unofficial anthem. Two years later, William Howard Taft began an annual tradition by becoming the first U.S. president to toss out a ceremonial first pitch before a game on opening day. During this same period, several clubs constructed new ballparks, abandoning wood as the primary building material in favor of steel-reinforced concrete. These ballparks proved to be safe, durable, attractive, and commodious, and over the decades, they earned legendary status. The Athletics opened the first steel-and-concrete ballpark, Shibe Park, in April 1909, and the Pirates followed with Forbes Field in June of the same year. Their success set off a construction boom, as clubs built new parks and refurbished older ones: Comiskey Park (Chicago) and League Park (Cleveland) in 1910; Griffith Stadium (Washington) and the Polo Grounds (New York) in 1911, Redland Field (Cincinnati), Navin Field (Detroit), and Fenway Park (Boston) in 1912; Ebbets Field (Brooklyn) in 1913; Weeghman Field (Chicago) in 1914; and Braves Field (Boston) in 1915. Biggest of all was New York's Yankee Stadium, a three-tiered ballpark seating at least 58,000 that opened in 1923.

Baseball's luminaries desired to link their sport's prosperity to the exuberant spirit of American nationalism. In particular, Albert Spalding, by now the prosperous owner of a sporting goods company and the embodiment of turn-of-the-century capitalist values, sought to prove that baseball was the quintessential American game, born in this country without English antecedents. Even though he had once acknowledged that baseball had developed from rounders, Spalding now argued that "baseball must be free from the trammels of English traditions, customs, and conventionalities." Henry Chadwick, born in 1824 and venerated as "the Father of Baseball" for all he had done to promote the game, had never shied from his rounders thesis. He had seen rounders played in England as a boy, and after coming to America, immediately recognized baseball's similarities. Over several decades, Chadwick presented his case repeatedly even as a series of other writers took the "no rounders" point of view. In 1905, Spalding created a commission chaired by Abraham Mills to settle the question, but over three years very little substantial evidence emerged. When the Mills Commission published its report, only eight paragraphs long, in 1908, its conclusion that baseball was unquestionably American rested on a letter sent to Spalding from Abner Graves, an otherwise insignificant retired mining engineer who later shot his wife and died in an asylum. He wrote that he had grown up in Cooperstown and was present when a friend named Abner Doubleday interrupted a game of marbles by drawing a diamond in the dirt with a stick and explaining a new game he had just devised.

Chadwick laughed off this explanation, but the Doubleday story proved so simple and attractive and patriotic that its veracity was accepted immediately. Doubleday, in fact, was not even present in Cooperstown in the summer of 1839. He was a West Point cadet who, after graduation, went on to military glory, fighting in the Mexican War, commanding the Ft. Sumter battery that first returned Confederate fire in April 1861, and leading troops that helped repel Pickett's Charge at Gettysburg. Doubleday knew both Spalding and Mills, but he had no connection with baseball whatsoever. The Doubleday story gained a boost, though, in 1935 when a farmer in Fly Creek, New York, a town near Cooperstown, rummaged through an old trunk he said had belonged to his distant relative, Abner Graves. Among the trunk's contents was an old, battered baseball that almost immediately became known as the "Doubleday baseball," supposedly used by the creator. Cooperstown was enshrined as the "birthplace of baseball," a designation made all the more resilient when the National Baseball Museum and Hall of Fame opened there in 1939. Neither Mills nor Spalding backed the findings of the commission forthrightly, but both were content that Graves's letter had helped accomplish their goal, demonstrating that baseball was an American game devoid of English influence. Scholars have been much less kind to the Doubleday tale. Beginning in 1909 with a magazine article by Will Irwin and then more extensively with the publication of Robert W. Henderson's *Ball, Bat, and Bishop* in 1947, the Doubleday myth has been thoroughly debunked. A coterie of scholars continue painstaking research into baseball's origins, grounded in a wide quest for solid evidence that connects baseball with prior stick-and-ball games.

The best player in the National League during the first decade of the twentieth century was Pittsburgh's shortstop, Honus Wagner. A superior athlete with short legs, big hands, and a barrel chest, Wagner played for 21 seasons, won eight batting titles, and hit for a career average of .328. Some experts consider him the best shortstop and one of the best players of all time. He led the Pirates to the pennant in 1901, 1902, 1903, and 1909 when they won the World Series. The best player in the American League's first years was Napoleon Lajoie. He started his career with the Philadelphia Phillies in 1896, jumped to the Athletics in 1901, and then accepted a trade to Cleveland early in the 1902 season. Lajoie won the Triple Crown in 1901, leading the American League in batting average (.426), home runs (14), and runs batted in (125). He led the league in batting in 1903 and 1904 and was involved in a disputed race for the batting title in 1910 with the cantankerous Ty Cobb of the Detroit Tigers. Cobb broke into the league in 1905 and won twelve batting titles, including nine in a row. The Tigers won pennants in 1907, 1908, and 1909 but lost the Series each time. The best pitcher of the decade was the Giants' Mathewson, renowned for his good looks and outstanding character. Matty, as he was called, won 373 in his career and led his team to additional pennants in 1911, 1912, and 1913. The Athletics won three American League pennants during the decade, plus three more in 1911, 1913, and 1914, and three World Series. The Chicago Cubs (formerly the White Stockings) won three straight National League pennants in 1906, 1907, and 1908, plus another one in 1910.

In 1906, they won 116 games, a total that no National League team has ever surpassed, against only 36 losses. Three members of those Cubs were immortalized in baseball's most famous piece of doggerel poetry, "[Joe] Tinker to [Johnny] Evers to [Frank] Chance."

The majors and minors re-fashioned the National Agreement in 1912, hoping to inaugurate a long period of stability, but a year later, a group of businessmen formed the Federal League, six teams that played as an independent minor league in 1913 and as a self-proclaimed third major league in 1914 and 1915 (i.e., outside Organized Baseball). Like the American League before it, the Feds, as the league was called, heeded the reserve clause at first, signing only players not yet under contract for the coming season, but later they targeted anyone willing to jump to the new league. Many contract disputes wound up in court, and in January 1915, the Federal League brought an antitrust lawsuit against the National Commission and all sixteen major league clubs. Hoping for a favorable decision, the Feds filed the suit in the U.S. District Court for Northern Illinois, where it was assigned to Kenesaw Mountain Landis, a trust-busting judge and avowed baseball fan. Landis heard testimony for four days but then delayed rendering a decision, hoping that the parties would negotiate a settlement. That is what happened. The upstart league ceased playing after 1915 while Organized Baseball compensated several Federal League owners and allowed two others to buy major league clubs. The Baltimore club in the Federal League refused to accept the settlement and filed its own lawsuit against Organized Baseball. This suit, *Federal League Club of Baltimore v. National League Etc.*, reached the U.S. Supreme Court in 1922. Its decision declared that baseball was not a business subject to antitrust regulation because it was "not trade or commerce in the commonly-accepted use of those words."

Baseball reacted to America's participation in World War I erratically. After the United States entered the war in April 1917, clubs demonstrated their patriotism. They showed an interest in preparedness by practicing close order military drill with bats instead of rifles, and Clark Griffith, owner of the Washington Senators, established a "bat and ball" fund to send equipment overseas. Yet, after the season, owners seemed to regard the war as an imposition. Ban Johnson suggested without success that eighteen players on each major league team be exempted from military service. When the government imposed a ten-percent tax on entertainment events, ball clubs raised ticket prices to the next highest nickel and pocketed the surplus. After Provost Marshal Enoch Crowder issued the "Work-or-Fight" order, club owners argued that baseball should not be classified as a non-essential occupation. When this request was denied, owners quickly truncated the length of the 1918 season to 140 games and concluded the World Series on September 11. After the Armistice, they played a second short season in 1919, only to be surprised when attendance more than doubled to over 6.5 million. Owners hastily expanded the World Series to a best-five-of-nine format to capitalize on the commercial opportunity, and the Cincinnati Reds beat the Chicago White Sox, 5 games to 3.

Over time, owners in both leagues had grown disenchanted with the structure of the National Commission and the governance it provided. The two league presidents sat on the Commission as permanent members, and they annually elected Garry Herrmann, co-owner of the Reds, as the third member, but Johnson's voice dominated the Commission's deliberations while Herrmann's position eventually proved untenable. On any question for which he supplied the deciding vote, critics disparaged his judgment for either favoring his league or acting as Johnson's pawn. Moreover, National League owners challenged the system that put an owner in a position implicitly superior to their league president. This dissatisfaction played into the hands of several American League owners who had also grown tired of Johnson's oppressive administrative style. Several American League clubs had changed hands since 1901, and Johnson no longer had the power to select new owners to his liking. Five owners called the "Loyalists" or the "Loyal Five" continued to support the president, but a coalition of three others, the "Insurrectionists" or "Insurrectos," sought to curtail Johnson's authority after he settled a series of disputes against them. Following the 1919 season, National League president John Heydler bowed to the Commission's detractors and refused to vote to re-elect Herrmann. He resigned, and the Commission, lacking a third vote, could no longer function.

A proposal to re-constitute the Commission with three members from outside the baseball establishment made little headway until a Cook County (IL) grand jury returned indictments in September 1920 accusing eight members of the White Sox of conspiracy to fix the 1919 World Series. Gambling had never completely disappeared from baseball, and these indictments suggested, among other things, that the Commission could no longer govern effectively. Confidential negotiations among all eight National League owners and the three American League "Insurrectos" produced a consensus that the old Commission had to be discarded. These dissidents considered a list of candidates to chair a new three-man commission, and they approached their first choice, Kenesaw Landis, the district court judge who had presided over the Federal League lawsuit. Landis dismissed the idea of a three-man panel, saying he would take the job if he could preside over baseball alone. The owners agreed, and Landis took office. In August 1921, a Chicago jury acquitted the White Sox after a curious trial. Not satisfied with this outcome, Landis asserted his considerable authority for the first time. He rendered his own version of justice by banning the eight players, called the Black Sox, from baseball for life. "Regardless of the verdict of juries," he said in a statement, "no player that throws a ball game, no player that entertains proposals or promises to throw a game, no player that sits in a conference with a bunch of crooked players and gamblers where the ways and means of throwing games are discussed, and does not promptly tell his club about it, will ever again play professional baseball."

The decade of the 1920s has sometimes been called the "Golden Age of American Sports." The national economy rebounded from the dislocations of wartime mobilization, and many middle-class Americans were able to spend more dollars on recreation, including on tickets to sporting events. Most sports had one or more stars that fans regarded as heroes, including Babe Ruth in baseball, Red Grange in football, Bobby Jones in golf, Bill Tilden in tennis, Jack Dempsey in boxing, and even Man o' War in thoroughbred racing. Attendance at major league games jumped to over nine million in 1920 and remained high until 1932. The game's popularity grew for other reasons, too. Daily newspapers, intent on increasing circulation, dramatically increased the amount of editorial space they devoted to sports. Most papers produced a self-contained sports section every day, and some papers featured coverage of big events such as heavyweight championship fights or the World Series on the front page. Pittsburgh radio station KDKA, generally acknowledged as the world's first commercially licensed station, broadcast a major league baseball game for the first time on August 5, 1921, and joined with two other stations to broadcast a World Series game that year between the Giants and the Yankees. Baseball embraced the new medium gradually because owners feared that having too many games on the radio would cut into attendance. The Reds tested this theory by broadcasting all their games in 1929, and a few years later, WMAQ in Chicago carried all Cubs and White Sox home games. In 1934, though, the three New York clubs signed a five-year agreement to ban all radio broadcasts of their games. Owners eventually realized that radio was not a liability but rather an asset, a good way to market their teams, and they began to charge fees for the right to broadcast games. Radio stations passed these fees on to advertisers pleased to associate their products with sports, and the announcers who handled each team's broadcasts not only became spokesmen for these products but also often became celebrities in their own right.

Batters gained an advantage in 1920 from a new rule forbidding pitchers to deface the ball in any way or to apply to it any foreign substance, including saliva. Following the death of Cleveland infielder Ray Chapman, who was hit in the head by a pitched ball on August 16 and died the following day, umpires began removing discolored balls from play more quickly. Whether these changes caused the ensuing boost in offensive production is a matter of debate, but batting averages, runs scored, and home runs increased throughout the decade. A more likely explanation for this upswing centers on the transformation in how the game was played wrought by the incredible abilities of Babe

Ruth. He made his major league debut for the Boston Red Sox as a pitcher in 1914 and was converted to a fulltime outfielder in 1919, one year before having his contract sold to the Yankees. Ruth's talents were prodigious. As a pitcher, he won 23 games in 1916, while leading the American League with a 1.75 earned run average, and 24 games in 1917. As a hitter, he led the league in home runs a dozen times, starting in 1918 when he hit 11 and climaxing in 1927 when he hit 60. Ruth was an offensive player unlike anyone the game had seen previously. He completely destroyed the common wisdom that batters should swing carefully, avoid striking out, and endeavor to put the ball into play so that teams could build runs through a combination of base hits, walks, sacrifices, and stolen bases. Ruth swung mightily and struck out frequently. He set his first home run record in 1919, hitting 29, and when he hit 54 in 1920, his total eclipsed that of every other American League team. When he finished his career in 1935, he had slugged 714 home runs, a record that stood until 1974. Yet he was so talented that his career batting average was .342, still the fourteenth-highest. Ruth changed baseball forever, and Yankee fans rewarded him with unprecedented adulation. New York's attendance more than doubled in 1920 to over 1.2 million, and the Yankees' owners compensated the Babe with a salary that grew to exceed that of the president of the United States.

With Ruth on their roster, the Red Sox won the American League pennant and the World Series in 1915, 1916, and 1918, but the Yankees became the league's dominant team in the 1920s. They won 3 consecutive pennants twice (1921–1923 and 1926–1928) and 3 World Series. Ruth was the game's best player, but New York's roster was so strong that its batting order was known as "Murderers' Row." With Lou Gehrig playing first base, Tony Lazzeri at second, and Bob Meusel and Earl Combs in the outfield next to Ruth, the Yankees led the league in home runs for 9 straight seasons, and they won the World Series in 1923, 1927, 1928, and 1932. Yet they were not the only club that could claim dynastic standing. The Philadelphia Athletics, owned and managed by Connie Mack, had not finished first in the American League since 1914, but they won 3 straight pennants (1929–1931) and 2 World Series (1929 and 1930) before the economic rigors of the Depression caused Mack to sell off the core of his club. In the National League, the Giants followed up their success earlier in the century by winning 4 straight pennants in 1921, 1922, 1923, and 1924 and the World Series in the first 2 of these years. The Giants were a team without a dominant star, but their long-time manager was John McGraw, perhaps the game's fiercest tactician. He managed for 33 seasons, and his teams won 10 pennants and 2,763 games, more than anyone else except Mack, who managed for 53 seasons and won 3,731 games.

The Giants' tenure as the best team in the National League was threatened first by the Pirates, who won the pennant in 1925 and 1927, and then by the St. Louis Cardinals. Their best player during the 1920s was second baseman Rogers Hornsby, who won six straight batting titles. The best hitter in National League history, Hornsby batted over .400 three times, including .424 in 1924, so that his average over six seasons (1920–1925) was an astounding .397. Hornsby managed the Cardinals to a World Series title over the Yankees in 1926, but the next season he was gone, traded to the Giants for their second baseman, Frankie Frisch. The St. Louis roster remained strong because executive Branch Rickey perfected a new way to develop major league players, an organizational strategy called the farm system. Working with little capital, the Cardinals had a difficult time acquiring and retaining young prospects. Rickey began assembling a network of minor league clubs where he could place young players safely. He signed "working agreements" with some clubs and bought others outright. In either case, St. Louis could assign players to minor league rosters, confident that other major league clubs could not draft them or purchase their contracts. Commissioner Landis opposed the concept of the farm system, but other clubs soon began to copy the Cardinals because they were so successful. The best St. Louis prospects advanced to the parent club and helped them win pennants in 1928, 1930, 1931, and 1934. By the late 1930s, St. Louis had an interest in more than thirty minor league clubs and controlled more than 700 players.

Commissioner Landis did nothing to void the unwritten understanding that African Americans could not play in Organized Baseball. Some individuals and a few all-black teams had bucked the restrictions imposed by Jim Crow and played in the minors before 1890, but after that, incidents of integrated play grew rare. Black players were confined to "colored" teams playing outside any league structure and only occasionally found opportunities to test their abilities against white competition. The Cuban Giants, formed in 1885 from the wait staff at the Argyle Hotel in Babylon, New York, were the first of several black teams, many of them called the Giants, that traveled throughout the country and gained national reputations. Although these teams barnstormed for most of the season, they tended to call as home the great industrial cities of the north, including New York, Philadelphia, and Chicago, and fans began to support the best African American players, often comparing them to the best white players in Organized Baseball. Thus, shortstop John Henry Lloyd was the "black Honus Wagner"; pitcher Jose Mendez, the "black Christy Mathewson"; outfielder Oscar Charleston, the "black Ty Cobb"; and slugging catcher Josh Gibson, the "black Babe Ruth."

The owners of all-black clubs had little recourse whenever any of their players jumped from one club to another, and they were often at the mercy of booking agents, often white, who controlled access to ballparks. Rube Foster, an outstanding pitcher and co-owner of the Chicago American Giants, tried to bring some measure of stability to black baseball by forming the Negro National League in 1920. Operating with most of its clubs in Midwestern cities, the league enjoyed some success. Other entrepreneurs tried to copy Foster, setting up the Eastern Colored League and the Southern Negro Leagues, but after Foster died in 1930, much of this organizational structure crumbled. Independent teams, especially the Kansas City Monarchs, Homestead Grays, and Pittsburgh Crawfords, thrived in the early 1930s as barnstorming outfits, with some of them being capitalized by the illegal numbers racket. In 1933, Gus Greenlee, owner of the Crawfords and an underworld figure of some renown, revived the Negro National League as an eastern operation and attracted other barnstorming clubs to become members. Four years later, a second circuit, the Negro American League, brought together clubs in the Midwest and South. Scheduling for these leagues remained haphazard, so their attempt to climax each season with a World's Series often fell short of expectations. The East-West All-Star Game, however, played annually in Chicago starting in 1933, became a centerpiece of the black game. Urban black communities took pride in their teams and players, and fans looked forward with great anticipation to post-season games between black clubs and touring squads of white players that often included stars. These encounters demonstrated that while the typical black club lacked the depth to compete at the major league level, individual African American players were certainly more than good enough to succeed against their white counterparts. With Landis at the helm of Organized Baseball, though no owners were eager to oppose him on this matter, any thought of erasing the color line remained far more dream than reality.

Baseball endured the Great Depression with difficulty and did not fully recover until after World War II. The increase in offensive production that had begun in the 1920s continued, aided perhaps by a change in how baseballs were manufactured. In 1930, American League batters connected for 673 home runs, more than ever before. National League teams scored 5.68 runs per team per game and batted .303, both records that have not since been surpassed. The Philadelphia Phillies batted .315, but they gave up 6.71 earned runs per game and finished last in the National League. Major league attendance topped 10 million for the first time in 1930 and fell off precipitously after that, bottoming out at 6.1 million in 1933 when the national economy was still in the doldrums. Attendance would not hit 10 million again until 1945, the year World War II ended. Baseball's worst financial years were 1932, 1933, and 1934. Most clubs lost money. Teams cut player salaries, and the poorest clubs sold their best players, making their situations on the field even worse. The minor leagues suffered even more as individual clubs and whole leagues succumbed to the effects of the Depression. A total of 26 leagues started the 1929 season, but that number fell to 23 in 1930, 19 in 1931, and 14 in 1933. Some leagues and clubs could not even finish what they started, going out of business in mid-season. The minors' governing body, the National Association, got new leadership in 1932, a North Carolina lawyer named William Bramham with experience running 4 minor leagues. He tightened the requirements for minor league club ownership, demanded guaranteed deposits to cover player salaries, and disagreed with Landis by supporting the expansion of farm systems. With the limited financial help major league clubs provided to these farm teams, the minors made a remarkable recovery. In 1940, no major league club had fewer than 5 farm teams, and 44 minor leagues started and finished the season.

After the Athletics completed their three-year run as American League champions, the Yankees re-asserted their primacy. As Ruth's skills waned, Gehrig replaced him as New York's star player. He appeared in a record 2,130 consecutive games (from June 1, 1925 to April 30, 1939), won the Triple Crown in 1934, and hit 23 grand slams in his career. Joe DiMaggio joined Gehrig in the Yankees lineup in 1936. Although he played only 13 seasons, missing 3 because of World War II, he won the league's Most Valuable Player award three times and is perhaps best known for hitting safely in 56 consecutive games in 1941. The Yankees won four straight pennants in the late 1930s (1936–1939) and took the World Series each time, losing a total of only 3 games. The National League had no club comparable to the Yankees, but the Cardinals and Giants were generally regarded as the league's best with the Cubs a close third. The 1934 Cardinals, later known as the "Gashouse Gang," were a colorful team that played scrappy baseball and won an exciting 7-game World Series over the Detroit Tigers. The Giants and Cubs won six pennants between them in the 1930s, but only one World Series. In 1938, Cincinnati pitcher Johnny Vander Meer accomplished a feat that has not been duplicated, throwing consecutive no-hitters against Boston on June 11 and Brooklyn four days later.

Several innovations helped baseball counteract the effects of the Depression. The advent of night baseball opened the game to fans who worked during the day and had previously been able to attend only weekend games. Playing baseball at night had been tried as early as the 1880s, but it was the barnstorming Kansas City Monarchs that developed a portable lighting system in the 1920s that could be erected quickly. Night ball came to the minors in 1930 and to the majors five years later. Cincinnati general manager Larry MacPhail pushed for permission to play games at night to help solve his club's attendance problems. On May 24, 1935, President Franklin Roosevelt pushed a telegraph key in the White House at 8:30 p.m. and illuminated Crosley Field so the Reds could play the Brooklyn Dodgers. Night baseball boosted attendance dramatically, but other clubs were slow to adopt it. Three American League clubs did not install lights until after World War II, and the Cubs did not light Wrigley Field until 1988.

In 1933, Chicago sports editor Arch Ward acted upon a decades-old idea and put together a proposal for a mid-season game matching the best players from each major league against one another. Commissioner Landis, who lived in Chicago, approved, but some club owners were lukewarm, opting to stage the game only as a one-time event in connection with Chicago's World's Fair, the Century of Progress Exposition. Fans voted for the two teams with some input from their respective managers, and the American League won this All-Star Game, 4–2. In 1934, the National League overcame additional owner opposition and hosted a rematch, and thereafter the All-Star Game became an annual event. The American League won 7 of the first 10 games and 12 of the first 16. The National League won 23 of 25 between 1960 and 1981, and the American League won 12 in a row starting in 1997. How the teams have been selected has varied over time. Fans voted from 1947 through 1957 and then again starting in 1970. From 1959 through 1962, 2 games were played each year, and after a tie game in 2002, the commissioner gave the game extra significance by declaring that the winning league would earn the extra home game for its representative in the World Series.

Shortly after the Mills Commission identified Cooperstown as the birthplace of baseball, the village's chamber of commerce suggested erecting a shrine to the sport. That idea came to fruition in a much grander form when the National Baseball Museum and Hall of Fame opened on June 12, 1939, the year in which baseball celebrated its supposed centennial. Founded by philanthropist Stephen C. Clark, the museum provided a home for artifacts documenting the game's history, while the Hall of Fame gallery housed plaques honoring the game's greatest players, managers, umpires, and executives. The first class of inductees included five players, Ty Cobb, Babe Ruth, Honus Wagner, Christy Mathewson, and pitcher Walter Johnson, who won 417 games from 1907 to 1927. Subsequent classes have been elected by a variety of procedures, always including participation by the Baseball Writers' Association of America, and the Hall of Fame has become a quasi-religious destination for baseball tourists.

When the United States entered World War II in December 1941, baseball officials wondered, as they had in 1917, what effect American mobilization would have on their business. Commissioner Landis wrote to President Roosevelt, whom he did not support politically, asking for guidance. The president responded with what became known as the "green light letter," writing, in part, "I honestly feel it would be best for the country to keep baseball going." The major leagues played full seasons during the war, but attendance suffered greatly, falling from 9.7 million in 1941 to 8.6 million in 1942 and 7.5 million in 1943. Baseball reduced the number of night games early in the war and canceled the 1945 All-Star Game after the government asked all sports teams to reduce their travel. The Phillies suffered perhaps more than any other club, losing half a million dollars during the war years and changing ownership twice. The number of minor leagues also fell, from 41 in 1941 to 31 in 1942 and just 10 in 1943 and 1944. The problem, of course, was manpower, as roughly 500 major leaguers and about 3,500 minor leaguers served in the military, depleting rosters and diminishing the quality of play. The St. Louis Browns, who won the American League pennant in 1944 and finished third the next year, used Pete Gray, a man with one arm, in the outfield for 77 games in 1945. With major league talent in short supply and no club owner willing to sign players from the Negro Leagues, the Cardinals, with their enormous farm system, won three straight National League pennants (1942–1944) and two World Series. Baseball supported the war effort in a variety of ways, including sending equipment overseas, giving stateside servicemen free admission to games, and helping to sell war bonds. Some players in all branches of the armed forces saw combat, but a large number played ball as their primary assignment in the service. Pitcher Bob Feller, for one, joined the navy right after Pearl Harbor and was stationed on the battleship *Alabama* throughout the war. On shore, he ran the ship's baseball team and recreation programs, and at sea, he was a gun captain, winning several commendations.

Baseball prospered in the immediate postwar period as never before. Major league attendance almost doubled in four years, jumping from 10.8 million in 1945 to 20.9 million in 1948. The Yankees became the first team to draw more than 2 million fans in one season, attracting 2.3 million in 1947, a total they would not surpass until 1978. Fans flocked to ballparks to see young players but also to watch those who had returned from the war. The Tigers' Hank Greenberg, who had hit 58 home runs in 1938, was one such veteran. He played only 19 games in 1941 before being drafted and did not return to baseball until July 1, 1945, but his home run on the last day of the season gave the Tigers the American League pennant and put them on the road to a World Series victory over the Cubs. Ted Williams of the Red Sox, who had batted .406 in 1941 and .356 in 1942, missed three seasons serving in the navy. He came back in 1946 to win the American League's Most Valuable Player award. Boston won the pennant that year, its first since 1918, but the Cardinals won the World Series, their third in five years, in 7 games. By the next season, though, the Yankees were on top again. They took the World Series in 1947, their first since 1943, and then, under new manager Casey Stengel, they won five straight World Series from 1949 to 1953.

The most extraordinary development of the immediate postwar years was the dismantling of baseball's color line. Commissioner Landis died in

1944, and his successor, Kentucky politician Albert B. Chandler, was receptive to ending segregation in his sport. Branch Rickey, having left the Cardinals to become president of the Dodgers, had the same goal. Over the objection of every other owner but with Chandler's blessing, Rickey signed Jackie Robinson, an African American, to a minor league contract late in 1945 and assigned him to the Montreal Royals, Brooklyn's top farm team. Robinson led the International League in batting in 1946, and Rickey promoted him to the Dodgers in 1947. Robinson had attended college, and he was a military veteran. More importantly, he possessed enormous personal courage and fortitude that allowed him to succeed despite the racist invective hurled at him. Several members of his own team did not want him added to the roster, and an enduring allegation has the Cardinals threatening to strike rather than play against a black man. Robinson bore this and much more with a steely resolve, and he played the game with fiery determination. Moreover, his triumphant debut paved the way for Cleveland owner Bill Veeck and outfielder Larry Doby to integrate the American League in July 1947. Robinson won the Rookie of the Year award that season and the National League's Most Valuable Player award in 1949. The Dodgers added other African Americans to their roster quickly, but most other clubs integrated more slowly, the Red Sox becoming the last to do so in July 1959. However, the end of the color line on the field did not signal the end of racial discrimination in other areas of the sport. Major league baseball did not get a black umpire until 1966 or a black manager until 1975, and clubs were even slower to hire African Americans for front office positions.

Some players began to press their rights as employees in the years after World War II. Like workers in other industries, returning veterans expected to get back their prewar jobs, and all players anticipated higher salaries as compensation for several seasons of fiscal restraint. When management balked at these demands, dozens of players filed lawsuits, and eighteen accepted offers to play for substantially higher salaries in the Mexican League, outside the structure of Organized Baseball, although their experiences in this league ultimately proved less than ideal. Other players, fully aware that some major leaguers still made less than $5,000 per year, consulted with Robert Murphy, a labor attorney interested in establishing a players' union. Murphy's effort, the American Baseball Guild, did not succeed, but club owners responded to its unsettling potential with a package of benefits including a higher minimum salary, meal money during spring training (called "Murphy money"), a pension plan funded from All-Star Game and World Series revenues, and the right to negotiate further through elected players' representatives. When the owners later tried to back away from their commitment to fund the pension plan, players reacted by forming the Major League Baseball Players Association.

Brooklyn's decision to integrate its roster, coupled with Rickey's astute player personnel moves, pushed the Dodgers to the top of the National League. Before Robinson's arrival, Brooklyn had won the pennant in 1941, its first since 1920, and finished second in 1942, even while winning 104 games. These clubs, though, were patchwork aggregates of youngsters seasoned by too many veterans to sustain a quest for excellence. By 1947, when the Dodgers returned to first place, the roster was full of young players on the rise. Brooklyn won the pennant again in 1949, 1952, 1953, 1955, and 1956. Robinson and shortstop Pee Wee Reese supplied leadership, centerfielder Duke Snider hit 40 or more home runs for five seasons in a row, and catcher Roy Campanella won three Most Valuable Player awards. These Dodgers became known as the "Boys of Summer," an affectionate nickname that did not ignore the fact that Brooklyn managed to win only one World Series in 1955. The Yankees beat the Dodgers in 1941, 1947, 1949, 1952, 1953, and 1956. Mickey Mantle, who replaced DiMaggio in centerfield, led the Yankees' offense. Catcher Yogi Berra won three Most Valuable Player awards of his own, lefthander Whitey Ford led a fine pitching staff, and Stengel managed his bench shrewdly. New York's third team, the Giants, rebounded from more than a decade of mediocrity when Willie Mays arrived to play centerfield in 1951. He won the National League Rookie of the Year award, took the Most Valuable Player award in 1954, and was generally regarded at the game's most exciting player. The Giants beat the Dodgers in a 3-game playoff to win the 1951 pennant, but lost the Series to the Yankees. In 1954, the Giants won the pennant again, this time sweeping the Series from the Indians, who had won a record 111 games.

The attendance bubble of the late 1940s burst in the 1950s, belying an oft-expressed opinion that the 1950s were a "golden age." Total attendance began to drop in 1949 and did not reach 20 million again until 1962, when both major leagues had expanded to ten teams. Many clubs drew fewer than a million fans in some seasons, with the Boston Braves recording the lowest attendance of the postwar period, 281,278, in 1952. Historians have ascribed this decline to several factors: population migration away from major league cities to the South and West, the rise of the suburbs, competition from other sports and new recreational opportunities, physical deterioration of the ballparks built four decades earlier, and the growing popularity of television. Baseball was slow to respond to these changes, especially to the growing economic power resident on the West Coast. In the first half of the decade, three major league clubs abandoned their longtime homes, but none of them went to California. The Braves moved to Milwaukee, the Philadelphia Athletics became the Kansas City Athletics, and the St. Louis Browns moved east to Baltimore and adopted an old name, the Orioles. Much more stunning shifts occurred after the 1957 season when the Dodgers abandoned Brooklyn for Los Angeles and the Giants moved to San Francisco. Their departure from New York left the nation's largest city with only one major league team, the Yankees.

On the field, baseball in the 1950s and early 1960s looked like a slow, ponderous game. The offensive upsurge that had begun in the 1920s and started to tail off after 1930 continued on a downward path for quite some time. Batting averages, doubles, triples, and stolen bases fell, while home runs and strikeouts rose. Widespread use of the pitch called the slider made things even worse for batters, as did teams' increasing reliance on relief pitchers. Managers employed a predictable offensive strategy: try to get someone on base and hit a home run. Nearly every roster featured one or more sluggers who were barely adequate in the field and on the base paths. Games got longer, and most pennant races lacked excitement. In the American League, the White Sox finished a disappointing third five years in a row and second twice before breaking through in 1959 to win their first pennant since 1919, but the Yankees remained dominant. They won additional pennants in 1957 and 1958 and then another five straight (1960–1964). In the National League, the Dodgers slipped from the top spot when the "Boys of Summer" got old. The Braves replaced them, finishing second in 1956 and first in 1957 and 1958 before losing a playoff in 1959. Each major league had individual stars, of course. In the American League, Ted Williams won the batting title in 1957 and 1958 while Mickey Mantle led the league in home runs four times, including 1956 when he took the Triple Crown. In the National League, Stan Musial won four batting titles in the 1950s (and seven overall) and was part of a league-wide home run–hitting cadre that included Mays, Snider, Ernie Banks, Gil Hodges, Ted Kluszewski, Eddie Mathews, and others. Warren Spahn won 202 National League games during the 1950s, and Robin Roberts won 199. Early Wynn won 188 games in the American League as he closed in on a career total of 300.

The minors suffered a decline worse than the majors. Forty-three leagues started the 1952 season, but by 1959, there were only twenty-one left. More than three hundred cities and towns lost minor league teams during the decade. Minor league officials felt helpless. They tried to lay the blame on the rise of television, especially after 1951 when major league owners lifted their ban against televising major league games into minor league markets. But that was only one factor among many. Minor league ballparks were deteriorating, pro football was becoming more popular, and the recreational pleasures of suburban life gave people alternatives to attending a minor league game. Baseball tried several schemes to revive the minors, but in the end, contraction proved to be the most viable. The Player Development Plan passed in 1962 used major league funds to guarantee the survival of roughly a hundred minor league clubs. Leagues were regrouped into just three classifications, AAA, AA, and

A, with major league clubs subsidizing player salaries. At the same time, major league clubs sought to control the escalating costs of developing players. Even before every organization had a farm system, several clubs would often bid against one another for the best prospects, paying signing bonuses that exceeded most major league salaries. In 1949, the first "bonus baby" rule tried to rein in this behavior. It dictated that any player receiving a bonus of $6,000 or more could play in the minors for only one season before joining the parent club. In 1952 and again in 1954, the rule was modified, requiring clubs to place bonus babies on the major league roster immediately after signing them and keep them there for two full seasons. Surreptitious disregard for the rule led to its abolition in 1957, but this sent player development costs soaring again. In 1965, owners implemented an annual draft of high school and college players, assigning drafted prospects' rights to one club only, thus clamping down on costs dramatically.

Baseball responded to the advent of television much as it had to radio, with fear and hesitation. Club owners believed that televising home games would cut into attendance and revenue. They were slow to realize that television could help market their product and pay them substantial rights fees. In 1951, the National League playoff and the World Series were telecast nationally, but clubs derived most television revenue in the 1950s from contracts with local stations. National networks competed for the right to broadcast the All-Star Game, the World Series, and selected weekend games packaged for years as the "Game of the Week." For a period of time, these weekend telecasts of regular season games were blacked out in all major league cities, but after a while, these restrictions were loosened. Television monies eventually became a substantial portion of each club's revenues, elevating the value of every franchise and supporting meteoric increases in player salaries and team profits. By 1980, when clubs were each earning nearly $2 million annually from network television contracts, baseball had started playing its most important games at night to boost the size of the television audience. The first World Series game played at night was Game Four in 1971, and the last daytime World Series game was Game Six in 1987.

In the late 1950s, as Branch Rickey hatched an idea to launch a third major league called the Continental League, Congressional hearings considered the sport's antitrust status. In reaction, major league baseball began to expand. Each league, though, acted independently since Chandler's successor as commissioner, former sportswriter and league president Ford Frick, declined to exert much authority over the game as a whole. In 1961, the American League transformed the Washington Senators into the Minnesota Twins while adding a new club in Washington and another in Los Angeles. The National League launched new clubs in New York and Houston in 1962. Established clubs profited from expansion in two ways. Both leagues charged their new owners huge fees just to join, and both used expansion drafts to fill the new teams' rosters, making available odd combinations of older players and untried youngsters at inflated prices. Expansion brought with it some complaints that the quality of play would be watered down, and when each league also lengthened its schedule from 154 games to 162, traditionalists howled that the sanctity of baseball's records would be compromised. This argument came to a head immediately when Roger Maris of the Yankees hit 61 home runs in 1961, one more than Babe Ruth in 1927, but in a longer season. This first round of expansion worked no economic miracles. Attendance remained fairly flat, perhaps because ten-team pennant races proved unattractive to fans whose teams fell far out of first place early each season.

While the Yankees' dynasty came to a halt in 1964, bringing some much-needed competition to the American League, the Dodgers and Cardinals reasserted their primacy in the National League by grabbing all six pennants from 1963 through 1968. During these same years, several clubs moved into new stadiums, financed in large part with public funds and designed to host professional football games and other events in addition to baseball. Quite similar in architecture and dimensions, these round "cookie cutter" parks featured large scoreboards, escalators and other modern amenities, and plenty of parking. The Houston club, originally the Colt .45s and later the Astros, built the world's first indoor baseball stadium to avoid playing games in the Texas climate. Since grass does not grow indoors, the Astrodome required the development of artificial turf, varieties of which were later installed elsewhere, primarily because of its durability. Two clubs that had moved in the 1950s moved again. The Braves gave up on Milwaukee and settled in Atlanta in 1966, and the Athletics left Kansas City for Oakland in 1968.

Baseball's initial stab at expansion was an experiment, a quick reaction to Rickey's challenge that did not come to fruition, but when expansion came again in 1969, there was a larger plan. The American League added clubs in Kansas City and Seattle, while the National League put new clubs in Montreal and San Diego. Moreover, trying to emulate the success of the National Football League, baseball divided each major league into two six-team divisions, East and West, mandating a round of playoffs called the League Championship Series prior to the World Series. The Seattle Pilots lasted only one season before becoming the Milwaukee Brewers, but baseball's path toward further growth was set. The American League grew to fourteen teams in 1977, adding the Seattle Mariners and Toronto Blue Jays. The National League responded by adding the Florida Marlins and Colorado Rockies in 1993. Five years later, the leagues worked together. The Arizona Diamondbacks commenced play in the National League, the Tampa Bay Devil Rays (later the Rays) started in the American League, and the Brewers switched leagues, giving the National League sixteen teams and the American League fourteen. Post-season play also grew in 1994 as each league's two divisions became three. This necessitated still another preliminary round of post-season play, the League Division Series, matching the three division winners plus a "wild card," the second-place team with the best won-lost record.

When Maury Wills of the Los Angeles Dodgers stole 104 bases in 1962, breaking the major league record Ty Cobb set in 1915, baseball appeared poised to end a long period of offensive lethargy. Following this season, though, the Baseball Rules Committee expanded both the top and bottom of the strike zone, a change that handicapped batters. Pitchers had additional advantages. No one regularly checked the height of pitcher's mounds, so groundskeepers tended to build them far taller than the rules allowed. Gloves had gotten larger. New ballparks not only allowed advertising on centerfield walls, impeding hitters' vision, but also had much more foul territory than their predecessors, turning many foul balls into outs. As a result, batting averages continued to fall, dropping to .242 in 1967 and .237 in 1968, the all-time low. In fact, during the twenty-five-year period from 1946 to 1970, the six seasons starting in 1963 recorded the six lowest overall batting averages ever. Individual offensive stars continued to shine, including Mays and the Braves' Henry Aaron, both of whom hit enough home runs to get within range of Ruth's career mark, but pitchers were dominant. Sandy Koufax led the National League in earned run average five straight years (1962–1966), won 25 or more games three times, and pitched four no-hitters, including one perfect game. The Tigers' Denny McLain won 31 games in 1968, called the "Year of the Pitcher," while St. Louis's Bob Gibson, a powerful righthander, finished 1968 with 268 strikeouts, 13 shutouts, 22 wins, 28 complete games, and an earned run average of 1.12. Gibson held opposing hitters to a composite batting average of .184, yet he lost nine times because the Cardinals scored only 17 runs in those 9 games. In 1969, rules makers reacted to this dearth of offense by reducing the size of the strike zone and mandating that pitching mounds be no higher than ten inches.

In 1966, the Major League Baseball Players Association hired its first full-time paid executive director, Marvin Miller, a labor economist who had worked for the United Steelworkers of America. He theorized that the players were employees similar to those in many other businesses, and he guided them through the complexities of federal labor law so that the players were able, over time, to transform what had been a loose association into a disciplined trade union. Initially funded by the proceeds from licensing agreements with Coca-Cola and the Topps baseball card company, the union bargained collectively with the owners for the first time in 1968 and negotiated its first contract. The basic agreement, as it was called, was a revolutionary document in a business that had been governed solely by the owners since 1876. It established the players' right to help formulate baseball policy through future negotiations, improved working conditions, instituted a grievance procedure, and set up two joint study committees, one of which was charged with discussing a possible alternative to the system by which clubs had been reserving players since the 1880s.

The era of division play got off to a stunning start when the New York Mets, an expansion team that had never finished a season with a winning record, won the National League East (100–62), swept the Atlanta Braves in the League Championship Series, and upset the favored Baltimore Orioles in the World Series. The Mets did not repeat as league champions, but the Orioles did, winning the American League East five years out of six and capturing the World Series in 1970. Division play proved popular. With the advent of the four new clubs in 1969, total attendance jumped to more than 27 million and grew steadily thereafter, except for seasons disrupted by labor-management disputes, until the severe economic downturn that began in 2008. Total attendance passed the 50 million mark for the first time in 1987, hit 70 million in 1993, and reached more than 79 million in 2007. The Dodgers became the first club to draw more than 3 million, in 1978, and the Blue Jays became the first to exceed 4 million, in 1991. Still, not every club was perennially successful. The Senators left Washington to become the Texas Rangers after the 1971 season, and the Montreal Expos moved to Washington in 2005, becoming the Nationals. For a period of time starting in the 1990s, due to a commonly voiced assertion that "small market" clubs could not compete economically with "large market" clubs, baseball gave some consideration to contraction, that is, to eliminating one or more clubs, but implemented no plan to do so.

Division play ensured that no club would finish tenth, but this new arrangement did not guarantee competitive balance. During the 1970s, each of the four divisions had one or two clubs that vied for the pennant almost every season. In the National League East, the Pirates won five division titles and two World Series while the Phillies took four straight division championships, plus one more in 1980 when they won the World Series for the first time. The Dodgers won the National League West three times, but the Reds won the division five times, and their most vaunted lineup, the "Big Red Machine," took the World Series in 1975 and 1976. This same pattern was repeated in the American League. Following the Orioles' run, the Yankees won the East three years in a row, added another division title in 1980, and took two straight World Series. In the West, the Oakland A's put together the most substantial streak, five straight division championships, three straight pennants, and three straight World Series championships. Yet they, too, were overcome by the Kansas City Royals, who won the division four years out of five, including 1980. The 1970s were also a decade of great individual achievements by outstanding players. Henry Aaron broke Ruth's career home run record in 1974 and finished his own career in 1976 with 755. Pete Rose tied Willie Keeler's National League mark, hitting safely in 44 consecutive games in 1978, and went on in 1985 to surpass Ty Cobb's record for most hits in a career. Lou Brock broke Maury Wills's record for stolen bases in a season in 1974 and Cobb's record for career stolen bases, finishing with 938. Nolan Ryan pitched seven no-hitters, the first two in 1973 and the last in 1991, and wound up with 5,714 strikeouts, exceeding Walter Johnson's career record by more than 2,200.

The only major rules change during the 1970s was the American League's decision in 1973 to allow the use of a designated hitter, a tenth player permitted to hit for the pitcher throughout the game without forcing the pitcher to be replaced. Introduced to boost offense, the rule had some noticeable effect, and it was copied by every other professional league except the National League, which remained adamantly opposed. The World Series did not incorporate the designated hitter until 1976 when the leagues agreed to begin using it in even-numbered years. This policy changed in 1986 when the DH was authorized in all World Series games played in American League parks. Similarly, starting in 1989, the DH was used in every All-Star Game hosted by an American League club.

Following the 1969 season, the Cardinals traded centerfielder Curt Flood to the Phillies. Flood objected to the trade, but since his contract, like all players' contracts, bound him to one club, he had no freedom to determine for which club he would play. When Commissioner Bowie Kuhn refused Flood's request to be made a free agent, the player filed a lawsuit in federal court challenging baseball's anti-trust exemption and sat out the 1970 season. The district court ruled against him, as did the federal appeals court and the Supreme Court. Nevertheless, Flood's action made other players notice the contradictions in the reserve system, and the Players Association searched for a way to end it. Meanwhile, the union made other gains. The second basic agreement, signed in 1970, raised the minimum salary to $13,500 and extended players' arbitration rights by granting final authority on grievances to an independent arbitrator instead of the commissioner. In the spring of 1972, after the owners rejected to the union's proposal that annual contributions to the pension fund be increased to $500,000, the players voted 663–10 to go on strike at the beginning of the season. The strike lasted thirteen days and caused teams to miss from seven to nine games each. It was settled when the owners agreed to the substance of the players' original demand.

The third basic agreement, concluded in 1973 after the owners locked out the players for seventeen days in spring training, included salary arbitration, an important change, but it made little progress on the players' desire to address the restrictions inherent in the reserve system. Resolution of this question did not occur until two pitchers, Dave McNally and Andy Messersmith, played the entire 1975 season without signing contracts and then filed a grievance declaring that they had become free agents. The players argued that the renewal clause in the contracts they had signed for the 1974 season bound them for one year only. Their clubs responded that the reservation system bound them and all players in perpetuity. Peter Seitz, the independent arbitrator, decided for the two players, and his decision was subsequently upheld in federal court. Thus, how to implement free agency, as it was called, for the rest of the players became the key discussion point as negotiations began for the fourth basic agreement. Owners locked out the players again in spring training, this time also for seventeen days, and the new agreement was finalized in July 1976. It allowed players with six years of major league service to become free agents and participate in an off-season re-entry draft.

Whether clubs losing a player to free agency would receive compensation remained a sticking point. Owners argued that clubs losing a player should receive a player in return, while the union countered that such a procedure would mark the effective end of free agency. During the next negotiation, the clubs also advanced for the first time a proposal for a wage scale for players with six or fewer seasons in the majors. This issue led to an eight-day strike at the end of spring training in 1980 and nearly another strike during the season, but the two sides agreed to continue negotiations, albeit fruitlessly. In the spring of 1981, without a new agreement, owners unilaterally implemented their plan for compensation, and the Players Association voted, 587–1, to go on strike beginning on June 12.

This work stoppage, the most disruptive to that date in the history of American professional sports, lasted fifty days and destroyed the integrity of the 1981 season. When the strike ended on July 31, the new agreement included compensation in a limited form. Clubs losing a player to free agency would receive either a draft choice or a player from a specially created pool. Most owners accepted the settlement reluctantly, but they were glad to salvage what was left of the season. Play resumed on August 9 with the annual All-Star Game, and regular season games began the next day. Owners voted to adopt a plan that split the season into two parts. Each division's first-half winner, the team in first place before the strike, met the second-half winner, in a mini-playoff, best two-of-three, prior to the League Championship Series. This scheme did not stimulate second-half attendance, and it infuriated the two National League clubs that finished with the best overall record in their divisions without winning either half.

For many fans, these incidents of labor-management strife and those to come stripped the romance from the game of baseball. Led by the sporting press, many of whose members expressed little sympathy for or understanding of ballplayers acting as union members, fans consistently sided with management, often complaining that free agency destabilized the game they loved and that players did not deserve the higher salaries their economic freedom conferred upon them. Attendance recovered quickly in the seasons after the 1981 strike, but fans who once felt a certain kinship with players voiced dismay as the average player salary increased dramatically from roughly $25,000 in 1970 to $185,000 ten years later. By 1984, thirty players had signed multi-year contracts making them millionaires, and just six years later, the average salary was more than a million dollars. Abetted by these remarkable increases in salaries and frequent appearances of every team on television, baseball players became celebrities with lifestyles far different from those of the average fan. The game at which they excelled had evolved from sport to business to entertainment. Club executives often explained that they were businessmen, not sportsmen, whose goal was to corner a greater share of the entertainment dollar by attracting casual fans and even people who were not fans to the ballpark. Clubs pushed season ticket sales and augmented the experience of watching a ball game with promotional schemes such as free gift days, incessant music, humorous mascots, and post-game concerts and fireworks. Teams donned colorful uniforms, and some players began to express their individual personalities by growing facial hair and engaging in various behaviors that called attention to themselves. The higher salaries fueling these developments created a psychological barrier between players and fans. Attendance continued to grow, but some fans, especially so-called traditionalists, began to measure baseball time not season by season, but labor dispute by labor dispute.

The basic agreement that ended the 1981 strike expired in December 1984. During negotiations, both sides argued over the fiscal health of the game, presenting wildly dissimilar analyses. Owners once again proposed a cap on wages, called a club payroll plan, as well as changes to the salary arbitration system. Players resisted, demonstrating their usual solidarity, and demanded enhanced contributions to the pension plan as a result of increased television revenues. Talks between the two sides made little progress, and the players went on strike on August 6. The walkout lasted only two days and was settled by the adoption of a five-year agreement substantially in line with the players' bargaining position. The owners dropped the payroll plan and consented to increased payments to the pension plan. The union agreed that players would need three years of service, not two, to be eligible for salary arbitration. Perhaps most importantly, the re-entry draft for free agency was abandoned so that all clubs would be able to bid for six-year free agents. During the life of this agreement, the Players Association filed grievances claiming that clubs had colluded to limit competition for free agents. Arbitrators found for the players three times and required the clubs to pay substantial damages. Nearly simultaneously, owners and players locked horns for the first time over the question of illegal drug use. In 1986, six players, admitted drug users, testified under immunity at the trial of an alleged dealer. Commissioner Peter Ueberroth, former head of the 1984 Olympic Summer Games in Los Angeles, pressed the Players Association unsuccessfully for a drug-testing program.

Negotiations to fashion a new basic agreement began in November 1989 but did not resolve the drug-testing issue. Management advanced a plan to share a fixed percentage of gate receipts and broadcasting revenues with the players coupled with a complex pay-for-performance system during a player's first six years, but the real issue dividing the two sides was the future of salary arbitration. Once again a work stoppage, a spring training lockout that delayed the start of the season, preceded a settlement. Accord on a four-year contract came when the two sides agreed that all players with three years' service plus 17 percent of those with two years' service would be eligible for salary arbitration. Yet, well before expiration of this agreement, both sides gave indications that the next negotiation would also be contentious.

Club owners continued to insist that the business of baseball was precarious, and in January 1994, they proposed a plan for revenue sharing and a salary cap. Players rejected this proposal, and after talks made insufficient progress, the Players Association went on strike on August 12. With an agreement nowhere in sight, Commissioner Bud Selig canceled the remainder of the regular season and the post-season on September 14. Three months later, owners declared a collective bargaining impasse and announced their intention to impose their salary cap proposal unilaterally and, if necessary, to play the 1995 season with so-called replacement players. The Players Association filed an unfair labor practices charge and sought an injunction against the owners' plan. The two sides began talking about a luxury tax on club payrolls above a certain level, and in March 1995, a federal district court judge issued the injunction the union had sought, forcing the owners to let the players play. The season, cut to 144 games, began on April 25 and was played to a successful conclusion, but a new basic agreement was not signed until December 1996. This new contract included revenue sharing, a luxury tax on high team payrolls, and a plan to begin inter-league, regular-season games in 1997. Despite the protracted and difficult negotiations that led to this agreement, the formula it established remained intact into the twenty-first century and brought baseball an extended period of labor-management peace.

In the years between the strikes of 1981 and 1994–1995, every team in the National League and all but three in the American League won at least one division title. In the National League, the Astros, Expos, and San Diego

Padres won their first division titles. The Cardinals won the World Series in 1982 for the first time since 1967, and the Giants, absent from the Series since 1962, returned in 1989 when play was interrupted for ten days because of the Loma Prieta earthquake. The Cubs, without a World Series championship since 1908 or a National League pennant since 1945, won their division twice, in 1984 and 1989, but failed to advance either time. In the American League, the Royals, Brewers, Twins, and Blue Jays played in the World Series for the first time. The Tigers won their first Series since 1968, and Toronto took two in a row in 1992 and 1993. The Cleveland Indians, Texas Rangers, and Seattle Mariners were shut out of post-season play entirely. Among outstanding individual performances, Kansas City's George Brett hit .390 in 1980, the highest batting average since 1941, the Dodgers' Orel Hershiser pitched a record 59 consecutive scoreless innings in 1988, and Cecil Fielder of the Tigers became the first player to hit 50 or more home runs in a season since George Foster in 1977 when he hit 51 in 1990. Steve Garvey played in 1,207 consecutive games, a National League record, and Rickey Henderson passed Lou Brock for the career mark in stolen bases, eventually finishing with 1,406. In 1981, Dodgers pitcher Fernando Valenzuela became the first rookie to win the Cy Young award, and Milwaukee's Rollie Fingers, who also won the Cy Young, became the first relief pitcher to win the American League's Most Valuable Player award.

Baseball tried to recapture the allegiance of fans soured by the prolonged labor dispute. Some clubs offered discounted tickets and other amenities called fan-friendly, but total attendance recovered slowly, not reaching its 1993 level until 1998. Many clubs, beginning with Baltimore in 1992, opened new ballparks featuring brick construction, quirky outfield dimensions, seats closer to the playing field, and better concessions. The first few of these, called retroparks, proved to be attractions by themselves and helped their clubs put together several consecutive seasons of sellouts or near sellouts. The Orioles played an additional part in baseball history when Cal Ripken, Jr., played in his 2,131st consecutive game on September 6, 1995, breaking Lou Gehrig's record. In 1991, the Atlanta Braves, a club that had loitered at the bottom of the National League West for several seasons, began an unprecedented streak of excellence. They qualified for post-season play in fourteen straight seasons (not counting 1995) and won the World Series in 1995, thereby becoming the first club to win the Series representing three cities (Boston, Milwaukee, and Atlanta). The late 1990s also marked the resurgence of the Yankees to a level of success they had not enjoyed for several decades. Starting in 1995, New York finished first in the American League East ten years out of twelve and made the post-season thirteen seasons in a row, winning the World Series in 1996, 1998, 1999, and 2000. Fans complained that the Yankees' achievements were inextricably tied to the club's large revenue base, allowing it to outbid rivals for free agents while absorbing the luxury tax assessments mandated by the basic agreement.

Attendance rose from 63 million in 1997 to over 70 million in 1998 in some measure because fans, old and new, flocked to ballparks to watch Mark McGwire of the Cardinals and Sammy Sosa of the Cubs engage in an epic contest to break Roger Maris's single-season home run record. Their competition, won by McGwire, who hit 70 homers to Sosa's 65, helped define a new era of offensive prowess that had begun in 1993 when the cumulative batting average jumped nine points, runs per game rose significantly, and five players hit 40 or more home runs for the first time since 1969. This was just the beginning. Prior to the strike of 1994–1995, only two players had hit 50 or more home runs in a season since the start of division play. Yet in the eight seasons beginning in 1995, ten players reached the 50-homer plateau eighteen times. Observers of the game advanced several reasons for this explosion, including changes in the way baseballs were being manufactured, dilution of pitching talent after the expansions of 1993 and 1998, new ballparks with more intimate dimensions, lighter bats, a smaller strike zone, and improved physical conditioning. What caused the most controversy, though, and became a source of great problems for the baseball business was the unavoidable suspicion that offensive performances were being boosted by players' use of anabolic steroids and other performance-enhancing drugs.

Sosa followed his 1998 feat by hitting 63 home runs in 1999 and 64 in 2001, yet in none of these three seasons did he lead the National League. He was overshadowed first by McGwire and then by the Giants' Barry Bonds, who put together baseball's greatest offensive season in 2001. Bonds batted .328, drove in 137 runs, led the league with 73 home runs and an on-base percentage of .515, and set major league records for slugging percentage (.863) and walks (177). Apparent changes in his physical appearance plus allegations by two former players that steroid usage was rampant in baseball led labor and management to approve random testing for all players during the 2003 season, but not the off-season, with testing to continue for the next two seasons if five percent tested positive. This tentative response to what some saw as a severe problem drew criticism from many quarters, including the World Anti-Doping Agency, the organization responsible for testing Olympic athletes. After a federal grand jury took testimony from several players and brought indictments against personnel from a laboratory alleged to have supplied steroids to athletes, baseball reacted again, announcing in January 2005 year-round testing with suspensions for those who tested positive. Several congressional committees held hearings on the testing program, and in November 2005, the union agreed with Commissioner Bud Selig's proposal to increase the penalties for testing positive and to begin testing for amphetamines. In an attempt to put the sport's drug problems behind it, the commissioner appointed former U.S. Senator George Mitchell to conduct a full investigation of baseball's past drug usage. Mitchell released his report in December 2007, a month after a grand jury indicted Bonds for perjury and obstruction of justice, but no one was quite sure how to deal with Mitchell's conclusions. Even as the commissioner expressed his hope that baseball's "steroid era" was over, doubt about the game's cleanliness remained, and additional allegations called into question the Hall of Fame credentials of several prominent players. Over time the Joint Drug Prevention and Treatment Program expanded the list of banned substances, adding a test for human growth hormone in January 2013. The penalty for a first failed test was an 80-game suspension followed by a 162-game suspension for a second offense and a lifetime ban for a third.

Baseball in the twenty-first century remained a game with a competitive balance between offense and defense that continued to please millions of fans on a daily basis. Once content to be identified as the National Pastime, modern baseball sought a global audience not only by attracting players from a growing number of nations, but also through the World Baseball Classic, a sixteen-team, international tournament played initially in the spring of 2006 and again in 2009. Talk of reducing the number of major league teams, a matter taken to an owners' vote in 2001 but not enacted, subsided, and the game's economics stabilized. Labor and management conducted negotiations quietly and reached collective bargaining agreements without rancor or disruptions in play. Some clubs still behaved as if they did not generate sufficient revenues to be competitive, but in the early years of the century, an array of different teams qualified for the post-season, and two clubs, the Red Sox and the White Sox, won World Series championships after having not done so for decades. In 2012, each league added a second wild-card team to post-season play, requiring the two wild cards to play an elimination game to advance to a division series. The following year, the Houston Astros moved from the National League Central to the American League West. This gave each league three five-team divisions and mandated at least one interleague game every day. Moreover, after a period of uncertainty, baseball came to terms with the implications of the digital age. Fans could still attend games in person, listen to them on the radio, and watch them on television, both over-the-air and cable; but they could also play fantasy baseball and follow the sport in many different ways on the Internet. Modern technology made its way into the ballpark, too, first by the introduction of certain tools to help evaluate umpires' performances and then, in 2008, by the approval of video review of certain calls by umpires in key situations. Baseball was a far cry from the folk games from which it evolved, but it still occupied a significant niche in the American cultural scene.

Suggested Readings

Serious readers of baseball history should begin with the three books written by Harold and Dorothy Seymour Mills, *Baseball: The Early Years* (1960), *Baseball: The Golden Age* (1971), and *Baseball: The People's Game* (1990). Students of the early game need to consult such books as David Block, *Baseball Before We Knew It: A Search for the Roots of the Game* (2005), Monica Nucciarone, *Alexander Cartwright: The Life Behind the Legend* (2009), and John Thorn, *Baseball in the Garden of Eden: The Secret History of the Early Game* (2011), as well as the classic Robert Henderson, *Ball, Bat and Bishop: The Origins of Ball Games* (1947). Readers should also consult the official baseball rules at http://mlb.mlb.com/mlb/official_info/official_rules/foreword.jsp

On the nineteenth century, see such works as Edward Achorn, *Fifty-nine in '84: Old Hoss Radbourn, Barehanded Baseball, and the Greatest Season a Pitcher Ever Had* (2010), Stephen D. Guschov, *The Red Stockings of Cincinnati: Base Ball's First All-Professional Team and Its Historic 1869 and 1870 Seasons* (1998), Peter Levine, *A.G. Spalding and the Rise of Baseball: The Promise of American Sport* (1985), Tom Melville, *Early Baseball and the Rise of the National League* (2001), and David Nemec, *The Beer and Whisky League: The Illustrated History of the American Association—Baseball's Renegade Major League* (2004).

The game in the first half of the twentieth century is covered well in such books as Charles C. Alexander, *Breaking the Slump: Baseball in the Depression Era* (2002), Lawrence D. Hogan and Jules Tygiel, *Shades of Glory: The Negro Leagues and the Story of African-American Baseball* (2006), Daniel R. Levitt, *The Battle That Forged Modern Baseball: The Federal League Challenge and Its Legacy* (2012), Eugene Murdock, *Ban Johnson: Czar of Baseball* (1982), Daniel A. Nathan, *Saying It's So: A Cultural History of the Black Sox Scandal* (2002), and David Pietrusza, *Judge and Jury: The Life and Times of Judge Kenesaw Mountain Landis* (2001).

For the second half of the twentieth century see Richard Crepeau, *America's Diamond Mind, 1919–1941* (1980), Mark Fainaru-Wada and Lance Williams, *Game of Shadows: Barry Bonds, BALCO, and the Steroids Scandal That Rocked Professional Sports* (2006), Charles P. Korr, *The End of Baseball As We Knew It: The Players Union, 1960–1981* (2002), William Marshall, *Baseball's Pivotal Era, 1945–1951* (1999), Jules Tygiel, *Baseball's Great Experiment: Jackie Robinson and His Legacy* (1983), and James R. Walker and Robert V. Bellamy, Jr., *Center Field Shot: A History of Baseball on Television* (2008).

Some ballparks have their own histories. See, for example, Bruce Kuklick, *To Every Thing a Season: Shibe Park and Urban Philadelphia, 1909–1976* (1991), Peter Richmond, *Ballpark: Camden Yards and the Building of an American Dream* (1993), and Glenn Stout, *Fenway 1912: The Birth of a Ballpark, a Championship Season, and Fenway's Remarkable First Year* (2011).

Baseball's many collective biographies trace their roots to Lawrence Ritter, *The Glory of Their Times: The Story of the Early Years of Baseball Told by the Men Who Played It* (1966). Among the massive number of individual biographies, these are a few that stand out: the quartet of works by Charles C. Alexander, *Ty Cobb* (1984), *John McGraw* (1988), *Rogers Hornsby: A Biography* (1995), and *Spoke: A Biography of Tris Speaker* (2007), Robert Creamer, *Babe: The Legend Comes to Life* (1974), and David Zang, *Fleet Walker's Divided Heart: The Life of Baseball's First Black Major Leaguer* (1995).

2

Economics

DAVID GEORGE SURDAM

Economists view the world of professional sports through the lens of scarcity. To a degree, fans do, too. Their favorite team never has enough talent. Ticket prices stretch their budgets too tight. The economists' fascination, even obsession, with scarcity makes them unpopular guests at cocktail parties and other soirees, but they do provide unique insights into human behavior.

Introduction

Many students consider economics courses difficult. Some dislike the equations and graphs, but I suspect the main impediment is the reliance upon abstract thinking. To learn and to practice economics requires an imagination. "What if?" is a pertinent question for people studying economics.

I tell my students that economics is not rocket science. I confidently predict that the average college student can acquire economic thinking. There are two reasons for my confidence. First, almost everyone is already practicing economic thinking before they ever grace my classroom. Second, everyone has an incentive to act according to basic economic principles.

Let me explain myself. Economics deals with scarcity. We live in a world of scarcity. Sports owners face scarcity, whether of talented players, stadium capacity, wealth, and knowledge. You face scarcity on a daily basis. There is never enough money, time, energy, ability, or knowledge to accomplish or to attain everything you want. Indeed, the only thing not in scarce supply is scarcity itself.[1]

Because of scarcity, any time you use a resource for one purpose, you are giving up the opportunity to use that resource for another purpose. Instead of spending $25,000,000 for the hard-hitting outfielder, a team owner might have purchased a slick-fielding shortstop and a dependable catcher. Since a resource can be used for different purposes, any particular use of the resource incurs an opportunity cost. The opportunity cost is the best foregone alternative.

The concept of opportunity cost is crucial for understanding economics. I am certain that all of my readers have at least an intuitive sense of opportunity cost. Think back to your childhood, when someone gave you ten dimes to spend in a candy store. So many candies, so few dimes. If you bought the licorice, you had fewer dimes left to purchase peppermint. I suspect all of you can recall a time when your lack of purchasing power was a frustrating experience. You had an incentive to learn how to allocate your limited resources judiciously. Therefore, all of my readers have behaved in an economic fashion, before they started an economics class.

In order to practice sound economic thinking, you must train yourself to identify the relevant opportunity costs and benefits. If you do so, your economic thinking will be superior to that of many of the talking heads parading as economists in the media. Many people call themselves economists, and it's not against the law to impersonate one.

Economists study professional sports because the industry offers several opportunities for economists. The abundance of player statistics helps economists determine player productivity. In many other fields, measuring productivity is difficult, and researchers often resort to less-than-optimal proxies (years of education is a good example of a crude measure of productivity). While most owners of professional sports teams hesitate to divulge information regarding franchise values, revenues, profits, and player salaries, enough information has seeped through their self-imposed embargo to enable economists to make educated guesses.

Economists employ examples from professional sports to illustrate economic concepts ranging from compensation of labor to the behavior of cartels. Some economists study the effect of a professional sports team on the local economy, while others study competitive balance and movement of players between teams. Some economists even offer courses in "sports economics." The reader should not think of such courses as "fluff" for athletes or for students looking for an easy course; many of the concepts are abstract and require considerable thought.

Some Basic Economic Principles

Those of my readers who have already taken a course in economics may skip this section, although there may be some novel applications of economic principles to sports-related situations.

What is economics? An elegant definition of economics is "the science which studies human behavior as a relationship between given ends and scarce means which have alternative uses."[2] We can illustrate this definition easily enough. Suppose you are in class, eyeing the clock as it nears noon. You dash out the door to grab some lunch. You have $8 to spend (your scarce resource). There are several places to dine (the alternative uses of your scarce resource). Your "given ends" in this situation is to get the best meal. I note that "best meal" means various things to different people. Some people stress nutrition, while others may emphasize taste. Your "given ends" are a mixture of objective and subjective aspects.

Economists frequently construct models to explain how economic actors behave. An economic model is a pared depiction of reality. Economists make assumptions that focus on the most salient points in order to make the model usable. People ridicule economists for their "unrealistic" assumptions, but this ridicule is misplaced. The icons posted on bathroom doors are a great example of a model. There are triangular figures for women and rectangular ones for men. No one has friends who resemble these icons, but the icons have proved useful. Even the dullest or most inebriated person can determine which door to enter so as not to experience social embarrassment. Economists trade simplicity for ease of use in their models. Making more realistic figures or adding more complexity often results in less ease of use.

As I assume (one of economists' favorite words, along with "rational," "equilibrium," "margin," and "efficient") that my readers have been spending money for decades, I can deduce that all of you are pretty good shoppers. There are competing tactics in allocating your scarce resources to best achieve your given ends. One is to buy items randomly. Of course, this approach is unlikely to provide much satisfaction. Another approach is to follow social norms. "Everyone eats at Joe's." You might, however, be a rare person who doesn't like Joe's food. Another, more fruitful, approach is to weigh the cost of the commodity versus your perceived benefit. "I like hamburgers more than pizza, but hamburgers cost $6.50 each versus two slices of pizza for $5."

Economists use the term *marginal* in analyzing situations. *Marginal* means the change in a variable with respect to a change in another variable. If you study calculus for that extra hour, what is the effect on your calculus grade? The change in your test score would be the marginal gain from studying one additional hour. What is the marginal (incremental) gain to your satisfaction due to buying the hamburger?

The marginal cost is the price you pay for an additional unit of consumption (in this case, the price of a hamburger). When the marginal benefit of consuming something outweighs its marginal cost, buying an additional unit is a good idea. When the marginal cost of consuming something outweighs its marginal benefit, you should not buy the additional unit. To optimize, you should keep buying or using something until *the marginal benefit equals the marginal cost.* The previous sentence is the fundamental decision-making rule.

Before I discuss the determination of prices in the market, let me discuss some more aspects of costs. The cost of your attending a baseball game includes not only the prices of the ticket, parking, and concessions but also your time spent at the ballpark. Instead of watching the game, you could be working and earning income. Even if you are in a salaried position, an additional hour of work may generate some marginal income in the form of a higher probability of getting a bonus. The foregone hourly earnings (perhaps adjusted by income taxes) is a good proxy for the time cost of attending a ball game. There are two other general costs to consider. There is a safety cost to attending the ball game. Sometimes people are injured at the ballpark; perhaps a foul ball conks them on the head. An afternoon spent golfing entails the risk of being hit by an errant golf ball or being injured by overturning a golf cart. Finally, there is what I call a prestige cost (or benefit). There's a prestige cost to being caught buying a designer piece of clothing at a discount warehouse rather than a trendy boutique. There could be a prestige cost of sitting in the bleachers rather than reserved seating. Conversely, there is a prestige benefit to attending a game in person instead of watching it on television. Perhaps that's why people keep their ticket stubs for memorable games to prove that they were there.

If an owner can make getting to the ballpark more convenient, install simple safety devices as nets to catch foul balls, or improve the social acceptability of attending a ball game, she will reduce the overall cost of being at the ballpark.

We turn to the determination of prices. In our economy, most markets are free to operate according to the dictates of supply and demand. The forces of supply and demand determine prices. The market works impersonally. In the standard situation, demand consists of millions of consumers voting with their scarce dollars on which commodities and services to buy. Consumers are trying to spend their dollars on the thousands of available commodities in such a way to maximize or to optimize their satisfaction. Supply consists of producers deploying their scarce resources (such as labor, capital, raw materials, time, and knowledge) among various uses to maximize their well being, usually measured in terms of profit. Consumers and producers are both trying to optimize—to do the best they can—given their available resources.

Because the market price of a commodity is a cost to the consumer, the higher the price, the smaller quantity consumers will want to buy, all other things held constant. The demand for a commodity has an inverse or teeter-totter aspect. When price increases, quantity demanded decreases; when price decreases, quantity demanded increases.

As the market price of a commodity is a reward to the producer, the higher the price, the more producers will want to supply, all other things held constant. The supply of a commodity has a positive aspect. When price increases, quantity supplied increases; when price decreases, quantity supplied decreases.

In both cases, scarcity drives consumers' and producers' behavior. The market-clearing price for a commodity is the price at which the quantity supplied equals the quantity demanded. In other words, the market clears in the sense that there are no unwanted surpluses or a shortage reflected by consumers who were willing to pay the price but who leave empty-handed due to a shortage. Because the market clears, people do not have to wait in line to get the commodity, and producers do not have to expend resources in storing unwanted inventory. The market-clearing price also has the virtue of being efficient in the sense that all of the mutually beneficial transactions have been made.

The market for tickets to championship games rarely clears. The presence of long lines of customers willing to pay the official price but being unable to get a ticket attests to the owner's setting a price below the market-clearing price. The low price gives rise to that colorful and slightly disreputable character, the ticket arbitrageur. The ticket arbitrageur believes the owner sets too low a price and buys a group of tickets, intending to resell them at a higher price. Sometimes the arbitrageur guesses incorrectly and takes a loss. Why owners don't charge a market-clearing price for championship games is an interesting question.

The reader will recall the phrase "all other things held constant." Underlying the relationship between price and quantity demanded or supplied are several factors. The demand facing an owner of a professional ball club is dependent not solely upon the ticket prices but also on rival forms of entertainment (reflected by the prices of these alternative venues), consumers' incomes, taxes and subsidies, the number of potential consumers, amenities at the stadium, quality of the team, and consumers' preferences. The supply of a commodity is not solely dependent upon its price. Some events that will affect the supply include prices of labor and capital, technology used in producing the commodity, other uses for the resources invested in the team, and taxes and subsidies. An example of "other uses for the resources" occurred during the late 1940s, when arena owners staged hockey games during the winter. As there were many open dates, these owners decided to launch a professional basketball league (the Basketball Association of America). If pro basketball had become more popular than hockey, the arena owners could have opted to reduce the number of hockey games while increasing the supply of basketball games.

Events that make the demand for a commodity increase will cause the market-clearing price to increase and the quantity to rise, while events that make the demand for a commodity decrease will cause the market-clearing price to decrease and the quantity to fall.

Events that make the supply of a commodity increase will cause the market-clearing price to decrease and the quantity to rise, while events that make the supply for a commodity decrease will make the price increase and the quantity fall.

Here are some examples. If an owner improves her team, more fans will want to attend the games; the demand for her team increases and the price (and number of tickets) will increase. If, instead, the owner pulls a "Florida Marlin" and sells most of her best players, then the fans will anticipate a poorer-quality team and will seek other entertainment. The demand for her team will fall, and the price (and the number of tickets) will fall. Since the owner is likely to have price-setting power over the ticket prices because potential owners cannot place a team in that city, she may opt to leave the ticket prices unchanged. In the case of an increase in demand, the stable ticket price will result in an even larger increase in the number of tickets sold. In the case of a decrease in demand, the stable ticket price will result in an even larger decrease in the number of tickets sold.

Taxes and subsidies affect the supply of demand for Major League Baseball games. When Congress began tinkering with corporate tax laws during the 1950s, baseball owners became nervous. The New York Yankees, for instance, sold a large number of season tickets to corporations. Because of the very high marginal tax rates on corporate profit—for every additional dollar of profit, the federal government took a large percentage of it—corporations received a significant tax deduction by buying tickets to baseball games with which to entertain clients. Owners feared that a more stringent regulation would erode corporations' willingness to purchase such tickets. Suppose corporations faced a 60 percent tax on every dollar of profit. Buying a season ticket for $200 meant that the company had $200 less profit to report, saving them $120 in tax liability. In a sense, the corporation got a 60 percent subsidy on baseball tickets. If the corporate tax rate decreased, the attractiveness of baseball tickets would have decreased, too. The demand for tickets would have fallen and so would have the quantity purchased.

Because owners of professional sports teams have discretion over the price they set, unlike producers in more competitive industries, they have to think about what price to set. If we assume owners are out to maximize profits, then they must weigh the effects on revenue and costs. Before we consider profit, let us examine revenue.

Suppose you are a sales manager, and your boss calls you into her office.

"Raise sales revenue or you're fired!" (Your boss has been watching that inane Donald Trump television show, *The Apprentice*.) You have two choices: raise or lower the price. If you lower the price, people will buy more of your product. You know that if you raise the price, people will buy less of your product. Total revenue is the price of the product multiplied by the number of units you sell. Let us first consider a decrease in the price. The price goes down, while the quantity demanded goes up. The key is whether the quantity demanded goes up more than the price goes down. Think about a grocery store. When they put something on sale, they are hoping for a large customer response; in other words, they are hoping to attract a crowd of shoppers, whereby the increased number of buyers more than offsets the decrease in price. In fact, the grocery store will encourage this outcome by proclaiming in advertisements that items are on sale: "Crazy Harry's cutting prices!" A sales manager hopes for a large consumer response to a reduced price. If, instead, you raise the price and get fewer customers, you are hoping not to lose too many customers. If you only lose a few customers, you will increase sales revenue. You are hoping for a limited consumer response. You are unlikely to proclaim your price increase: "Crazy Harry's raising prices!" (In this case, the adjective is probably accurate.) The question is which effect is greater.

Economists characterize the consumers' response as being the price elasticity of demand. The price elasticity of demand can be elastic, inelastic, or unitary elastic. If customers are sensitive to changes in the price, then the price elasticity of demand is elastic. In the case of the price cut, you are hoping that demand is elastic, as the significantly greater number of units sold more than offsets the price decrease, so your sales revenue will rise and you will keep your job. If customers are not very sensitive to changes in the price, then the price elasticity of demand is inelastic. If you raise your price, you are hoping that the price elasticity of demand is inelastic. You'll lose few customers and your sales revenue will increase. If the price elasticity of demand is unitary elastic, the proportional change in the price is exactly offset by a similar proportional change in the quantity demanded. Your sales revenue will not change, and, in fact, your sales revenue is maximized when the price elasticity of demand is unitary elastic. In many situations, the price elasticity of demand is elastic for "high" prices, as substitute commodities become more attractive. As the price falls, the price elasticity of demand falls (in absolute value) to a point of unitary elasticity and then into inelastic demand.

There are two extreme types of price elasticity of interest. If consumers are completely insensitive to price, they will buy the same quantity regardless of the price. In this case, they are exhibiting perfectly inelastic demand. Due to scarcity, though, no consumer can be completely indifferent to prices. Even a drug addict will have to reduce consumption as increases in the price eventually exhaust his income. Although no commodity is likely to have perfectly inelastic demand, some items have fairly inelastic demand. People with diabetes are usually somewhat insensitive to changes in the price of insulin. Most major medical procedures face inelastic demand. If a hospital had a "blue-light special" on appendectomies, most people would ignore it; appendectomies are not something that people will stock up on when the price is low. If consumers are completely sensitive to changes in price, then they have perfectly elastic demand. If the price of such a commodity rises above the existing price, consumers will switch to some other commodity.

The two key factors affecting the price elasticity of demand include the availability of close substitutes and income effects. Coca-Cola and Pepsi-Cola are very close substitutes, although most readers probably have a preference between them. In blindfold taste tests, though, most people cannot distinguish between them. If the two colas were perceived as being identical, then they would be perfect substitutes for each other and the price elasticity of demand would be perfectly elastic. In this case, the producers would have no discretion over price; they would take the market price as given, and they would be price takers. Being a price taker is not a very desirable state of the world, so companies such as Coca-Cola and Pepsi-Cola work very hard to get consumers to believe there is a (positive) difference between their product and rival products. You can now understand why insulin has a relatively inelastic demand, since there are few suitable substitutes for it. If you are suffering from appendicitis, there are few suitable substitutes for an appendectomy. Appendectomies face inelastic demand.

An interesting question arises: Are two Major League Baseball teams sharing a city close substitutes for each other? In Chicago, the very question of whether Cubs and White Sox games are substitutes is anathema. A White Sox fan figures a good day is when the Sox win and the Cubs lose, but not all fans are so rabid; the teams are undoubtedly substitutes. They are unlikely to be perfect substitutes, as they play in different parts of the city and feature different talent. In the past, the two teams shared a stadium; presumably this might render them closer substitutes for each other (Yankee Stadium and the old Polo Grounds were just a river's width apart). A related issue deals with fan loyalty. When the Boston Braves, Philadelphia Athletics, St. Louis Browns, New York Giants, and Brooklyn Dodgers relocated, did the remaining team capture most of the disaffected fans?

Commodities are affected by changes in consumers' incomes. As their incomes rise, consumers buy more of some items and less of others. Normal goods are goods whose consumption varies positively with income, while inferior goods are goods whose consumption varies inversely with income. When baseball fans' incomes rise, they often migrate from bleacher and general admission seats to reserved or box seats; when baseball fans' incomes fall, they move to bleacher and general admission seats and away from reserved and box seats. Luxury goods are commodities whose consumption increases proportionally faster than income. In other words, if you got a 10 percent raise at work and increased your consumption of box seats by 15 percent, then box seats are luxury goods for you. If the consumption of a commodity increases but less rapidly than the proportional change in income, the commodity is a necessity. All things equal, luxury goods tend to have a greater price elasticity of demand than necessities, and both tend to have greater price elasticities of demand than inferior goods.

Economists usually assume that businesspeople are keenly interested in maximizing profits. When economists think about profit, they think in terms of economic profits: revenue minus economic (opportunity) costs. Economic and accounting profits differ. Accounting costs are incurred, historical costs. An owner of a team incurs some opportunity costs with respect to his team that do not show up in the ledgers. If he paid millions of dollars for the franchise, those millions could have been invested in some alternative investment. The owner is giving up the opportunity to earn interest on bonds, dividends and capital gains on stocks, and so on. If the owner takes time away from his other business endeavors to operate his team, then he is incurring an opportunity cost for his time. Because of competition, businesspeople in most industries face the prospect of earning zero economic profits in the long run. You may think this is a pessimistic statement, but you need not shed tears for them. Earning zero economic profits simply means that you are doing as well in your current endeavor as you would in your best foregone alternative. Calculating economic profits are crucial for making good decisions; ascertaining accounting profits are important for satisfying Uncle Sam's IRS.

While owning a professional sports team complicates defining an owner's goal, as the satisfaction from winning a championship undoubtedly is a strong second-place and perhaps even paramount goal, owners must pay attention to profitability. Too much exuberance in pursuing a championship may result in unsustainable losses. Such baseball owners as Connie Mack, Charles Comiskey, and Clark Griffith had few assets outside of baseball. While they liked to win, their limited capital forced them to pay more attention to profits and losses than their better-endowed peers.

How does an owner choose a price that will maximize profits? With regard to the price elasticity of demand, an owner maximizes profits by setting a price in the elastic region of demand. If an owner set the price in the inelastic region of demand, he could improve his profits by raising price. First, by raising price, his revenue would increase. Second, by raising price, he would sell fewer units. Producing fewer units typically means that costs are lower than producing more units. By increasing the price, the owner simultaneously increases revenue while decreasing cost. Things don't get much better than that. The owner should raise his price into the region of elastic demand. Although the owner maximizes his revenue when the price elasticity of demand is unitary, the presence of costs induces him to set a price in the region of elastic demand (readers who have taken a course in economics will recognize the principle that marginal revenue equals marginal cost). Owners should, therefore, price their tickets in the region of elastic demand, although there is a caveat. If the owner also sells related goods such as concessions and parking, it may be profitable to reduce the price into the inelastic region of demand. A movie theater owner faces a similar decision. If all she sold were tickets, then she'd price them in the elastic region of demand. If she also sells popcorn and sodas, then she might be better off dropping the price into the inelastic region of demand in order to induce a larger crowd of concessions-loving fans.

I now turn to voluntary trade, where no one coerces either party to make the transaction. Voluntary trade benefits both the producer and the consumer (unless someone makes a mistake); voluntary trade is mutually beneficial. If you pay $50 to attend a Major League Baseball game, you prefer watching the game to the $50. You are better off attending the game than keeping the $50. The Major League Baseball team owner prefers the $50 to the empty seat. In a sense, consumers are better off when they buy things. By "better off" I mean in both objective and subjective ways. The dollar amount a consumer is better off after buying so many units at a given price is called consumer surplus. The dollar amount a producer is better off after selling so many units at a given price is called producer surplus. Most students have little difficulty understanding producer surplus, as it is closely related to profits. The idea of consumer surplus is less obvious. In any event, voluntary trade is a positive-sum game; both parties are better off. This is a key point. Many people think that trade is a zero-sum game, whereby what one person gains is a direct loss to the other person.[3] The neat thing about the market-clearing price is that it maximizes the *combined* consumer and producer surplus. Economists call this an economically efficient outcome. Another way to think about economic efficiency is that the market has reached a point where no one can be made better off without making someone worse off; all of the gains from trade have been exhausted. Anything that makes the market deviate from the market-clearing price is probably going to be inefficient.[4]

Markets are not always economically efficient. If producers have price-setting power (monopoly power), they will not set the market-clearing price. While they are better off when charging a higher price than the market-clearing price, they are foregoing potentially mutually beneficial trades. Therefore, monopolists that sell output at a single price to all customers are inefficient.

This aspect is the key reason why economists dislike monopolies. A second reason for market inefficiency is if there are externalities. An externality is a third-party effect from a transaction, whereby the third party is not involved in the transaction but is affected by it. If you buy meat from a slaughterhouse and the slaughterhouse dumps the waste into the river, thereby fouling the beach of a downstream resort, the resort owners suffers an external cost. If you open a boys' and girls' club in a disadvantaged neighborhood, businesses near your club may experience an external benefit because of your club. If there are externalities, the market may not be efficient, although economist Ronald Coase demonstrated how the market might resolve externalities. He won a Nobel Prize for his insight. His theorem, which I'll discuss in greater detail later, has application to the world of sports.

If you are a monopolist (and who wouldn't want to be), you may not be satisfied with your economic profits that are above normal profits. Like the small child on her birthday, who having unwrapped all her presents, says, "Is this all?" a monopolist may ask, "Is this the most profit I can make?" The quick answer is "No!" By setting different prices for different consumers based on their differing demands for a product, a monopolist can reap more profit and producer surplus than by setting a single price. There are some challenges before a monopolist can practice what economists label "price discrimination." First, the monopolist must have price-setting power in the market. Second, the monopolist must face consumers with different price elasticities of demand for his product. Third, the monopolist must be able to easily distinguish who has the greatest willingness (least elastic demand) to pay and who has the least willingness (most elastic demand) to pay. This is not always obvious. Finally, the monopolist must be able to prevent resale of his product.

Sports teams have long charged different prices for seats. Part of the differential may be due to cost considerations. It costs the owner more to provide a luxury box seat than a bleacher seat, but most of the differential is due to different willingness to pay. Some fans are willing to pay more for a seat with a better view of the action or with the prestige of being "exclusive." The owner can set a higher price for seats at midcourt or behind home plate. In a sense, the seats in a stadium or a ballpark are substitutes for each other. Today's owners have sophisticated ticket pricing schemes. A couple of years ago, the Chicago Cubs website listed fourteen different classes of seats and three different kinds of game. Fans paid more for premium games with the St. Louis Cardinals than for the mundane games with the Washington Nationals.

Economists love sports for both personal and professional reasons. Applying some economic principles to sports results in, as the cliché goes, "a whole new ball game."

The Dirty Little Secret of Professional Team Sports: Cartels and Collusion

Baseball owners promote and sell competition. The uncertainty surrounding each game and varying effort and performances make baseball different from motion pictures (where each showing is a perfect substitute for the previous day's showing). Off the field, though, baseball owners are implacable foes of competition. Their actions are predictable; they are always striving for less competition: for players, for fan dollars, for taxpayer dollars. To reduce competition, they are willing to trample on players' basic civil liberties; heck, they are willing to trample other owners' civil liberties, if need be. To reduce competition, they are willing to employ tactics against rival leagues that would make even the most ruthless of the robber barons blush. While owners band with their league peers to stamp out competition from outside their cartel, their organization is a hydra. Each owner desires to relegate his fellow league owners to the nether region of the league standings. To prevent such competition from becoming ruinous, owners pass edicts seeking to tame their basic competitive instincts. Of course, such behavior is rarely completely sublimated.

Let me state an unpleasant reality: Professional team sports leagues are cartels. Major League Baseball is the granddaddy of all American sports cartels. In most instances, a cartel is forbidden under the country's antitrust statutes.

Major League Baseball gained an explicit exemption from antitrust legislation when the Supreme Court ruled in 1922 that baseball was not interstate commerce and, therefore, was not subject to antitrust action.[5] Because of the importance of this controversial ruling, it will be discussed in greater detail in another chapter.

Economists are keenly interested in how cartels operate. Since many countries prohibit collusive agreements facilitating cartels, most cartels operate clandestinely. No one writes a book called *How to Build and Maintain a Successful Cartel*. Because Major League Baseball has an explicit immunity from antitrust laws (and the other professional team sports have somewhat more modest immunity), more of its behavior can be scrutinized.

Businesspeople would love to collude to fix prices, thereby creating a cartel. If the members of a cartel can maintain their collusive agreement, they stand to make economic profits by charging higher prices than would occur in a free, competitive market. Cartels face three obstacles. First, members have to decide how to split the economic profits. Since each member desires the largest slice of the pie, reaching an agreement may be difficult. If the members reach an agreement, they face a second obstacle: monitoring and enforcing the agreement. Once there is an agreement, each member has an incentive to cheat. By selling to customers in another member's territory, the cheater can increase his profits. If a member is caught cheating, the cartel's legal options are limited. The offended members cannot go to their local magistrate and say, "This person cheated on our collusive agreement." The magistrate may well be very interested in the story, but not to the desired effect. Collusive agreements are, in general, illegal in the United States. The members would run afoul of the Justice Department antitrust investigators.

Readers who are also aficionados of gangster movies will readily understand the ways that enforcing a cartel agreement can spiral out of control. During Prohibition, various mobs controlled the bootleg alcohol market in large cities. The gangs would meet and assign territories. Of course, once the agreement was reached, each gang had an incentive to cheat on the agreement and poach on another gang's territory. To enforce the agreement or to punish cheaters, a careening car with Tommy-gun-wielding goons served well. Of course, violating the nation's antitrust laws via their collusive agreement was probably the least wicked of the gangsters' sins.

Suppose, though, that cartel members have maintained their agreement. They should be doing handsomely, earning economic profits. As economic profits are rare, if our successful cartel members choose to flaunt their enhanced prosperity, they run the risk of intriguing others. For this reason, a cartel's third obstacle is minimizing the risk that other businesspeople will enter a profitable market, or, as economists put it, preventing entry.

For a bunch of multimillionaires, owners of sports teams are notoriously modest. They don't like to brag about making profits. For many years, baseball owners refused to release even such basic information as attendance. If they were fighting a rival league, such as the Federal League in 1914–15, they might publicize attendance figures. Under these conditions, the attendance figures would likely be inflated, so as to make it appear that the established teams were more popular than the upstarts. Bragging about profits, though, can usually only lead to trouble. First, publicizing profits may excite other wealthy people. Owning a professional sports team can be glamorous, but some potential owners may hesitate to purchase a team, fearing losses. Second, if the public believes owners are doing well, they may not be as willing to ante up tax dollars to pay for new stadiums. Owners have discovered it is best to plead poverty when begging for a new stadium.

Are professional sports teams profitable? Assuming adequate demand for such games, an owner would have to be spectacularly inept to negate the advantages accruing to owners of sports teams. Marvin Miller, the baseball players' labor leader during the 1960s and 1970s, once satirized the owners in his *A Whole Different Game* by penning a "mock advertisement"

Your methods of operation, your business practices—such as the use of blacklists, group boycotts, and conspiracies in restraint of trade, including combinations with foreign associates—are free of legal restraint. The United States Supreme Court has determined that the industry is not subject to the antitrust law of the United States or of any state, *unlike your closest competitors, who are subject to such restraints* [italics in the original]. You are therefore free to utilize what would otherwise be illegal sanctions to enforce your will in controlling the entire skilled labor complement of the industry, to deprive cities and entire areas of your product when you choose to do so, to maintain with your associates a complete monopoly by barring would-be competitors, to fix prices and to allocate divisions of the market.[6]

Miller aptly described the owners' advantages. No wonder so many businesspeople want to own teams. But there are additional advantages. Anyone buying a team after 1945 received a tax break. Thanks to a fortuitous IRS ruling, owners who have just purchased a team can depreciate the value of the player contracts obtained in the purchase. This ability to depreciate player value can save the owners much of the cost of purchasing the team via tax reductions and raises the value of the franchise. Players are not allowed to depreciate themselves, even though their skills deteriorate with age.

Those owners who own other business entities besides their sports team can sometimes switch expenses and profits between their entities to serve their needs. WGN television station carries Cubs games. The parent company of WGN used to own the Cubs. The reader might think the deal was pretty sweet for WGN, since it no longer had to pay for the rights to televise Cubs games. Such thinking neglects the role of opportunity costs; instead of telecasting the games itself, the parent company could have sold the rights to another television station. Therefore, WGN's parent company incurred an opportunity cost of televising Cubs games. For tax or publicity purposes, WGN's parent company could have the station pay a large broadcasting fee. The fee would show up as an expense for WGN and would reduce its tax liability. If, instead, the Cubs were making a good profit, due, in part, to its television revenue, the parent company could have the team charge WGN only a nominal amount of money for broadcasting rights. By doing so, the Cubs' profitability would appear to be reduced (less tax liability) and any argument for public financing of a new stadium or more parking would gain traction. An overly profitable team is a poor candidate for public largesse.

Owners can also reduce profits by paying themselves salaries (of course, they have to pay income taxes on the salaries), or they can put their ne'er-do-well relatives on the payroll instead of giving them cash gifts. An owner putting her wastrel nephew Engelbert on the payroll incurs an expense that reduces her tax liability; giving Engelbert a gift does not help her tax liability.

Although owners frequently plead poverty, there is another check on their claims. Franchise prices reflect current and future profitability. When franchise prices are rising, then prospective owners feel optimistic about the future profitability of a team. These prospective businesspeople and their lawyers and accountants demand access to the financial ledgers of the team they are considering purchasing, so there is less chance of camouflaging profits. Current owners would, of course, have an incentive to privately exaggerate profitability in order to entice prospective owners.[7] In any event, rising franchise values imply that professional sports earn healthy profits, even if the accountants demur.

Members of a sports league cartel divide territories, set minimum ticket prices, determine property rights to players, establish (or not) revenue sharing rules, and set rules on who can be a member of the cartel, whether in terms of being a new buyer of an existing team or joining the league/cartel via a new expansion team. Many of their actions are self serving, at best, and outrageous violations of players' civil liberties at worst.

So far I've painted a dismal picture of professional team owners and their cozy cartels. While cartel members are largely self interested, they do provide some benefits for consumers. By the nature of their product, some overt cooperation is necessary. Unlike owners of other businesses, owners of professional sports teams produce a joint product: It takes two (teams) to tango. While teams could stage intra-squad games, fans largely eschew such efforts as being similar to the sound of one hand clapping. Owners of sports teams, then, have to cooperate by arranging to play games at set times and places. Professional sports leagues set uniform rules. In the early days of football and baseball, there were radically different versions of the game. In baseball, there were the Massachusetts and New York styles.[8] A league settles on one style, rendering moot arguments between its member teams as to the rules. Although Major League Baseball has one large exception to uniformity—the designated hitter rule—National League fans attending an American League game can readily understand what is going on. While some social critics scorn uniformity, in many contexts uniformity is a valuable trait. When you are traveling America's interstate freeway system and get hungry, the known quality of McDonald's is a blessing. Hotel chains in the 1950s began stressing uniform standards. When I watch Alfred Hitchcock's famous movie *Psycho*, I often think that Marion, the unfortunate woman who has a fatal encounter with Norman/his mother, should have looked for a Holiday Inn.

Leagues also centralize and rationalize schedule making. In the pre-league days, a team captain or promoter would have to make arrangements for games, often playing a motley of opponents. The nascent National Football League had such haphazard scheduling that the owners voted on which team was the champion. Having balanced schedules (an equal number of home and road games; an equal number of games against each rival) lent legitimacy for crowning as champions the team that won the most games.[9]

Shed no tears for owners of professional sports teams, for they enjoy advantages denied common business people.

A Jaundiced View of Baseball History: How the Baseball Cartel Worked

Sports league cartels serve to reduce competition between members and competition from outside the league. Sports fans can benefit by viewing the history of Major League Baseball from the perspective of cartel behavior.

Incumbent teams rarely welcomed new teams or leagues. More teams meant increased competition for players, pushing salaries higher. More teams meant greater competition for fans, especially in cities with multiple teams. The diluted demand could depress ticket revenue. Faced with a squeeze upon profits from rising costs and falling revenues, incumbent owners were churlish towards potential new owners. While it would have been too much to ask the incumbents to have gracefully accepted the new teams, it is not outrageous to expect them to have avoided violating antitrust legislation (once passed) regarding restraint of trade.

The Cincinnati Red Stockings team of 1869-70 was the first overtly professional team. Harry Wright, a British immigrant and cricket player, quickly adopted his new land's pastime. He had a flair for organization and recognizing talent. The Red Stockings won three score and ten games in a row (the actual number is in dispute), mostly on the road. The team actually turned a profit, despite the players' salaries and travel expenses.

While Wright demonstrated that a barnstorming team of professionals could be viable, if not wildly successful, other entrepreneurs were willing to take professional baseball a step further. These entrepreneurs believed that a team of professional players could stage many games at a home park throughout the summer and be commercially viable. As time went on, this model meant that significant capital would be needed to build ballparks. Enclosed ballparks precluded people from watching for free, as witness the controversy surrounding Wrigleyville apartment dwellers who can see the Cubs' games from their rooftops. The men providing the capital naturally wanted control of the teams.

The National Association of Professional Baseball Players was a ramshackle affair. Teams paid a $10 fee to join the association. Teams also scheduled games, leading to competition for the best dates. Teams came and went, and there was little continuity. The Boston club, run by Wright, after failing to win the championship in 1871, dominated the next four seasons, possibly accounting for the high rate of attrition among teams. Many of the Boston players had toured with Wright's team in 1869-70.

William Hulbert raided the Boston team for several key players. His Chicago White Stockings were prepared to contend for the championship. There was a problem, though. Hulbert anticipated that the other owners in the National Association would not acquiesce to his raiding and would punish him. He decided to enlist some other owners of western teams to form a new league. The genius of Hulbert's scheme was his list of rules. He wanted to rationalize professional baseball, just as industrialists, such as John D. Rockefeller and Andrew Carnegie, were rationalizing American industry. Hurlbert, living in Chicago, was familiar with the meat packers' attempts to consolidate their industry. His rules for the nascent National League of Professional Baseball Clubs (note the subtle change in the name, reflective of the shifting power from players to owners in the game) included a minimum city population of 75,000 (immediately violated with the inclusion of Hartford), territorial protection (future membership had to be approved by a super majority of owners), centralized scheduling, and a central administration. Territorial protection kept other league members from invading another member's territory. Of course, teams in other leagues could simply ignore another team's territorial protection and poach upon lucrative territories. The rules also stipulated a minimum ticket price of fifty cents. Hulbert and his confederates hid their more ruthless control of baseball behind a facade of reform. Players were not allowed to gamble or to drink; alcohol was not allowed at the ballpark; and games were not scheduled on Sundays. Hulbert brazenly flaunted his vision via the *Chicago Tribune* newspaper. None of his ideas violated any antitrust laws, since there were no such laws until 1890.

While the National League may or may not have had all of the best players and teams in professional baseball in 1876, the league definitely was a pioneering effort. When the Philadelphia and New York teams opted not to make their final western trip in order to save travel costs, the other league owners voted to banish them. The two teams had offered western teams payment to switch home fields but to no avail. While the banishment certainly gave the league president, Morgan Bulkeley, credibility, in retrospect the league undoubtedly erred by not fielding replacement teams in the two cities. By leaving New York and Philadelphia open, the National League was tempting other entrepreneurs to enter.

Despite further turmoil resulting from players and even entire teams being kicked out for gambling, the National League was a more stable entity than the National Association had been. Other entrepreneurs, including owners of banished National League teams, quickly decided to emulate the league's success by fielding their own league. The American Association was the National League's most serious rival during the nineteenth century. The owners comprising this league introduced several innovations: Sunday baseball, beer at the ballpark, and twenty-five-cent admission. St. Louis was an anchor team for the league, and the city's German population scandalized the staid, if not puritanical, Anglo-Saxons with their penchant for having fun on Sunday afternoons, including patronizing beer gardens. The lower admission price infuriated the National League owners, but they did not follow suit.

The owners in the two leagues suffered from escalating salaries due to the increased bidding for players. Eventually, they reached an accommodation under the "National Agreement."[10] Owners learned that peace between them produced prosperity. They were so successful that yet another league, the Union Association, set up shop in 1884. The Union Association proclaimed it would not have a reserve clause, making it attractive to disgruntled players. Of course, readers are entitled to wonder how long these new owners would have maintained this stance. Henry Lucas, owner of the aptly named St. Louis Maroons, had acquired sufficient talent to run away with the league title with a 94–19 record (twenty-one games ahead of the second-place Cincinnati club), which did not help the league's viability. Some of the teams folded midway through the inaugural season. To help stymie the Union Association, the National League induced the American Association to expand to twelve clubs. The National League and American Association owners conspired to destroy Lucas. The National League invited Lucas to join their league, with the stipulation that he had to charge fifty-cents' admission. They also stipulated that he could not sell beer at his ballpark or stage games on Sunday. Since the American Association St. Louis team charged just twenty-five cents and fielded a superior team, this effectively doomed the Maroons. John T. Brush bought the team and moved it to Indianapolis, where it folded a few years later.

After destroying the Union Association, the National League and American Association continued to work under a détente. The two leagues' champions even met in a world series of sorts. All the while, National League owners devoutly desired the demise of the American Association (and the feeling was surely mutual).

Because the two leagues honored each other's player contracts, players suffered reduced leverage in bargaining for salaries, leading to diminished salaries. The Brotherhood of Professional Base Ball Players, an early players' union, was chafing under the owners' plan to set up a salary classification based not only on performance but on off-the-field comportment. In this, the owners were similar to many American titans of industry, who felt their workers would be dissipated without guidance. George Pullman's famous company-housing project required workers to be temperate, among other desirable habits. Henry

Ford employed corporate spies to pry into his workers' behavior. The owners may have consoled themselves that paying players more money would have only further demoralized them. Today's drug testing is an echo of employers' past scrutiny of workers.

Under fellow-player (turned lawyer) John Montgomery Ward's tutelage, the players revolted, and set up the Players' League. The Brotherhood planned to set up a league in which they would be owners. While the players had entrepreneurs backing them with capital, the resulting financial bloodbath killed the revolutionary league and weakened the American Association. (The National League owners helped weaken the rival league by getting it to absorb some marginal franchises.) By 1892, the National League was the sole "major" league, fielding an unwieldy twelve teams. While the 1890s might have been the "Gay Nineties," for the National League, they were anything but. Twelve teams meant that too many teams were out of contention. Only teams in "B cities" won pennants: Brooklyn, Baltimore, and Boston. No one appears to have thought of splitting the league into two divisions.

The league was riven with dissent. By 1899, Andrew Freedman counseled his fellow owners that syndicate ball was the answer. Some owners wanted interlocking ownership, whereby owners had interests in more than one team. Taking this idea to an extreme, a couple of owners pushed for corporate ownership of all the teams. The league would then apportion players, presumably building stronger teams in the biggest cities. The owners of teams in the smaller cities wanted no part of this plan. After some legislative chicanery, including two presidents, the conservatives won out.[11]

While the National League was engaged in a civil war of sorts, the league was threatened by a new entity. Ban Johnson saw an opportunity when the National League shrank to eight teams. There were some viable cities left open, so his American League walked in. Eventually, the American League, desiring a presence in New York City, transferred the Baltimore Orioles to New York. The American League was successful in raiding the National League for players and also featured tighter pennant races for most of the first decade of the twentieth century. The two leagues reached an accommodation, just as the National League had done with the American Association. In a sense, the American League was the best thing to happen to the National League, as the two leagues together were able to withstand the Federal League, the Mexican League, and the Continental League.

The success of the peace between the National League and the American League led to growing profits and owner willingness to invest large sums of capital into more elaborate and permanent ballparks. The older ballparks were largely cheaply constructed of wood and had an unfortunate tendency to burn down. A building wave went through Major League Baseball, as new concrete and steel stadiums became de rigueur, including such venerable ballparks as Fenway Park, Comiskey Stadium, Briggs Stadium, Ebbets Field, and the Polo Grounds. These stadiums conferred an unforeseen advantage on Major League Baseball: they constituted a literal barrier to entry by new teams or rival leagues. Any prospective interloper needed suitable places to stage games. Naturally, the Major League owners refused to lease their stadiums to such newcomers nor should they have been compelled to do so. When the Federal League challenged the established leagues in 1914, these owners had to hastily construct ballparks. Chicago's Wrigley Field is the most lasting physical legacy of the league. While the Federal League owners signed a few major league players, many of these were aging stars. The chief ramification was the inability of the Philadelphia Athletics' owner, Connie Mack, to match Federal League offers to his star pitchers, Chief Bender and Eddie Plank. Mack dispersed his star players from his 1914 pennant-winning team; the Athletics went into a prolonged funk, matched only by the Boston Red Sox' banishment to the league's nether region after owner Harry Frazee stripped the club (including the infamous sale of Babe Ruth).

Although the Federal League caused much distress for the two older leagues, it was unable to compete. The league's owners decided to file an antitrust suit against Major League Baseball, citing restraint of trade. The presiding judge, Kenesaw Mountain Landis, urged the parties to reconcile their differences, while he delayed rendering a verdict. Major League Baseball owners would later gratefully remember Landis and would choose him to be the commissioner of baseball in the wake of the Black Sox Scandal. Landis was, in many ways, a sanctimonious fraud, but he cowed the owners sufficiently that they left him alone.

Major League Baseball owners eventually bought out four of the Federal League teams and allowed two of the owners, Phil Ball and Charles Weeghman, to buy the St. Louis Browns and Chicago Cubs, respectively. Whether the owners did Ball a favor is debatable; the Browns, except in 1922, were among the dregs of the American League. One team, the Baltimore club, was dissatisfied with Major League Baseball's offer and continued to press its antitrust suit. As will be discussed in greater detail in the chapter on law and baseball, the Supreme Court made a bizarre ruling that baseball was not interstate commerce and therefore was exempt from antitrust laws. Since Major League Baseball owners are the only professional team sports owners to have an explicit antitrust exemption, this ruling was an important milestone. The other leagues have de facto exemptions granted by legislation, especially with regard to negotiating for selling national television broadcast rights.

One of the Federal League's legacies was a temporary increase in player salaries, giving players a glimpse of their true market value.

How did established leagues combat new leagues? Incumbent owners could attempt to deny new teams players by threatening to blacklist any player who switched leagues. The blacklist could boomerang. Having too many blacklisted players meant creating a pool of players for a new league. In many cases, blacklisted players were reinstated, especially if they challenged the reserve clause in court as happened during the Mexican League raids during the late 1940s. It is breathtaking, though, to see how extensive the blacklist could become. So-called Organized Baseball extended up and down the major-minor league ladder. No team in Organized Baseball could hire a blacklisted player without running the risk of being branded an outlaw team. Thus, a player blacklisted in Major League Baseball could not play anywhere in Organized Baseball. Motion picture moguls held and abused similar powers over actors and actresses.

The established owners could also appeal to their friendly local aldermen for help in obstructing new teams by denying building permits for new stadiums or re-routing mass transit lines away from a prospective owner's ballpark. Ty Cobb, with his razor-sharp spikes, had nothing on the owners in terms of ruthless competitiveness.

During the struggle to stymie the proposed Continental League in the late 1950s, Major League Baseball owners could have used the player pension plan to discourage players from thinking about jumping to the new league. Instead they used it as a barrier to entry, stating that they'd welcome the Continental League if it offered a similar pension (along with "Major League" stadiums, as stipulated by current Major League Baseball owners).

Former Dodgers and Pirates general manager Branch Rickey recognized an opportunity for a third major league, the Continental League, when the Dodgers and Giants vacated New York City. Major League owners proved that they practice recycling, as they reuse mistakes. Once again, with only one team in New York City, the opportunity arose for a new league. The United States Congress also added an impetus for more major league teams by holding annual hearings into baseball and other professional team sports cartels. Fearing for their antitrust exemption, the major league owners started talking about expansion. At first they claimed they would welcome a new league, assuming such a league met certain criteria: minimum stadium capacity, similar pension plan as the existing major league plan, and other requirements. The incumbent owners presented a benign face. Of course, the absurdity of established businesses determining entry requirements for new entrants should not have been lost on legislators and fans. The audacity of this becomes clear if you imagine that two grocery store chains in your town told the city government what requirements a new chain would have to satisfy before opening. Then again, the Democrats and Republicans were in no position to cast aspersions on baseball owners' cartel behavior, since the two-party system is even more brazen about keeping new entrants out (and note the competitive imbalance in congressional elections, with incumbents winning 90 percent of the races). Rickey, being a staunch foe of player rights and bemoaning sharing television revenue ("there's no socialism in baseball"), was somewhat hypocritical in his gnashing of teeth. Major league owners were also coy about sharing players with the nascent league.

Congressional pressure induced major league owners to preempt the Continental League by expanding to twenty teams. The four new teams filled slots vacated by the Giants, Dodgers, and Washington Senators (the team that became the Texas Rangers). These new teams ended any hopes of Continental League success, so the league was stillborn.

Ways to Improve Competitive Balance

Sports fans can certainly appreciate scarcity in the context of competitive balance. Year after year, the Kansas City Royals and Pittsburgh Pirates finish in the nether region of the standings, while the New York Yankees and Boston Red Sox spend lavishly to field the best teams money can buy. A scarcity of talent haunts all teams.

The assertion that the reserve clause promotes competitive balance retains its status as dogma, even though economists have challenged it for over fifty years. The assertion has been the primary defense for the reserve clause: no reserve clause and chaos would ensue (if you think chaos means the New York Yankees winning every pennant).

There are two interesting questions about competitive balance. First, what would be an optimal level of competitive balance? No one seems to have an answer. While fans and pundits leave unanswered the question, "What is the optimal amount of parity," they are certain that the New York Yankees win too often. Hockey has its Montreal Canadiens, while basketball has its Los Angeles Lakers, Chicago Bulls, and Boston Celtics. You rarely hear people say, "Break up the Lakers, Celtics, Bulls, or Canadiens." The Yankees are sports' bête noire. The reader will notice that I have left professional football out of the discussion so far. The Cleveland Browns during the postwar era, the Green Bay Packers during the early 1960s, and the New England Patriots during this millennium have been dominant, but none of these teams has sustained its superiority for decade after decade as did the Yankees of 1926–64 (with no losing seasons). My guess is that in the absence of the New York Yankees, the question would be of less interest. Second, why, despite reverse-order drafts, revenue sharing, and free agency, do some teams remain mired in ineptitude for years while other teams without any obvious advantages consistently win?

Researchers use different statistics to measure competitive balance. The standard deviation of the win-loss percentages is a common place to start. To compare standard deviations across leagues, researchers adjust for the different lengths of seasons. The issue of stability is crucial, too. If the Superbas always win the pennant with a 59 percent win-loss record, while the Bums always finish last with a 41 percent record, this might be less preferable than a situation where there is a bigger spread in the win-loss records but churning of pennant winners. While researchers think the NFL has more competitive balance, they rarely factor in the NFL's deliberate attempt to use its schedule to rig the standings. Weak teams get an easier schedule in the following season. This rigging may compress the standard deviation.

Many people think the change from the reserve clause to free agency benefited teams such as the New York Yankees. Under free agency, the Yankees could "buy the pennant." Most of these commentators ignore the fact that prior to free agency, the Yankees did quite well, aside from the 1965–1975 period (proving that sportswriters and fans have short memories, forgetting fourteen pennants in the sixteen seasons 1949–64). Some of these commentators also wax nostalgic about how the home team's stars used to stay put. Let me dispel this comforting myth. Even before free agency, star players rarely stayed put. Hall-of-Fame baseball players moved frequently. By 1999, there were 137 players in the Hall of Fame who had started their careers in 1903 or later, of whom only 38 spent their entire careers with their original major league team, while another 18 spent all but the last year or two years with their original team. Even without free agency, the flow of talent was from teams in smaller cities to teams in medium-sized and larger cities. Free agency might have increased the amount of movement, if players exercised location preferences, but in terms of net redistribution of talent, the general flow from smaller to larger cities existed before and during free agency in baseball.

Here's the shocking theory: Most economists believe that competitive balance is relatively unaffected by the switch from the strict reserve clause to free agency. They base their belief upon a theory developed by Nobel Prize–winner Ronald Coase. According to Coase, if property rights are well defined and transaction costs are low, then it doesn't matter who has the legal right in determining how property will be allocated. The legal rights matter only as they affect who gets the economic rent from the scarce property. The issue is: Who owns the property rights to a player's labor? Under the reserve clause, once a player signed with a team, the team owned the rights to the player's labor. Under complete free agency, players would own the right to their labor and would be able to freely contract with any team they desire. Does this affect the overall distribution of talent, as reflected by teams' win-loss records? Economist Simon Rottenberg wrote a seminal paper on the distribution of playing talent in Major League Baseball in 1956, presaging the Coase Theorem. His thesis suggested that the distribution of players under a free market would probably be similar to that under the reserve clause.[12]

The reserve clause gave owners inordinate bargaining power against their players, as did other collusive agreements. These advantages increased the value of their franchises. During congressional hearings in the 1950s, some senators understood this aspect, with Senator Karl Mundt stating regarding granting antitrust exemptions:

> We should do it with our eyes open that we are thereby expanding tremendously the financial value of a baseball franchise. We are giving to the fortunate owner an exclusive right which increases vastly his economic investment, and his economic opportunity, and increases vastly the resale value of the investment that he already has. Now I ask you, sir, whether in good conscience we can, by legislative fiat, make dollar bills out of 50-cent pieces for the people who own these baseball clubs without assuming some responsibility to be sure that public service is considered by the owners of the club.[13]

The reader should remember the apt phrase, "make dollars out of 50-cent pieces."

Suppose Peyton Manning is under the reserve clause. The Indianapolis Colts might generate an additional $5 million with Manning playing for them. If Manning played for the New York Jets, he might add $7.5 million to that team's revenues. Since Manning is more valuable to the Jets, the two teams have an incentive to transfer him via trade or sale to New York. The Colts' owner could pocket the economic rent, the payment for Manning's scarce talent. If, instead, Manning had the rights to his labor via free agency, he could offer himself to the highest bidder. The Jets would likely outbid the Colts, and Manning would play in New York. The difference is that Manning would capture the economic rent for his talent.

The above is a simple story. Much depends on the original situation. A New York Jets team that already possessed a star quarterback might get less marginal revenue from acquiring Manning than if it had a nondescript quarterback. The result, though, is that Manning is likely to end up in New York regardless of who has the property rights to his talent.

With free agency, the fear was that rich teams would corral every star. Will the Yankees sign every all-star free agent available? The team faces several restrictions. First, while the Yankees are a wealthy team, they do not have unlimited resources. The team might afford even a $300 million payroll, but a $400 million payroll ($16 million per player on a twenty-five-man roster) is probably too much. Second, the benefits of adding more all-stars begin to diminish, both on the field and in the stands. Suppose the Yankees' current roster could win 90 games. Adding the clone of Mickey Mantle might mean 99 wins. Getting the clone of Ted Williams might further increase the wins to 106. The ghost of Lefty Grove in his prime could mean a near-record 112 wins. Adding Walter Johnson, Christy Mathewson, and Napoleon Lajoie might bump the total to 121 wins. Each additional all-star is likely to boost the number of wins, but at some point, the number of additional wins begin to fall. Economists designate this as diminishing marginal productivity.

Aside from diminishing benefits on the field, what about the effects on attendance and revenue? Although the gate is usually boosted by winning games, too much winning can eventually squelch demand. Fans tire of runaway pennant races and repeat champions. Even the Yankee faithful grew tired of the team's repetitive pennants during the 1930s, 1940s, 1950s, and 1960s. Therefore, no team will sign every top player.

If the reserve clause is not too useful for promoting competitive balance, what other palliatives exist? Some leagues have salary caps. While these caps are intended to thwart rich teams from becoming too powerful, in practice their main effect is to reduce payrolls. A binding salary cap, one that affects owners' behavior, is similar to a minimum wage. Usually a binding rule makes people do something they don't want to, so it creates some dissatisfaction. Before imposing a minimum wage of, say, $8 per hour, business owners were free to pay their workers $8 per hour but chose not to. Imposing a minimum wage will make business owners react, often to reduce the number of workers. A binding salary cap, too, forces owners to do unpleasant things. Naturally, owners attempt to mitigate the effects of a salary cap by getting exemptions. The evidence that salary caps promote greater parity is lacking.

Many people think that revenue sharing will create parity in professional sports. Revenue sharing has existed from the beginning of professional sports. Hiring top players costs money, and the owners or promoters needed to recoup the player salaries. When the Cincinnati Red Stockings of 1869 became the first overtly professional baseball team, their team captain and manager, Harry Wright, needed to arrange matches with all comers, or at least those who guaranteed a sufficient payday. Because the Red Stockings were becoming famous for their undefeated string of games, Wright could arrange for favorable shares of the gate.

When baseball team owners decided to create formal leagues, they often argued about gate sharing. Many historians and sports pundits believe that gate sharing exists to "level the playing field" by transferring money from strong teams, usually based in the largest cities, to weaker teams based in smaller cities. Owners appear to have disagreed. An equally plausible rationale for gate sharing was to reward strong teams that attracted large crowds on the road.

For most of baseball's history, fans preferred to see strong visiting teams. After the purchase of Babe Ruth, the New York Yankees became a powerful magnet for fans across the American League as well as out in the hustings on the exhibition circuit. According to the Yankees' financial records, Ruth received handsome bonus payments tied to exhibition game crowds.

The Robin Hood depiction of revenue sharing, whereby the plan takes from the rich and gives to the poor, is not applicable to all sports at all times. Since the Yankees (and later the Dodgers) were popular on the road, there were many years when that team was a net beneficiary from gate sharing. In 1962 the nine other American League teams gave the Yankees enough net revenue-sharing dollars to pay Mickey Mantle, Roger Maris, and Whitey Ford's combined salaries. So much for revenue sharing promoting competitive balance.

Some people laud the NFL's "generous" revenue sharing plan vis-à-vis Major League Baseball's. During the 1950s, the NFL's plan transferred roughly one-third of gate receipts to the visiting team, while baseball's plans transferred about one-sixth or one-seventh. The fault of baseball's plan was not in its "stingy" rate but in the patterns of attendance. The postwar NFL's season-ticket holders comprised a larger proportion of its audience than did baseball's season-ticket holders. Baseball had a marked relationship between a team's win-loss record and its ability to draw on the road. While football had a similar relationship, the magnitude was not as large. Had baseball doubled its rate of gate sharing during the postwar period, it would have simply meant the Yankees' getting twice as much net revenue from the plan in the late 1950s as they actually did.

Both football and baseball's plans had what economists call regressive features, in that the best-drawing teams paid a smaller proportion of their home revenue to visiting rival teams than did teams with weak drawing power. While football's plan called for a one-third split, there was the pesky fine print: a $20,000 minimum payout per game. The Chicago Cardinals, a notoriously weak franchise, often had to pay the minimum. In effect, this meant that the Cardinals sometimes paid 40 percent or more of their gate revenue to the visiting teams. Baseball's plan was a fixed amount per attendee. The Yankees received higher average gate receipts per attendee, so they shared a smaller proportion than other teams.

Had Major League Baseball been serious about transferring larger sums of money from the haves to the have-nots, the owners could have altered the rules. The simplest approach would have been to pool all gate-sharing revenue into a common pool to be divided equally. Such a division would have severed the link between a team's win-loss record and its share of the gate. In this fashion, the Yankees would no longer be net beneficiaries of gate sharing. The current

Major League Baseball revenue-sharing plan has this pooling mechanism. I suspect, however, that some owners are disgruntled about this new, improved plan.

Throughout the history of gate sharing, owners, usually of teams in larger cities, complained or worried that gate-sharing, like public assistance, was potentially demoralizing. An owner could decide to slash his payroll and live off the gate share revenue, just as some politicians believe that indigent Americans mulct the public by accepting public assistance. A more interesting aspect of gate-sharing plans is that they can make it more difficult for teams in smaller cities to improve their teams, just as public assistance plans make it difficult for jobless, impoverished Americans to improve their financial condition. Any improvement means less gate-sharing revenue, just as working and earning income means less public assistance. Gate sharing may erode the marginal benefit of improving your team.

Many economists believe that gate-sharing rules have minimal effect on competitive balance, although some rules may help poor teams survive. These economists believe, however, that gate-sharing rules may tamp down salaries. Under some conditions, gate-sharing rules can reduce the marginal benefit of improving any team's talent, so owners are encouraged to bid less for top players. This effect helps keep salaries lower than they might have been. In a sense, then, clever revenue-sharing rules can solve the owners' quandary of bidding "too much" for the best players. Sports economists don't know whether owners are conscious of this potential aspect of revenue sharing.

Major League Baseball has implemented a luxury tax on payrolls deemed excessive. The New York Yankees and Boston Red Sox have frequently incurred such a tax. The rationale for the luxury tax is that, in addition to the hefty salaries paid to top talent, an overly enthusiastic owner has to pay a penalty, thereby making acquiring too much talent less desirable. While today's fans bemoan the Yankees' financial edge versus the Kansas City Royals of the world, they can, at least, be cheered by the fact that the Yankees must pay relatively more to win than in years past.

There are no "New York State of Mind" problems outside Yankee Stadium, as basketball, football, and hockey's Knicks, Giants, Jets, and Rangers have only occasionally won championships. The Knicks teased their fans by getting draft rights to Patrick Ewing. The result was one appearance in the NBA Finals. The Jets have Joe Namath's magical game and little else.

The best way to improve competitive balance would be to place more teams in New York and Los Angeles, but incumbent owners would surely howl at the injustice and fight any such attempt. Since they bought their franchises with the understanding that there would be no additional teams in their cities, they would have justice on their side ... sort of. Moving teams from small cities to larger cities would also help.

Labor-Management Strife at the Old Ball Game

The public is fascinated by the multi-million-dollar salaries owners pay athletes. Throughout professional sports history, players made more than the average worker. Players were also among the most exploited workers in America. How can I reconcile these statements? The issue of player compensation is of keen interest to economists.

Modern player-owner relations have often been rancorous. In the past, players occasionally made a bid for freedom, such as John Montgomery Ward with his aborted Players' Brotherhood League of 1890. Like Spartacus, chattel players had no chance against the owners. Through the 1950s, players largely accepted the reserve clause. Some owners were benign; others were patronizing. Yankees owner Jacob Ruppert lauded Lou Gehrig for his decorum, in contrast to the ribald but savvy Babe Ruth. While Gehrig was "The Pride of the Yankees," he was a docile negotiator. Players may have chafed at being caged, but at least they were in gilded cages.

Ballplayers earn higher salaries than most Americans, but they represent the apex of a large pyramid of participants in high school and college sports. Major League Baseball, the National Basketball Association (NBA), and the National Football League (NFL) employ fewer than 3,000 players. These athletes represent perhaps less than one-tenth of one percent of all participants in sports. Hollywood stars and bestselling novelists are comparable talents, but few people complain about Tom Cruise's or Stephen King's mega-dollars. After all, tens of millions of fans pay to see Tom Cruise's movies.

You may have heard the argument that it is wrong for professional athletes to make more money playing a game for one season than a dedicated school teacher makes in his entire career. "A teacher is more valuable than a professional athlete." I won't debate the statement, but I can help explain why this occurs.

Technology affects the amount of money players earn. George Mikan, a dominant center during the NBA's early years, won five NBA titles in six years (he was injured during the playoffs the one season his team didn't win the title). You could argue that relative to his peers, he was as productive as Michael Jordan. Mikan's top salary was around $25,000 per season (not per game). Even adjusted for changes in the price level between 1950 and 2010, his salary's purchasing power would barely equate with the current NBA minimum salary.

The NBA played in such small cities as Fort Wayne, Rochester, and Syracuse until the late 1950s. Their stadiums could accommodate fewer than 10,000 fans each. The league owners struggled to remain solvent. They did have a national television contract paying $3,000 to $5,000 per game.

Early NBA owners were between Scylla (low gate revenues) and Charybdis (high player reservation wages, i.e., the player's best foregone wage). Professional basketball rarely attracted large crowds, and most teams averaged fewer than 5,000 attendees per game. George Mikan and Bob Cousy struggled to get $30,000 salaries at a time when baseball star Ted Williams could get $100,000. Like most owners, NBA owners wanted to slash player salaries. While NBA owners boasted that their teams featured collegiate stars, this fact was a mixed blessing; in general, college graduates earned more than most people. NBA owners could not slash salaries much below $5,000 before many potential players would choose for jobs with companies sponsoring "amateur" teams, such as the Phillips 66ers.

As basketball became more popular, the NBA began commanding larger fees for television rights. The introduction of cable television increased the competition for NBA games and drove up the telecasting fees. The demand for NBA games and, hence, NBA players rose. Sending Michael Jordan back to 1950 would have impoverished him; even though he would have dominated the league, America was apathetic about the NBA. Jordan would have probably made a salary similar to George's.

A good teacher, someone who cares about and who provides a good deal of individualized attention to a student, can only interact with a few dozen students at most at any given moment. Your parents certainly would have been willing to pay perhaps even thousands of dollars to guarantee that you got an excellent teacher. The demand for a gifted teacher is strong, but it is narrow, given a teacher's inability to teach more than a few students at a time. A star athlete, even before radio and television, could entertain thousands of people at once. The star athlete also represents the pinnacle of a multitude of talent. Fans are willing to pay a premium to see the very best athletes perform (just as they are willing to pay a premium to see, say, the Chicago Symphony instead of the Podunk Symphony).[14]

Before television, only tens or hundreds of thousands of people could see Ted Williams swing a bat during the 1940s. With the wide diffusion of television during the 1950s, millions could see Ted hit. Many of these people were only lukewarm fans, perhaps willing to pay only twenty-five cents to watch Ted play in a game. Ted faced a broad but shallow demand for his services. Perhaps most people would not have been willing to pay even three dollars to watch Ted, but if millions of people were willing to pay twenty-five cents to see him play ball on television, he stood to make far more money than the best school teacher.

Today's top stars can entertain millions and even billions of fans. No school teacher is likely to attract anywhere close to that size crowd. While there are DVDs and telecasts of top professors delivering lectures, few professors can hope to fill Yankee Stadium with patrons eager to see them deconstruct a novel, describe a black hole, or espouse a new theory of fiscal policy. The best plumber in the world is unlikely to generate more than a few hundred thousand dollars a year in revenues. Technology has enabled athletes to reach a vastly wider audience than ever.

Sure, players make more money than most people, but they've faced economic exploitation from the start of professional leagues. Aside from the capital costs of erecting and maintaining large stadiums, owners faced significant costs in paying supremely talented athletes. The owners naturally wanted to rein in player salaries. The owners used their cartel to establish property rights to the players' labor. After the formation of baseball's National League in 1876, owners gradually developed the reserve system. At first, owners could "reserve" five players on their rosters; other owners agreed not to approach these players. Eventually the owners extended the reserve clause to their entire roster and also to some minor league players. They inserted a clause into the standard player contract. The owners interpreted the clause as tying a player to a particular team for his entire professional career unless sold, traded, or released at the behest of the owner. The reserve clause gave owners single-buyer bargaining power against the players that resulted in lower salaries than under a free market.[15] The reserve clause is such an important facet of professional team sports that it will be covered in greater detail in another chapter.

In order for the Coase/Rottenberg theorem to work, property rights have to be well defined. Socialists charge capitalists with being obsessed with private property. Capitalists should cheerfully plead guilty. Of course they are enthusiastic about property rights.

You are considering buying a house. When you purchase a house, you are purchasing a set of property rights. These property rights include the right to use, and use up, transferability, inheritability, and exclusivity. You don't have total control though. You cannot burn down your house (although you can, of course, "de-construct" it). If you do not pay your property taxes, the government can take ownership. Property rights affect your incentives. If you did not have the right to exclude people, you might hesitate to improve your house, lest interlopers be encouraged to usurp your space on the couch in your living room. The ability to transfer property means that it can end in the hands of people who place the highest value on it. For instance, if your property sat atop an oil reserve, you might want to sell it to someone with expertise in extracting oil.

For baseball owners, having a well-defined, broad set of property rights to players was crucial. Minor league owners might be hesitant to train callow youth, if they were worried about their ability to retain their players for sale or trade. Transferability is a crucial property right.

The owners quickly lorded their power over the players. While they could not drive salaries too low, as players would either turn to other employment or become so disgruntled as to impair morale, they did exploit them. In the early days of professional sports, most players did not possess college degrees. The opportunity cost of playing sports was the best foregone job in other industries. For ill-educated players, this alternative job was often semi- or unskilled labor. While players made more than the average working stiff, their playing careers were often just a few years. Few players during professional sports' early days could afford to loaf during the off-season playing golf or retire immediately after their playing days ended.

The owners also needed a mechanism to trade players. Owners benefited by being able to transfer players to teams where they'd be more valuable. Initially, two owners seeking to trade players released the players and then re-signed them. The owners were taking a risk, though, that a third owner would swoop in and sign one of the players. In at least one case, an owner was willing to purchase an entire team just to get the player he wanted. The owners then implemented a gentlemen's agreement not to sign players who were in the process of being traded. These owners, however, were not gentlemen, and a more ironclad arrangement was needed. Owners eventually decided to interpret player contracts in such a way that they were transferable. Voila! Problem solved (but at the expense of the players).

As with all management-labor relationships, management must arrange the pay structure to create incentives for labor to work in the owners' best interest. Professional sports owners want players to exert themselves in pursuit of victory (except, perhaps, when a valuable draft spot can be had by compiling a slightly worse record than the opponent's). Owners worry about players shirking, being overly sensitive to pain and injuries, or engaging in outright malfeasance (such as throwing games). Owners, as with employers in many industries, can erect a system of positive and negative incentives to ensure labor behaves in a fashion beneficial for the owners. In many cases, the system of incentives is not perfect. Paying players based on their statistics may create "selfish" players, who do not sacrifice themselves for the betterment of the team. You hear sportscasters discuss how virtuous are those baseball players who place a sacrifice bunt or hit to the opposite field to advance runners; in basketball it might be a player who sets the pick to free a teammate for an open shot. At contract time, these self-sacrifices may or may not be rewarded. I suspect that few players are paid for having more successful sacrifice bunts than a teammate.

To combat these issues, some owners have initiated bonus payments, based on a team's position in the standings. Most of the sports leagues have since banned such bonuses, as owners of teams in smaller markets complained that they were at a disadvantage for such bonuses. These standings-based bonuses are similar to companies offering profit-sharing plans. The bonuses suffer from the same defect as the profit-sharing plans: a player's effort is only loosely tied to the team's outcome. If you become "Charlie Hustle," you bear the cost of the extra effort, but the gains, if any, will be shared by all of your teammates. The reader can readily see how a similar argument applies to company's offering profit-sharing plans.

Player pension plans also serve to keep players in line. Players now worried about playing long enough to be vested in the pension plan. The owner now had yet another stick to wield over the players.

Many of you have seen *Eight Men Out*, *The Natural*, or *Field of Dreams*. In these movies or in boxing movies, an athlete is tempted to "throw a game" or to "take a dive." While player performances take place under the scrutiny of thousands, if not millions, of pairs of eyes, detecting player malfeasance is difficult. As sportswriter Leonard Koppett discussed years ago, the evidence against players accused of fixing games rarely consists of on-the-field or court documentation.[16] Instead, it is based on evidence pertaining to conspiracy to fix games. Exposing clandestine conversations is the key to indicting and convicting players and gamblers of fixing games.

Bookies, many, if not most, of whom are honest, are a vigilant bunch. They prefer an orderly, rational market, where the odds are correctly set in such a way that bettors line up evenly on each side of the bet. In this fashion, a bookie earns his or her commission with little exposure. A rigged game puts the bookie at risk, so the profession is sensitive to large, unusual bets. Of course, a person willing to make the effort to fix a game is interested in placing a large bet, usually well against the odds. Such bets attract attention.

The point spread was tailor made for crooked gamblers. Instead of asking players to throw the game, which runs counter to an athlete's pride and ethos, the crooked gambler now merely asks the player to "go a little easy on the rival."

In the motion picture *Field of Dreams*, one of the key characters is "Shoeless Joe" Jackson. In fact, the movie is based on a W.P. Kinsella novel entitled *Shoeless Joe*. I suppose Hollywood moguls tested the title *Shoeless Joe* and found it lacking. Jackson was a talented hitter for the Chicago White Sox. The team's owner, Charles Comiskey, a former player, was notoriously stingy in paying his players. Star hurler Ed Cicotte was disgruntled, ostensibly because, in addition to his lousy pay, Comiskey had promised him a bonus in 1917 if he won thirty games. Comiskey then arranged for the manager to stop using the pitcher as he neared the thirty-win mark. If there was an agreement, it must have been verbal, since Michael Haupert, an economist studying professional sports, has indicated there is nothing concerning such a bonus payment in the player contract file at the National Baseball Hall of Fame and Museum.

Comiskey could get away paying lousy salaries because of baseball's reserve clause. In baseball, Jim "Catfish" Hunter became a free agent after an arbitration board ruled in his favor against owner Charlie Finley, after the latter botched an annuity payment on Hunter's behalf. Baseball players won the right to salary arbitration in the early 1970s. While this right has not been as heralded by sports historians as free agency, the arbitration process contributed greatly to salary escalation. Hunter's arbitration board ruled him a free agent. Just as pundits feared, the Yankees signed him. Free agency has changed the property rights to a player's labor. The change in property rights raises questions. How will free agency affect player salaries? Do higher salaries trigger higher ticket prices? In the wake of more general free agency, salaries escalated rapidly, evidence that the reserve clause artificially curbed salaries. No team owner went out of business, and franchise values continued to rise. Miller was concerned about setting up complete free agency, as this would be disadvantageous for players' bargaining.

Fans often complain that the fabulous salaries paid to athletes causes ticket prices to rise. Older fans hearken to a more bucolic era when Dad could take the family to a ballgame for less than $20. Today's Fan Cost Index reveals that it costs a couple of Ulysses Grants just to get Mom, Dad, Billy, and Buffy into the ballpark and into reserved seats, after paying an Andrew Jackson for parking. To feed the family four hot dogs, two beers, two sodas, and a tray of nachos, you can kiss another Ulysses Grant au revoir (hey, you might as well learn a few foreign phrases while studying sports). "It's getting so the average fan can't afford to attend a game," wail fans and pundits.

An economist might demur. First, you must adjust 2010 prices to the 1955 prices that Grandpa paid, using the Consumer Price Index (CPI) calculated by federal government statisticians. The twenty dollars Grandpa spent in 1955 would be equivalent to about $177 today. Poor old Ulysses and Ben Franklin don't command as much respect as they use to (we've graduated to Ben Franklins—the currency statesman that drug dealers prefer).

There is another aspect to consider in discussions of affordability: the number of hours a worker must sacrifice to pay for admittance. As hourly wages and salaries have risen faster than prices in general, it is possible that, even with higher prices after adjusting for changes in the Consumer Price Index, a fan needs fewer hours of work to take the family to the ball game.

So far, we've made the standard adjustments to make today's prices comparable to the prices of Grandpa's halcyon youth. There is yet another adjustment to make. Today's ballpark experience is very different than the 1955 experience. Reserved seats are much better today than those of fifty-five years ago. The seats are wider and made of more comfortable material that is contoured to the human body. The stadiums no longer have structural obstructions, such as those that annoyed fans at Chicago's "old" Comiskey Park or New York's defunct Polo Grounds. Los Angeles' Chavez Ravine was revolutionary in 1962: clear sight lines and comfortable seats. Today's ballparks are clean; the restrooms are no longer filthy pestholes. Bill Veeck, Jr., admitted that the restrooms at old Comiskey Park were so terrible that he forbade his wife to use them. I haven't even alluded to those climate-controlled dome stadiums that some teams use; no more sweltering or shivering.

In addition to improved physical comfort and ambiance, today's fans consume much larger sodas and hot dogs. "Super size" did not exist in 1955. Most sodas were eight or ten ounces, and I suspect 1955-style hot dogs would be but an hors d'oeuvres to today's fans. There were no nachos or sushi at the ballpark during your grandpa's days. Today's fans are eating and drinking machines.

Comparing affordability, then, requires much more than constructing a Fan Cost Index. Such indices are useful for comparing year-to-year changes but become less useful for comparison across several years. This point is important for general comparisons of living standards. Members of one political party like to portray American living standards as stagnant or even receding. The raw numbers may support their claims, but theirs is an unsophisticated use of the index numbers. The CPI tends to overstate the change in the so-called cost of living. The CPI does not allow for substitution between goods, as their prices change at varying speeds. Substitution between goods mitigates price changes. The CPI also has difficulty incorporating the ad copy writer's quaint phrase: new and improved. Consumers change their spending patterns as new products become available.[17]

We return to the original question. Your favorite team, the Bay City Cry-Babies, has just signed Roy "The Natural" Hobbs, the best there ever was, for $60 million per season. The owner immediately raises ticket prices in excess of the change in the CPI. Do I need say more?

I do, in fact. The owner, knowing fans anticipate a better team (a better product), anticipates that the demand for tickets to Cry-Babies games will increase, thereby triggering a higher price. The team's local media revenue is likely to increase, too, as the owner can claim the television and radio audiences will be larger than before, as the CB's win more games. Even if the owner somehow induced Hobbs to play for free, she would still raise prices. The answer to which comes first, the big-bucks salaries or the higher ticket prices, is a red herring. Owners usually pay bigger salaries only if they expect greater revenues.

Not satisfied with the reserve clause, some owners have concocted another outrageous violation of young athletes' civil liberties.

In spring, a young athlete's fancy turns to the various professional sports drafts. Will Whatsamotta U's slinging quarterback go in the first round of the NFL draft? Will its playmaking guard go in the first day of the NBA draft? At least these athletes are mostly consenting adults. Major League Baseball's draft plucks seventeen- and eighteen-year-old players barely past their senior proms.

In the good old days, owners had to chase after callow youth in a free market. By the 1950s, baseball owners were offering untried high school players in excess of $100,000 to sign, and this was in an era when $100,000 meant something. Owners tried a variety of solutions, but most of these foundered on the shoals of self-interest. Owners attempted to discourage lavish bonuses by requiring a team to keep a "Bonus Baby" on the twenty-five-man major league roster. Many owners attempted to circumvent this rule by subterfuges such as paying the bonus over several seasons or outright lying about the amount of the bonus. The amateur draft helped owners solve their Prisoners' Dilemma problem, whereby all owners are worse off by competitive bidding for talented amateurs, even though each individual owner is acting rationally in pursuing such youth. As Tom Jones used to sing, "Can't help myself." Their football and basketball peers, though, had already closed this loophole for players. They had instituted reverse-order drafts of amateur players. Repeat after the owners: "The free market is a good thing ... for the other guy." While these owners likely boasted of being self-made, rugged individualist men (and they were mostly men), they abhorred paying market prices for talent.

The reverse-order draft does two things. The first generates good publicity: The draft allows woebegone teams first dibs on talented youngsters and thereby promotes "better" competitive balance. The stories of how Lew Alcindor (soon to be known as Kareem Abdul-Jabbar), Larry Bird, and Tim Duncan immediately transformed lackluster squads into title contenders lends credence to the idea of the reverse-order draft creating competitive parity.[18] The reality is more ambiguous, as witness the Detroit Lions, Los Angeles Clippers, and, until recently, the New Orleans Saints. Some teams languished for decades, despite a plethora of number-one draft picks. Those teams that adroitly selected productive players may well have had difficulty keeping such players. A talented player, who can produce more marginal revenue product by playing in a larger city, tends to gravitate to such cities. Abdul-Jabbar and Shaquille O'Neal eventually left Milwaukee and Orlando for the bright lights of Los Angeles. The benign competitive balance story, then, is partly, and perhaps predominantly, a comforting myth. The owners, though, like to trumpet this aspect of the draft, as it provides the fig leaf covering their naked self-interest or greed, as some people label it.

The second purpose, rarely articulated in polite company, is that the reverse-order draft provides owners single-buyer bargaining power vis-à-vis players. If Milwaukee selects you, you cannot bargain with New York or Colorado; you can opt to sit out a season and get drafted again, but few players have sacrificed a season. Because of this single-buyer aspect, known to economists as monopsony power, young athletes are exploited by being paid less than they would have been under a free market. Once again, a group of (wealthy) older men (and occasionally women) are exploiting athletes. I am not sure why fans don't recognize this exploitation. Certainly a top draft pick will get millions of dollars, but they would have gotten even more millions if all the teams could have bid on them. The fact that they become instant millionaires should not distract you from the reality. Rather than waving those outlandishly large number-one foam-rubber fingers, fans should be protesting their college's star player's exploitation.

If you don't believe me, consider the following thought experiment. You are a top Ph.D. in English. Rather than being able to negotiate with every university in America, suppose there was a reverse-order draft for newly minted English Ph.D.s. You'd be invited to the obligatory tryout camp, where you'd be exposed to a battery of tests, purportedly to measure your prowess at deconstructing obscure novels or inserting such words as "trope," "paradigm," and "post-modern" into a 1,000-word essay (written within an hour). Learned professors would create likely draft-day scenarios: "Harvard is really weak in early American novels, but they might opt for the best Ph.D. available rather than fill their gaping weakness." My guess is that, the glamour and excitement aside, you might feel aggrieved. You would be exploited financially, and you would be unable to express your preference as to location. Stated this way, I suspect some of you are beginning to discern the gross violations of your civil liberties.

The reverse-order draft is, along with the reserve clause, a legally and morally dubious enterprise. A friend of mine dislikes Eli Manning, because his father stated that his son would not play for San Diego. My friend thought Manning, Sr., was being arrogant. I say, "Hooray for Archie Manning for trying to protect his son from being exploited."

Professional athletes can make a lot of money. They could make even more money if the owners hadn't colluded to deny them basic human rights. No wonder athletes and owners are frequently at each other's throats; it is hard to be magnanimous when you are being exploited.

It Ain't a Perfect World

White owners conspired to keep black players out of Organized Baseball. Although some blacks played in Organized Baseball during the 1880s, a so-called gentleman's agreement ended overt integration. There is a strong likelihood that players who were part-black clandestinely played in Organized Baseball before Jackie Robinson. Several Cuban players raised eyebrows. By the goofy racial mores of the time, a person with a black grandparent or great-parent could be considered a "Negro." Today, marketing forces have induced Tiger Woods, who is half Asian and only one-quarter African, to identify as black. Isn't irony wonderful?

Economists find professional sports a fertile field for studying discrimination. Are black players paid less than similarly talented white players? Where is discrimination most likely to occur? Does it matter whether the owners, the fans, or the players are the ones who prefer discrimination?

Major League Baseball proudly touts Jackie Robinson's legacy. Certainly Robinson's courage and grace under grueling conditions is worthy of admiration and respect. Larry Doby, the first African-American player in the American League, persevered under difficult conditions, too, but has never received the acclaim that Robinson did.

Because they could not play in Organized Baseball, black players formed barnstorming teams. To induce larger crowds and to allay any racial animosity, black teams often introduced clowning and other entertainment. Eventually some entrepreneurs decided to form leagues composed of all-black players. These owners often had scant capital, and few owned ballparks. The Negro Leagues teams often rented stadiums from such major league teams as the New York Yankees. While there is a romanticism attached to these teams, the reader must never forget that conditions were harsh. While the salaries, when paid, where above what most blacks made, few players became wealthy.

Negro Leagues teams were highly susceptible to changes in the national economy. Because many of the Negro Leagues team owners did not own stadiums, it was easier, in a sense, for them to exit the industry when times were hard. The owners also lacked some of the white owners' reserves of capital with which to weather economic downturns. Owners of major league teams with stadiums may have decided to endure losses and keep playing because this was a better outcome than leaving stadiums empty. Black players also toiled knowing that they would not get a chance to play top white players in meaningful games. While there were supremely talented players in the Negro Leagues, given that whites made up roughly 90 percent of the population, there remains doubt as to the abilities of the rank-and-file black players. In any event, black players persevered under an unjust system. The William Brashler novel, *The Bingo Long Traveling All-Stars and Motor Kings*, recreates the conditions under which black players played. Robert Peterson's *Only the Ball Was White* was an early attempt to chronicle the black experience in baseball. Much of his work has been superseded by a wave of new scholarship, but he performed a great service by stoking interest in these entities.

The NFL had black players during the 1920s, including the amazing Paul Robeson (lawyer, thespian, singer, athlete, and activist). Some owners objected to black players, so the league tacitly banned them for a number of years. When the upstart All-American Football Conference debuted after World War II and employed some top black talent, the NFL owners grudgingly began hiring black players. The Washington Redskins outlasted baseball's Boston Red Sox in placing a black player on their roster.

The fledgling NBA had an ambiguous record for integrating its team, although all of its teams integrated before baseball and football completed their integration. Its rival, the National Basketball League, had black players and an entirely black team. After a fight between a white and a black player, the NBL owners, fearing more interracial strife, agreed to drop their black players. Their decision, while pragmatic, was lamentable, especially as the players involved in the fight denied any racial overtones. Given the frequency of fights in professional basketball, their claims were plausible and even probable.[19]

In all of these leagues, though, being a pioneering African-American player was stressful. These players frequently suffered indignities for years after Jackie Robinson's debut, such as being unable to stay in the same hotels as their teammates or eat at decent restaurants. Some of the black basketball players believed that they were assigned to guard each other and also were subtly instructed not to be too flashy or take too many shots. With the advent of the 24-second clock in the NBA, though, a wave of dominant black players unshackled by any constraints dominated the league in terms of championships and in terms of statistics. The white player who led the league in scoring or rebounding became noteworthy. Black baseball players rewrote the home run and stolen base records, while black running backs and wide receivers quickly became de rigueur in the NFL. While these players dominated, their prevalence in only a few positions created controversy. Observers and players alike accused the owners of "stacking." Lest the reader believe that stacking is purely a racial phenomenon, French-Canadians predominantly fill some hockey positions.

Black players in all sports also experienced subtle and not-so-subtle pressure to conform. White sportswriters, like most fans, held misconceptions about black players. Such baseball stars as Vic Power and Richie "Dick" Allen became controversial, while Ernie Banks became beloved. Power and Allen asserted their dignity in different ways than did Banks. A particularly tragic example of white misperceptions arose with J.R. Richard, a flame-throwing pitcher for the Houston Astros. Richard suffered a stroke during his prime, but most observers, including this author, thought he was malingering. Partly because of the misperception, he did not get the help he needed. Jackie Robinson's and Larry Doby's performances loom more impressively when considered against the mores of their times.

There are different forms of discrimination. Statistical discrimination is relatively common. On a number of metrics, blacks and whites' means or medians differ. In some cases, these differences are not inherent but are reflective of societal forces. Whether or not differences are "organic," the reader is cautioned to remember that in almost every case, there is a great deal of overlap in the distributions. Statistical discrimination occurs when, for instance, owners rely on differences in the means of groups in making decisions. Rather than expend some resources investigating differences in individuals, a lazy basketball owner might simply opt for height, always choosing the taller of any two potential players (a similar phenomenon occurs on playgrounds all across America when choosing among strangers). The owner knows the old slogan, "You can't coach height." The owner's tactic may be useful over a large number of decisions, but it is unlikely to be the best approach. Depending on how expensive obtaining additional information such as scouting reports is, the owner can probably do better by considering individual characteristics.

For many years, owners used a crude form of statistical discrimination to justify the absence of black players. Using euphemisms, owners claimed that African American players weren't good enough to compete with whites. Even when black teams beat white teams, owners pointed out that these contests were mere exhibitions and that the white players were goofing off. Many players, however, were not fooled. Dizzy Dean, as shrewd a player as you could find, even if his grammar was eccentric, recognized Satchel Paige as a fellow talent. Many postwar white basketball players readily admitted that black stars were just as talented. I suspect that anyone tackled by Paul Robeson would agree he belonged on the field. When the owners' fairy tale that blacks weren't good enough dissipated in the face of the evidence, they resorted to new arguments. Signing black players would ruin the Negro Leagues, or "blacks preferred to play with their own kind." Ironically, they were correct with regard to the Negro Leagues, although they contributed to those leagues' demise by running roughshod over those owners' rights to their players.

A second form of discrimination is based solely on preferences. Owners might have elicited more sympathy if they had argued that they were catering to their players' or fans' preferences, although they had precious little evidence on how fans would react to integrated teams. If employing black players alienated white fans, owners would understandably, if not justifiably, hesitate to integrate their teams. Certainly many fans were hostile to integrated teams, although I suspect in their heart of hearts, these misguided fans secretly enjoyed integration so they could hurl their epithets at black players. In the main, though, fans accepted integration. The Brooklyn Dodgers, although not enjoying much of an attendance boost with the debut of Jackie Robinson, quickly became the National League's best-drawing team on the road.

Owners might also face player preferences as to teammates (or opponents). Some of Robinson's Dodger teammates were hesitant, if not downright opposed, to having black teammates. When team leaders such as Pee Wee Reese embraced Robinson, only a minority dared to voice their opposition. Opposing players viciously attacked Robinson, although a proportion of their vitriol may have been of the standard variety meted out to all rookies.

In football, black players suffered considerable physical abuse. A lot of shenanigans can occur during a pileup. Referees can't see eye-gouging, ear-pulling, biting, and spitting. The NBA integration does not appear to have been as nasty as baseball's or football's. One possible explanation for basketball's relatively benign integration process is that most of the NBA's players were college graduates from northern universities. While there was certainly racial animosity in the North, at least northern universities frequently either had black players on their teams or played teams using black players. Teams in the Deep South often refused to play teams with black players.

Suppose the owners have a preference for players from Group A. In economic terms, if players from Group A are preferred to players from Group B, several things occur. First, the greater demand for players from Group A boosts their salaries, while the lesser demand for players from Group B lowers their salaries. So far the analysis is exactly as readers would anticipate. Where economists differ from popular opinion is their recognition that owners have to pay to indulge their preferences. If the labor market initially cleared, then the owners favoring players from Group A would end up paying more. If all owners preferred players from Group A, this might not be too detrimental. However, if some owners didn't have a marked preference, they could hire players from Group B on the cheap and field equally talented teams as the owners with a preference. Such an event would put the owners preferring players from Group A at a disadvantage. No wonder those owners with an animus towards black players worked to get all of their fellow owners to agree, actually to collude, against black players. One might wonder whether the owners of the Philadelphia Phillies, with their lousy records and terrible finances, would have considered hiring Negro Leagues players to go against the established National League talent.

Owners with a preference might evade the deleterious effects of their preference if there was slack in the labor market because of, perhaps, a minimum wage law. One of the unintended consequences of minimum wage laws is that they create an excess supply of workers. Rather than have exactly enough workers for the available jobs, employers now have a surfeit of workers. In order to allocate their relatively scarce jobs, owners can rely on irrelevant employee characteristics in assigning jobs.

Turning to the second question, once teams integrated was there equal pay for equal performance? Determining whether players' salaries reflect discrimination has proven frustrating. The player salary information rarely has been accurate. Quantifying player productivity has also proven more difficult than first thought. Various studies have come to differing conclusions.

Some studies found that up to the 1980s, blacks were paid less than equally talented white players. In hockey, there were findings suggesting that French-Canadian players received less pay. More recently, though, it appears that equally productive black and white players receive similar salaries amounts.[20]

Although such studies are useful, they may leave out aspects of the discrimination process. While stars may paid the same regardless of color, journeyman players may not. An owner may realize that it is costly to discriminate against star players, but may choose to replace black reserves with white reserves. The cost of discrimination to an owner is probably lower with regard to second-line players. If there are fan preferences for white players, an owner may appease them by making sure not to have "too many black players" and thereby discriminate against the less-talented black players.[21]

Even if owners and fans appear to be color blind, there still could be differences between outcomes by races in baseball. Apparently, while black and white males' mean heights are identical, the distributions are different. There are much higher proportions of extraordinarily tall and extraordinarily short men among the black population. Some observers also believe that African Americans have better "twitch" muscles, but this author has not investigated the scientific research pertaining to this controversial topic. Members of some groups may have less access to the initial training for a particular sport or occupation. The lack of tennis courts in poor neighborhoods may keep talented but poor children from becoming tennis stars. Individual sports such as tennis, ice skating, and gymnastics require a sizable financial investment by parents. Although those few members of a disadvantaged group who attain major league status may not be directly discriminated against by owners and fans anymore, they may represent success against lengthened odds.

Demonstrating that discrimination exists is more difficult than most observers surmise. Aside from a telltale sign, such as an explicit law prohibiting hiring a member of a particular group, discrimination frequently exists in more subtle ways. Even if overt prejudice has been driven underground, other factors may still lead to undesirable outcomes. Sports mirror the larger society, so it should be no surprise to find discrimination in our stadiums and ballparks at times.

Conclusion

What have you learned in this whirlwind tour of the economics of Major League Baseball? Major League Baseball owners are as competitive as their hired guns. Their cartels are ruthless and remorseless in combating rival leagues or potential upstarts. They have employed labor practices that would make the Gilded Age industrialists envious. They have usurped the political process to enrich themselves at the expense of the taxpayer, and they are adept at making dollars out of fifty-cent pieces. In return, though, they provide the public with ongoing storylines rife with twists and turns that few novelists would dare put to paper. For all the owners' foibles, I suspect the public is willing to forgive them, as long as the games go on.

Notes

1. As an aside, it is interesting that many of the world's religions posit the existence of a reality without scarcity.

2. Lionel Robbins, *An Essay on the Nature and Significance of Economic Science* 2nd ed. (London: Macmillan, 1945), 16.

3. There are negative-sum games, where both parties are worse off; often these are involuntary, coerced trades sometimes mandated by the government.

4. Efficiency is not the only virtue out there. Some people may dislike the equity of an economically efficient outcome. Since equity lies in the eyes of the beholder, economists often skirt this issue.

5. See *Federal Base Ball Club of Baltimore, Inc. v. National League Professional B.B. Clubs and American League of Professional B.B. Clubs*, 259 U.S. 200, 42 Supreme Court 465 (1922).

6. Marvin Miller, *A Whole Different Ball Game* (New York: Birch Lane Press Book), 168–69.

7. Prospective buyers of professional sports teams sometime hope for synergy between the ball club and their other businesses. For years, beer and baseball mixed very well. Many breweries owned ball clubs and festooned the outfield walls with advertisements for their liquid product. Some people figure the brewery owners gained by getting "free" advertising. Here is yet another case of opportunity costs. Rather than put beer advertisements on the outfield wall, a brewery owner could have sold the space to another company. The opportunity cost of advertising remains the same for the brewer. Other companies sought synergy because they were in the same line of business. Disney owns a hockey team; both entities are in the business of entertaining folks. The idea of synergy is more difficult to achieve than most people think. For synergy to work, the merger of the two companies must bring about some increase in productivity. A tanner that buys a slaughterhouse might capture synergy by eliminating the need to transport hides from the slaughterhouse to a separate tannery. Not all attempts to reap synergy are successful. The most famous sports disaster involving synergy was the Columbia Broadcasting System's purchase of the New York Yankees in 1964. At first pundits and fans thought CBS

wanted the team so it wouldn't have to pay broadcasting fees. As with the cases of our brewery and Cubs/WGN examples, CBS would face the same opportunity cost of broadcasting Yankees games as before. No, CBS probably thought that having the Yankees would boost its television business and its television business would boost the Yankees. Too bad the team flopped for the next decade. By the time George Steinbrenner bought the team in 1973, he paid a pittance for a once-proud franchise.

8. David Voight, *American Baseball: From Gentleman's Sport to the Commissioner's System* (Norman: University of Oklahoma Press, 1966), 8.

9. Up until 1969, Major League Baseball was scrupulous in having balanced schedules. The National Football League had balanced schedules in terms of home/road games, but during the 1950s, the Chicago Bears got a break by getting to play the woebegone Chicago Cardinals twice each season, even though the Cardinals were in the other division and usually would have played the Bears only once every three seasons. The league countenanced this imbalance because the Bears were far and away the Cardinals' best draw; having two games with the Bears helped keep the Cardinals solvent. A few decades later, the NFL purposely rigged the schedule to promote "competitive balance." Last-place teams got a couple of games against other last-place teams from the previous season. Fans don't appear to mind the overt manipulation of the schedule, and "strength-of-schedule," that bête noire of college football, is proudly publicized by the league. Major League Baseball's inter-league games have introduced a measure of bias in the schedule; pity the poor New York Mets, who must now face the powerful Yankees for six games every season. Of course, the Mets' owners can cry all the way to the bank under the arrangement.

10. Major league owners were not satisfied with territorial protection and strict player control for their leagues; they also wanted minor leagues to make obeisance to them. They either coerced or not-so-gently persuaded minor league owners to acquiesce to one-sided agreements whereby minor league owners respected major league territories and player control, as well as major league purchase at favorable terms of top minor league players. In return, the major league owners pledged to protect their "little brothers."

11. Chicago owner James Hart stated in 1901, "We are the only paradoxical business institution in the world. My good is your ill; your good is my ill. We compete for players, we compete for points, we compete for games; it is an antagonistic business from start to finish. If it was not, we would not be in business (National League and American Association of Professional Baseball Clubs 1901, *Annual Meeting of the National League and American Association of Professional Baseball Clubs, December 10 to 14, 1901* [no publisher], 104).

12. Ronald Coase, "The Problem of Social Cost," *Journal of Law and Economics* 3 (1960): 1–44; Simon Rottenberg, "The Baseball Players' Labor Market," *Journal of Political Economy* 64 (1956): 242–58.

13. U.S. Senate, *Organized Professional Team Sports: Hearings Before the Subcommittee on Antitrust and Monopoly of the Committee on the Judiciary*, 85th Cong., 2nd sess. (Washington, D.C.: Government Printing Office, 1958).

14. Being the very best is highly rewarding. Number one often reaps much greater rewards than a runner-up. Huge disparities in prize money, such as those found in golf tournaments, inspire athletes to play extra hard. The drive to be the best is costly. If all youngsters spent equal time practicing, the overall ranking might not differ much from

the initial distribution of natural ability. Although the absolute quality of play might fall if the youngsters spent less time practicing, the youngsters would have been collectively better off doing something else with their time.

15. In many ways, the reserve clause system was similar to Hollywood's "star system." An aspiring thespian would sign a contract with a motion picture studio. From then, the actor would be the chattel of the studio. Movie stars could be loaned out to other studios, relegated to cheap, less-prestigious "B" pictures, or cut outright. Bette Davis and Olivia de Havilland led the fight against the system.

16. Leonard Koppett, *The Essence of the Game Is Deception* (Boston: Little Brown, 1973), 209–210, 214.

17. As many of my readers are of college age, they may recoil in shock when I report that college students, circa 1979, did not have laptop computers, iPods, cell phones, or Facebook (Twitter, either, but I still don't know what in the world it is). These products, as well as DVDs (excuse me, Blu-Ray), CDs, plasma-screen televisions, artificial hips, and myriad other products were not available for my chums and me. A price index comparing 1979 and 2010 would, in a sense, be incomparable. Even products existing in 1979, primitive desktop computers (boasting 64K of memory), clunky VCRs, televisions, and phones were primitive predecessors of their 2010 incarnations. Again, the statisticians calculating the CPI have difficulty making adjustments. For all these reasons, a presidential blue-ribbon commission concluded during the late 1990s that the CPI overestimated the rate of change in the cost of living to be between a half of a percent to a percent per annum. Now you might think the difference between 3.0 percent and 3.5 percent per annum too trivial to occupy your attention. Thanks to the "magic of compound interest," over 30 years it means either paying Social Security beneficiaries 2.86 or 2.43 times the amount today's recipients are receiving (of course, assuming continued congressional lethargy with regard to the program's insolvency; when the system goes "broke" in 25 or so years, beneficiaries will be getting 75 percent of their promised benefits). In other words, 30 years from now, when you working stiffs are financing the Baby Boomers' retirement, you could be paying either 2.86 or 2.43 today's current rate. I see that I've caught your attention.

18. The discerning reader may be thinking, "Wait a minute, those are all basketball players!" Baseball's number-one draft picks have had a lesser impact on the standings than the other two sports.

19. The basketball owners had another reason to hesitate before integrating their teams. They often relied on appearances by Abe Saperstein's Harlem Globetrotters to give them a badly needed full house. Saperstein had cornered the market on African American players, and the owners feared antagonizing him by signing any of his players or any promising young black player. Until the late 1940s, the Globetrotters certainly held their own with the very best professional white teams, including some hotly contested games with the Minneapolis Lakers and their stars George Mikan and Jim Pollard. Eventually, though, NBA owners began raiding the Globetrotters and signing graduating black collegiate players. Saperstein's last coup was signing Wilt Chamberlain for a season. As Saperstein's control over the pool of black players diminished, the Globetrotters began emphasizing showmanship and clowning. Black basketball players, though, had one big advantage over their baseball and football peers: offers to play on Saperstein's Globetrotters gave them more leverage in negotiations with NBA owners than white players possessed, an ironic but seemingly just situation.

20. Rodney D. Fort, *Sports Economics*, 2nd ed. (Upper Saddle River, NJ: Pearson-Prentice Hall, 2006), 242–43.

21. Years ago, in a reversal of "token blacks," the Cleveland school district mandated that every high school basketball team had to have a white player (too bad it didn't stipulate an Asian player, so I could have played on the varsity). The news report panned down one team's bench: African American after African American player until the last kid on the bench—the token white kid.

Suggested Readings

Miller, Marvin. 1991. *A Whole Different Ball Game.* New York: Birch Lane Press Book. A surprisingly even-handed view of Major League Baseball's labor-management strife. Miller raised baseball players' consciousness and succeeded in raising player salaries beyond anyone's imagination.

Quirk, James, and Rodney Fort. 1992. *Paydirt: The Business of Professional Team Sports.* Princeton, NJ: Princeton University Press. Dated but loaded with historical data. The authors explain the basics of sports economics in lay terms. Fort maintains a website with a large amount of data.

Surdam, David. 2010. *The Ball Game Biz: An Introduction to the Economics of Professional Team Sports.* Jefferson, NC: McFarland. This book provides a more detailed examination of the topics covered in this chapter.

Veeck, Bill, Jr. 1962. *Veeck—As in Wreck.* New York: Putnam. A clever, witty, and controversial look at Major League Baseball, circa 1950s and 1960s. Veeck sometimes believes his own myth, such as in his "attempt" to integrate baseball in 1943, but his charm overcomes this. It's too bad that Larry MacPhail and Walter O'Malley failed to produce similar books, as they were seminal baseball promoters if more staid.

3

Media

John A. Fortunato

Baseball is just a game, as simple as a ball and bat, yet as complex as the American spirit it symbolizes. A sport, a business and sometimes almost a religion. —Ernie Harwell[1]

Introduction

From the moment that baseball games first received coverage in the newspapers, to listening to games on radio, watching games on television, and now through the use of the Internet and wireless handheld devices, mass media have played a prominent role in fans' experience and enjoyment of the game of baseball. While the technology has changed, the various kinds of mass media provide fans with the capability of experiencing baseball, helping make the game a major part of the American culture as well as an endless topic of conversation. Gumpert and Drucker simply explain, "Sports coverage has always been linked with the specific media environment of its time."[2] Many fans use all of these media sources at various times, because unless they have a ticket to the game one of these sources of media is necessary to witness the event. Even having a ticket to one singular game, to follow the entire sport and all of its happenings the mass media are needed. Some fans watch one game on television while following others online. So whether fans are planning to watch or listen to a live game or simply go to the Internet because they want to learn about the latest player and team news or check their fantasy team, some form of media will be used.

While a fan probably has a vivid recollection of his or her first trip to a major league ballpark, it is the media that have provided the shared experiences and memories of the game of baseball. Barwind comments, "Baseball is historical; its story is cultivated and refined through the experiences of a community of individuals who are bound by a common history."[3] The media have given us the video images of Willie Mays making an over-the-shoulder catch on Vic Wertz's 460-foot blast, wielding and making a throw back to the infield in game one of the 1954 World Series; of Yogi Berra jumping into the arms of Don Larsen after Larsen's perfect game in game five of the 1956 World Series; of some fans running on to the field to congratulate Henry Aaron on April 8, 1974, in Atlanta as he rounded the bases after hitting his 715th home run to break Babe Ruth's record; and of Carlton Fisk waving fair his 12th inning home run in game six of the 1975 World Series.

The television announcer adds to these visual images, such as Vin Scully describing a "little roller up along first, behind the bag, it gets through Buckner, here comes Knight and the Mets win it!" culminating what a few minutes prior was thought to be an impossible Mets win in game six of the 1986 World Series. The legendary radio calls of the baseball announcer are also a vivid component of baseball history, such as Russ Hodges exhilarating, "The Giants won the pennant!, the Giants won the pennant!" when Bobby Thomson's three-run home run in the ninth inning lifted the Giants into the 1951 World Series; and, Jack Buck telling fans, "I can't believe what I just saw," when an injured Kirk Gibson came off the bench to provide a pinch-hit, ninth inning, game-winning home run in game one of the 1988 World Series.

In addition to being the vehicle that allows fans to experience the game, the mass media affect the sport of baseball in other profound ways. For example, the mass media greatly influence the economics and the competitive balance structure of Major League Baseball. Conversely, baseball influences several different media practices and the decision-making of media organizations, such as television networks working with Major League Baseball to establish the programming schedule of when games will be played.

The overall objective of this chapter is thus to demonstrate the many ways that the media are intertwined with and influence the game of baseball. This chapter is separated into eight sections: (1) The Sports Audience, (2) Experiencing Games, (3) Media and Economics, (4) Television Networks, Sports Leagues, Advertisers, and Audience Relationship, (5) Media Providing Baseball News and Information, (6) Major League Baseball Produced Content, (7) Fantasy Baseball, and (8) Media and the International Audience.

The Sports Audience

In order to understand the prominent role that the mass media play in the game of baseball it is important to understand the characteristics of the sports audience. The sports audience is unique in comparison to product consumers in other industries. Sloan contends the term *fan*, short for fanatic, is more descriptive of people who watch sports than *spectator* or *viewer*, stating, "If people who do watch sporting events do so to satisfy a particular desire, then it is likely that only a few are merely spectators in its strict sense (i.e., watchers, observers)."[4] Tutko emphasizes the emotional characteristic of sports fans. He claims:

> There can be little doubt that the athletic area has become a center for taking care of our emotional needs. We participate in and are spectators of the emotional charge. If athletics did not provide excitement it would be gone in a short period. We look forward to indulging in the joys of victory but all too often steep in the agony of defeat. Without the occasional emotional charge, life would be a little bit duller—a little bit less alive and perhaps even have less meaning.[5]

Scholars have identified numerous individual motivations of sports fans with the intention of satisfying multiple emotional needs. Wann, et al., offer a succinct summary of the various motivations for why people watch sports; these motivations include fan identification, self-esteem, group affiliation, and entertainment.[6] Many of these motivations overlap, and experiencing one game can simultaneously satisfy many emotional needs.[7] One can easily be entertained watching a game while at the same time through his or her fan identification feel a part of a group, which may indeed raise the self-esteem of an individual.

Motivations of fans that involve identification and group affiliation are inspired by the desire to feel a sense of belonging to a larger community and being able to share the experience of sports with other fans. Sutton, et al., describe fan identification as an emotional involvement or bond that develops between fans and a sports team.[8] The group affiliation normally involves the team in the city where people reside. Trujillo and Krizek describe the importance of the local sports franchise to the community, claiming it is "experienced as a public trust that engenders a powerful sense of identification and identity for fans."[9] Hogg and Abrams point out, "Support for the home team is more than an act, it is part of identification with that team and/or what it represents."[10] While Lewis claims that through technology "fans now find it easier to follow any team they choose, without necessarily having any connection to the city that team represents,"[11] it could still be logically concluded that the majority of Chicago Cubs fans reside in Chicago.

In trying to provide some ranking of emotional needs in motivating audience behavior, Wenner and Gantz claim that the unknown outcome of the game is the motivation that generates the most interest and drives the behavior of watching games. They point out the strongest motivation for watching sports on television deals with resolution of ambiguity, stating, "Concerns with seeing 'who wins' and how one's 'favorite does' are among the strongest individual motivations for sports viewing. These tend to combine with the enjoyment that comes with experiencing the 'drama and tension' and the excitement of 'rooting' for a player or team to win. Indeed, seeking these experiences, along with looking forward to 'feeling good' when wins occur, round out the strongest motives for sports on television."[12]

The focus of winning as the most important behavior motivation is obviously increased when the fans' favorite teams are involved in the game. While many sports fans will watch a game regardless of who is playing, Wann, et al., point out that sports fans are obviously most interested and their motivations are greatly heightened in games when their favorite team is playing.[13] Thus, the opportunity to see a favorite team win has been identified as the number one fan motivation for watching sports.[14] Wenner and Gantz claim, "While watching sporting events, viewers' feelings of euphoria or sadness (and even anger) are accentuated when the focus is on a favorite team or player. 'Nervousness' about the contest appears heightened as well when favorites are involved."[15]

Zillmann, et al., recognize the sports fans' prominent characteristic of having favorite teams and the desire to see those teams win in their description of a disposition theory of sports-fan-ship. The disposition theory, however, presents another characteristic of a sports fan: love of one team means taking on the characteristic of having an interest in the games of rivals, as the results of those games can also have a direct impact on a fan's favorite team (i.e., a Yankees fan having an interest in the outcome of Red Sox games). Zillmann, et al., point out, "Spectators are known 'to root' for players and teams, hoping and wishing that their party will succeed in defeating the opposition. By the same token, spectators appear to wish that the players and teams they dislike be defeated, and they seem to take pleasure in seeing the opposition humiliated and 'destroyed'" (Zillmann et al. 1989, 256).[16] This interest leads to fans watching not only their favorite team's games, but also having such an interest that it might lead to the behavior of watching rivals' games.[17]

The summary of the disposition theory is that the enjoyment of watching sports contests and athletic excellence "depends to some extent at least, on the particular person displaying such excellence, and on the particular team to which this person belongs. People applaud great play on the part of their favorite athletes and teams. The same excellence, the same mastery of skills, seems to be far less appreciated, possibly even deplored, when it is exhibited by disliked athletes or resented teams."[18] For example, fans in Boston would applaud the skills of Red Sox players, but then deplore the same skills of the players they once cheered when these former Red Sox players, such as Wade Boggs,

Roger Clemens, and Johnny Damon, later played for the Yankees. According to Zillmann, et al. the ideal outcome for enjoyment would be a favorite team defeating a rival opponent, with the losing to a rival being the worst condition for enjoyment.

Because satisfying the emotional needs of the sports fan comes only when the necessary behavior of experiencing games has occurred, the sports audience is very loyal in its behavior.[19] Funk and James indicate that the emotional and loyalty characteristics of the sports fan can result in enduring and consistent behaviors, such as attendance at games and experiencing games or sports-related content through the mass media.[20] Even though there are a variety of individual reasons why all of these people might be choosing to experience sports, and though the audience motivations and behaviors can fluctuate depending on a number of variables, when all of these people engage in the same behavior, the result could be a very large audience.

Because of the nature of sports with games within a league being played simultaneously and in many geographic regions (even the local team obviously plays half of its games away from its home city), it is not a question of whether the media are going to be used to experience sports. It is merely a matter of which form of media will be used based on a person's desire to experience the content and his or her ability to utilize a certain media source at a given time. For example, if a fan cannot be in front of a large, high-definition television to watch the game, he or she would use a handheld device to follow the action. Ball-Rokeach and DeFleur explain in their theory of media dependency that there is a necessity on the part of the audience to use the media to satisfy information goals, to understand one's social world, to act meaningfully and effectively in that world, and to escape from daily problems and tensions.[21] Media use is prevalent and purposeful because there are so many needs satisfied through this behavior. It is the satisfaction of needs that predicts the media use behavior. The theory also stipulates that the greater the dependency on the mass media to satisfy their needs, the increased likelihood of media use by the audience.

The theory of media dependency recognizes that in some instances the audience does not have any options beside the mass media to satisfy their emotional, informational, and entertainment needs. Halpern emphasizes the availability or lack of a functional alternative to the mass media in creating a dependent relationship. Functional alternatives are simply options that an individual has at his or her disposal to obtain the content that can satisfy particular needs. It is the lack of functional alternatives to the mass media that have created the initial and most vital audience dependency factor.[22] For sports, the lack of a functional alternative is best explicated in how fans experience live games.

Experiencing Games

The most important interaction between the sport of baseball, the media, and the fans is through the experience of live games. Attending a game is certainly one option. In 2013, more than 74 million fans attended a Major League Baseball game. This marks the tenth consecutive season that more than 73 million fans attended a game, with the highest total coming in 2007 when Major League Baseball attendance reached more than 79.5 million.[23] Attending a baseball game is, however, obviously not the predominant way that fans experience the sport.

Williams contends that there are three events coexisting at the time of a singular live game: (1) the game event, featuring "the actions taking place on the field plus directly related activities taking place on the sidelines," (2) the stadium event, which is "the total sequence of activities occurring in the stadium," and (3) the medium event which is "the total telecast of which coverage of the game event is part."[24] With only a small number of fans having access to tickets to the stadium, it is the medium event that is the most important, as more people experience games through the media than in the stadium. While thousands may be attending one singular game, millions could be experiencing that game through some form of the mass media.

Watching games on television continues to be the dominant way that fans experience the sport of baseball.[25] The first Major League Baseball game on television occurred on August 26, 1939, as Ebbets Field in Brooklyn, between the Dodgers and the Cincinnati Reds.[26] The game aired on station W2XBS and was announced by Red Barber to the approximately 400 television sets in the New York area. The game was televised at the same time the World's Fair was being held in New York City, with the television being one of its featured exhibits. The coverage of the game featured two camera angles. One was down the third base line to show the infield throws to first. The second was high above home plate to give a full view of the field.

In 1940, with radio broadcasts being a constant, there was an increase in stadium attendance for baseball games. There were, however, greater concerns that televised games could adversely affect stadium attendance. In 1950 paid attendance dropped from almost 21 million to 17 million.[27] Branch Rickey, who had become the general manager of the Pittsburgh Pirates in 1950 after his years with the Brooklyn Dodgers, commented, "Radio created a desire to see something, television is giving it to them. Once a television set has broken them of the ballpark habit, a great many fans will never acquire it."[28]

One of the early staples of baseball on television was the Saturday afternoon Game of the Week, which began in 1953 on ABC. The game was blacked out within 50 miles of the ballpark in which the game was being played so as to protect home attendance. The local blackout was lifted in 1965. The Major League Baseball Game of the Week has produced pennant-clinching games at the end of the season, and on April 7, 1984, it featured Jack Morris of the Detroit Tigers pitching a no-hitter against the Chicago White Sox.

Since 1996 Fox has televised baseball and is currently the exclusive free, over-the-air broadcast partner with Major League Baseball. In its contract ending after the 2013 season Fox telecasts the Saturday afternoon Game of the Week with a game almost every Saturday during the regular season. In the 2013 season Fox used four different starting times for the twenty-four broadcast windows during which it televised games. On eight occasions games started at 4:05 and 7:15 eastern time. On six occasions games started at 1:05, and on two occasions games started at 3:05. Fox also has the broadcast rights to the All-Star Game, one of the League Championship Series, and the World Series. Beginning in 2014 and running through 2021 Fox will televise twelve regular-season games on its over-the-air network, the World Series, one League Championship Series, two Divisional Series, and the All-Star Game. Fox will televise another forty games on its Fox Sports One cable channel.[29]

Major League Baseball has two cable television partners. ESPN televises an exclusive, national game of the week on Sunday night as well as games on Monday and Wednesday nights in both its contract that expires in 2013, and its contract that runs through 2021. ESPN obtains the rights to one of the Wild Card playoff games beginning in 2014. In its contract that expires in 2013 Turner televises a game on Sunday afternoon, has the broadcast rights to one of the League Championship Series (Turner and Fox rotate televising the American League Championship Series and the National League Championship Series each year), and has the exclusive rights to the Division Series round of the playoffs. In the contract that begins in 2014 and runs through 2021, Turner will carry thirteen regular-season Sunday afternoon games, one League Championship Series, and two Division Series.[30]

In addition to these national broadcasts, every Major League Baseball game is televised in the local markets of the two teams involved in the game. The large majority of these games are televised on local cable and only a few games are offered on free, over-the-air television. For example, in New York, where there are two teams, aside from the games on Fox, only another forty to forty-five games over the course of the season are scheduled for broadcast on free, over-the-air television.

Currently, the lack of free, over-the-air television exposure of baseball in comparison to football and basketball is significant. The NFL is the only league in which all games are available on free television. Even if the NFL game is broadcast on ESPN or the NFL Network, the NFL mandates that it is provided on an over-the-air channel in the two cities of the competing teams.

The NBA is more similar to Major League Baseball in that much of its programming is broadcast on cable television. The only over-the-air televising of NBA games is the Sunday afternoon Game of the Week, some playoff games, and the NBA Finals on ABC.

Beyond professional leagues, however, baseball is at a disadvantage in comparison to football and basketball, which have the promotional luxury of collegiate athletics constantly being on free television. Autumn Saturdays are littered with college football, with games potentially airing on ABC, CBS, Fox, and NBC; while in the winter, the weekend features many college basketball games on free television and the NCAA college basketball tournament has predominantly been on free television. (It should be noted that portions of the NCAA college basketball tournament are on cable television as Turner in a joint bid with CBS are now the broadcast rights holders. The Regional Finals and the Final Four will remain on CBS through 2015.)[31]

Communication technology has allowed baseball to be more than a regional sport, since fans are able to watch games and obtain content about all teams. The initial growth of baseball on television nationally involved cable superstations. WTBS in Atlanta, WGN in Chicago, and WOR in New York provided Braves, Cubs and White Sox, and Mets games, respectively, to parts of the country other than those teams' home markets. Fans, therefore, had an option to watch a game other than their local team's almost daily.

Satellite television packages expanded this dynamic by offering fans the opportunity to see almost all of the league's games. The satellite package allows fans not living in the geographic region of their favorite team the opportunity to pay to see that team play its games (i.e., a Boston Red Sox fan living in Chicago). Major League Baseball has agreements with satellite providers such as DirecTV and Dish Network.

To further its cable television offerings the MLB Network was launched on January 1, 2009, with a distribution of approximately fifty million homes. The launch was the largest network debut in cable television history, exceeding any other network's launch by approximately twenty million homes. The network began broadcasting at 6:00 p.m. with the debut episode of *Hot Stove Live*, the off-season program that airs nightly and focuses on the latest free agency and trade news. On its premier night, MLB Network televised the original broadcast of Yankees pitcher Don Larsen throwing a perfect game in the 1956 World Series, defeating the Brooklyn Dodgers 2–0.

MLB Network features a combination of live game broadcasts, original programming, news and analysis shows, and historical baseball programming. Live games are televised regularly throughout the regular season as long as there is not a conflict with one of Major League Baseball's broadcast partners televising a game at that time. So if Fox has a game on Saturday at 4:00 eastern,

MLB Network will televise a game on Saturday night. In another example, during the spring and summer months ESPN televises games on Monday evening, so the MLB Network will not simultaneously broadcast a game on its air. However, in the autumn ESPN televises *Monday Night Football*, providing an opportunity for the MLB Network to televise games on that day. In the final week of the regular season on Monday, MLB Network has regional broadcasts of games with playoff implications opposite ESPN's televising its *Monday Night Football* game. The MLB Network also has great flexibility in that when the Texas Rangers and Los Angeles Angels were forced to play a doubleheader late in the 2012 season on a Sunday, the MLB Network was able to televise the second game. Beginning with the television rights contacts of 2014, Fox will sell two divisional series games to the MLB Network each year for $30 million.[32]

Technological capabilities have also clearly improved the quality of game production on television. Multiple camera angles provide replays in super-slow-motion, allowing fans to see the intensity and difficulty of certain plays as well as if a player were safe or out on a close play. The extent of instant replay usage has become a contentious issue for Major League Baseball officials and umpires. Advances in on-screen graphics provide a permanent score box on the screen that indicates the score of the game, the inning, the number of outs, the number of pitches thrown by the pitcher (pitch count), if runners are on base, and the count on the batter. Simulations of the strike zone provide viewers with a closer look at whether a pitch was a strike or a ball. During its playoff broadcasts Turner keeps its strike zone simulation permanently on the screen when pitches are thrown. All of these technological advancements allow more information about the game to be conveyed and fans to better enjoy the game.

Beyond television, the Internet has expanded visual options for experiencing the game of baseball. Major League Baseball offers its MLB.TV option through its Web site at www.mlb.com. MLB.TV offers games live or on-demand in HD quality on the Internet. In-game highlights automatically load moments after they occur, and games are archived in full-game or condensed versions. MLB.TV premium members have the choice of either team's local broadcast, DVR controls such as pausing or rewinding the game's broadcast, and a multi-camera-view option.

Every sports league has also created content offerings for wireless hand-held devices. Some of the prominent sports leagues have decided to provide exclusive content of their league to the sponsor in their wireless distribution category (e.g., the NFL offers exclusive content to Verizon subscribers). Major League Baseball does not offer exclusive content for a singular wireless provider; instead, it has built applications and devices for multiple carriers. For example, the MLB At Bat application is the official application for Major League Baseball. The application for Apple's iPhone, iPad, and iPod Touch offers audio from both teams for every game, a live telecast of at least one game per day, live look-ins of games, in-progress video highlights, and a pitch track system. The MLB At Bat application is free for MLB.TV premium members.

To supplement the television broadcast coverage of the playoffs, Major League Baseball Advanced Media (MLBAM), created to manage all of Major League Baseball's digital content offerings, offers Postseason.TV, an initiative that began in 2009. In 2013 Postseason.TV cost fans $4.99 and provided multiple live camera angles of each playoff and World Series game, including being able to watch up to four camera angles simultaneously, as well as live batting practice. Postseason.TV offers a variety of fan participation games. There is the Bracket Challenge, in which fans have to pick the winner of each series and the number of games it will take to win the series, and the MLB PrePlay, in which fans can select the outcome of every at-bat in real time.

To experience games live, fans still have the option of listening on local radio to the local team's broadcasts or to satellite radio systems that provide all Major League Baseball games. Since August 1921, when the first baseball game was broadcast on radio over KDKA from Forbes Field in Pittsburgh, and 1923, when WEAF in New York became the first station to broadcast the World Series, baseball on the radio has always had a prominent role in fans' experience of the sport.[33] In 1924 WMAQ in Chicago was broadcasting the home games for both the Cubs and the White Sox and in 1935 William Wrigley of the Cubs became the first owner to allow all of his team's games to be broadcast on radio. Because of the 162-game season, the fan is simply not able to watch every game; thus baseball on radio provides the background soundtrack to summer barbeques, driving the car, working in the yard, or spending days on the beach and in the park. Several teams have both radio and television broadcasts of games available in Spanish as well as English. In addition to games being on local radio, ESPN has a contract to broadcast games on its national radio affiliates, including all playoff and World Series games. ESPN will be the radio broadcast rights holder for Major League Baseball until 2021.

In 2004, XM Satellite Radio signed an eleven-year, $650 million deal with Major League Baseball to make available on its system all games as well as *MLB Home Plate*, a twenty-four-hour, seven-day-a-week channel devoted to Major League Baseball. The contract between Major League Baseball and XM was signed when XM and Sirius were competitively negotiating for content that would attract subscribers. With the number of games and the length of the baseball season providing more daily content, the XM annual average payment of $59 million per year to Major League Baseball was considerably more than the NFL's contract with Sirius for $31 million per year and NASCAR's contract with Sirius for $21 million annually. In 2008 XM and Sirius merged. While the NFL and NBA allowed for their content previously exclusive to Sirius to now be available to XM subscribers, Major League Baseball has not allowed its content to be available on the Sirius system without a new agreement and an increased fee paid to Major League Baseball. With the Major League Baseball contract with XM expiring in 2015 and there now only being one satellite radio provider with which to negotiate, Major League Baseball is trying to exercise its last source of bargaining power. Sirius subscribers could pay an additional fee to receive all major league games. The *MLB Home Plate* channel is also available to Sirius satellite subscribers.[34]

It is the baseball radio announcer that has historically been an inextricable part of the fan experience. For example, in 1929, it was Cincinnati Reds' announcer, Harry Hartman, who first used the phrase, "going, going, gone" to describe a home run.[35] The earliest broadcasts on radio had live play-by-play for home games, but away games were broadcast through re-creations with Morse code signals being sent from the city where the game was being played back to the city of the visiting team. The visiting team's announcer would get a description of the play handed to him on a piece of paper and he would then re-create the action for the audience.

While players get traded, sign with other teams as free agents, and retire, it is the team's announcer who remains through different generations and leaves an indelible mark in that city. The announcer becomes a major, identifiable personality of that team. Regan comments, "When filtered through the voice of a great announcer/storyteller, baseball broadcasts have increased the game's popularity and community identification with the game."[36] He adds, "In an age when sports heroes are seemingly less consistent, less devoted to the sport and the community, and less heroic, the fan can perhaps, better identify with the announcer. After all, he is a fan at heart; he remains loyal to the team and the community."[37] Smith also contends, "If a baseball voice is good enough, lasts long enough, and has an easy familiarity, he becomes an extended member of the family."[38]

One such announcer was Dave Niehaus, who was the lead play-by-play announcer for the Seattle Mariners from the team's inaugural season in 1977 until his death on November 10, 2010, at the age of 75. Niehaus was chosen by the Seattle Mariners to throw out the first pitch when the team played its first game at Safeco Field. At the time of his death a press release issued by the Mariners stated, "Dave has truly been the heart and soul of the franchise since its inception in 1997. Since calling Diego Segui's first pitch strike on Opening Night in the Kingdome some 34 years ago, Dave's voice has been the constant with the franchise. He truly was the fans' connection to every game."[39] *Seattle*

Times columnist Steve Kelley commented, "Words that always seemed to come so easily to him don't seem sufficient today to explain the impact of our loss. He was a Seattle icon, bigger than Junior or Edgar or Randy or Felix [Mariners' star players Ken Griffey, Jr., Edgar Martinez, Randy Johnson, and Felix Hernandez], because he was enduring." Kelley added, "For 34 years Niehaus was the Mariners' one consistent element of excellence. Before the franchise had a starting nine, it had Dave Niehaus. Before it had a win, it had a voice."[40]

In recognizing the importance of the baseball announcer, the Ford C. Frick Award, named for the former Major League Baseball commissioner from 1951 to 1965, is presented by the Hall of Fame to a broadcaster for "major contributions to baseball." Winners receive the award but are not elected to the Hall of Fame. Recipients are, however, often referred to as Hall of Famers and recognized with a plaque in the Hall of Fame library. Recipients are also invited to give a speech at the Hall of Fame induction ceremony. In 1978, Mel Allen and Red Barber were the first recipients of the Frick Award.

Media and Economics

The mass media not only provide the vehicle to experience the games; they have always been a major factor in the economics of baseball. By 1939 radio income represented, on average, 7.3 percent of a club's revenue.[41] Television money quickly surpassed radio as the primary source of media revenue. Parente points out, "Once a sport, league, or team has had its 'product' brought by television for use as programming that entity can seldom exist thereafter, at least in the same style or manner, without the financial support of television."[42] By 1950, television was providing baseball with $2.3 million, a number that would top $12 million in 1960 and grow to over $25 million by 1967. In 1980, television was accounting for 30 percent of all of baseball's $500 million in revenue and the average player was earning $185,000.[43] Bellamy summarizes, "Television could survive without professional sports, but professional sports could not exist in their present form without television monies."[44]

Television networks and leagues sign broadcast rights contracts in which the network agrees to pay the league a certain dollar amount over a certain number of years for the right to broadcast that league's games. The system of leagues collectively pooling the broadcast rights for all teams and selling the broadcast rights to the highest bidding television network was legally established in the Sports Broadcasting Act passed by the United States Congress and signed into law by President John F. Kennedy in 1961. In what Congress termed "special interest legislation" for this single industry of sports leagues, an economic system that provides Major League Baseball with one of its greatest revenue sources was established.[45]

In their national television contracts that ended after the 2013 season, Fox paid Major League Baseball a total of $1.8 billion in a seven-year agreement, ESPN paid Major League Baseball $2.37 billion in an eight-year deal, and Turner paid Major League Baseball $700 million in a seven-year deal. In national television contacts scheduled to begin with the 2014 season and run through 2021, Fox will pay Major League Baseball $4.2 billion, ESPN will pay MLB $5.6 billion, and Turner will pay MLB $2.6 billion.[46] Cable television networks continue to be a major factor in the acquisition of broadcast rights as they have the dual revenue source of advertising income and monthly subscription fees. ESPN is the most expensive cable network. Cable providers pay more than an estimated $5.54 per month per subscriber to have ESPN as part of the package of channels they can offer to customers.[47]

Rights fees can be increased if there are several networks bidding for the league's broadcast rights and if the league creates extra packages of games that a network might be interested in. For the 2012 season, Major League Baseball added a fifth team in each league to its playoffs, creating a Wild Card playoff game in each league. These games became another component of a rights package for networks to bid. ESPN, for example, in the broadcast contracts beginning in 2014, will broadcast one of the Wild Card playoff games.

The next vital step in the management of a sports league is the distribution of the television revenues. While sports leagues are not necessarily concerned with which team wins, they are concerned with creating an economic system in which each team has the opportunity to compete.[48] How revenue is distributed can have a major influence on the competitive balance among teams in a league. Concerns about revenue sharing thus emerge as a factor in addressing competitive balance. Zimbalist explains, "Team sports leagues are different from other industries in one fundamental way. The teams (companies) that compete against each other on the playing field must also cooperate with each other to a certain degree as businesses. General Motors can produce cars by itself; it does not need Chrysler. The Yankees, however, cannot play a game without another team. In the team sports industry, then, it takes at least two companies to produce the desired output."[49] It is competitive balance and the thought that at some point a fan's favorite team can win a championship that helps maintain fan interest in all cities throughout the league and can increase the behaviors of attendance and viewing games on television.[50]

The rules implemented by Major League Baseball are designed to facilitate, although not guarantee, competitive balance among its thirty franchises. In Major League Baseball money earned through its national television contracts is shared equally among all teams (it should be noted that all league-wide radio contracts and sponsorship contracts, too, are shared equally). Competitive balance for Major League Baseball is, however, largely impacted by local television revenue. Major League Baseball has a revenue sharing system through the collective bargaining agreement that ends after the 2016 season in which all teams pay a percentage of their local revenues into a fund. In the collective bargaining agreement that ended in 2011, the money from the local revenue fund was evenly distributed among all teams. Franchises in larger markets such as New York, Chicago, Boston, and Los Angeles obviously contribute more to this fund than clubs in Pittsburgh or Kansas City. By the end of the collective bargaining agreement in 2016 the teams in the fifteen largest markets will not be allowed to receive revenue sharing money.[51] There is also a luxury tax whereby if a team's payroll exceeds a certain amount, scheduled to be $178 million through the 2013 season, it has to pay a tax on the salary amount that exceeds the limit. The tax threshold rises to $189 million for 2014 through 2016. The tax rate for teams that spend more than the threshold also increases. The New York Yankees have perennially paid the luxury tax with the tax increasing based on the number of years that the team is over the threshold. In 2013 the Yankees had to pay a 50 percent tax rate, for a total of more than $29 million. The Los Angeles Dodgers, with 2013 being their first year over the tax threshold, had to pay at a tax rate of only 17.5 percent, totaling just under $10 million.[52] This economic system largely defined by local broadcast revenue creates large disparities in the revenues generated by the New York Yankees or Los Angeles Dodgers as opposed to the Oakland Athletics or the Tampa Bay Rays. For example, Time Warner Cable and the Dodgers have agreed to a twenty-five year, $8 billion contract, an average of $320 million per year.[53] This disparity is reflected in the teams' payrolls (see table 3.1).

TABLE 3.1
2013 Opening Day Team Payrolls[54]

Team	Payroll
New York Yankees	$228,835,490
Los Angeles Dodgers	$216,597,577
Philadelphia Phillies	$165,385,714
Boston Red Sox	$150,655,500
Detroit Tigers	$148,414,500
San Francisco Giants	$140,264,334
Los Angeles Angels	$127,896,250
Chicago White Sox	$119,073,277
Toronto Blue Jays	$117,527,800
Washington Nationals	$116,056,769
St. Louis Cardinals	$115,222,086
Texas Rangers	$114.090,100
Cincinnati Reds	$107,491,305
Chicago Cubs	$104,304,676
Baltimore Orioles	$90,993,333

Team	Payroll
Atlanta Braves	$89,778,192
Arizona Diamondbacks	$89,100,500
Milwaukee Brewers	$82,976,944
Kansas City Royals	$81,491,725
Pittsburgh Pirates	$79,555,000
Cleveland Indians	$77,772,800
Minnesota Twins	$75,802,500
New York Mets	$73,396,649
Seattle Mariners	$72,031,143
Colorado Rockies	$71,924,071
San Diego Padres	$67,143,600
Oakland Athletics	$60,664,500
Tampa Bay Rays	$57,895,272
Miami Marlins	$36,341,900
Houston Astros	$22,062,600

Unlike in the NFL, where every game is televised by a national network, in Major League Baseball the large majority of games are televised on local television. The games televised on the Fox national over-the-air network and the ESPN Sunday Night Game of the Week are only televised on those channels, while the other nights' ESPN games, the Sunday afternoon Turner game, and the MLB Network games are televised on the teams' respective local channels. If the game is not televised by Fox or on ESPN's Sunday Night Baseball, the rights revert back to the teams for local sale. There is a limit on the number of times that teams can appear on Fox and on ESPN Sunday Night Baseball during the season. The reason for this limit is that Fox and ESPN would continue to want to put the more popular teams and matchups on their air (e.g., New York Yankees vs. Boston Red Sox or Chicago Cubs vs. St. Louis Cardinals). Because these games cannot be carried on the teams' local channel, the package of games that the teams can sell to their local channels has less appeal. The owners of the more popular, bigger market teams have thus worked to limit the number of network appearances that their teams can play in so that their local rights maintain value.

Understanding local cable broadcasts as a potentially huge revenue source led to the creation of team-owned and -operated cable television networks. In the mid–1980s George Steinbrenner, owner of the New York Yankees, was the first owner to sell most of the team's local broadcast rights to a local cable operator, selling the rights at the time to Cablevision's SportsChannel in New York.[55] The Yankees later sold their broadcast rights to the Madison Square Garden (MSG) Network for the 1989 season. In 2001, the MSG Network paid the Yankees $52 million for their broadcast rights.

Recognizing an opportunity to further increase income from cable television by obtaining subscriber fees and advertising revenue, on Monday. September 10, 2001, the Yankees announced the formation of the Yankees Entertainment and Sports (YES) Network. The primary programming of the regional 24-hour all-sports network would be New York Yankees baseball, beginning in March 2002. On March 19, 2002, the YES Network launched its broadcast schedule by televising a spring training game between the Yankees and the Cincinnati Reds. On April 1, 2002, YES had its first regular season telecast as the Yankees opened the season against the Baltimore Orioles. At the time of the network's launch, cable companies agreed to pay YES an average of $2 per subscriber within the New York designated market area and $1.65 per subscriber outside the New York area to make YES a part of the basic cable package that was offered to subscribers.[56] One estimate is that the YES Network earned over $435 million in 2010.[57]

Little League Baseball has even capitalized on the money that is available from cable television by signing a deal with ESPN. The network will pay approximately $7.5 million per year in a contract that will expire in 2022. Little League has expanded its viewing options to broadband as well signing a two-year contract with Youth Sports Live in July 2009 that will stream most of Little League's non-televised tournament games over the Internet. Customers pay $14.95 for their subscription with Little League Baseball receiving a small percentage of every subscription.[58]

Television Networks, Sports Leagues, Advertisers and Audience Relationship

While the sports leagues receive their money from the networks, these networks that made the investment in the sports leagues are then selling commercial time during their games to advertisers. Despite broadcast rights to prominent sports leagues reaching into the billions, one of the reasons that sports programming remains attractive for the networks is that it delivers a difficult-to-reach audience demographic that is desired by advertisers. Wenner contends that sports programming is a good proposition because this type of programming offers the desirable, and relatively hard-to-reach, male audience between the ages of 18 and 49. He claims that the sports programming demographic tends to be well-educated with considerable disposable income and "advertisers are willing to pay top dollar for this audience because they tend to make purchase decisions about big-ticket items such as automobiles and computers."[59] Bellamy adds, "With a seemingly endless proliferation of television channels, sport is seen as the programming that can best break through the clutter of channels and advertising and consistently produce a desirable audience for sale to advertisers."[60]

In baseball, commercial breaks are well defined with in-between inning switches as well as pitching changes, whereas other sports have to force their commercials into the action (e.g., in college basketball media timeouts are called at the first stoppage in play after the 16-, 12-, 8-, and 4-minute marks in the half). The fee that advertisers pay the networks is determined by the size and demographics of the audience watching the game on television, commonly referred to as the television ratings. Television ratings measure the number of households viewing a particular program in comparison to the total number of television households. Webster and Lichty describe ratings as "a fact of life for virtually everyone connected with the electronic media. They are the tools used by advertisers and broadcasters to buy and sell audiences."[61]

Networks are attracted to sports programming because these games generally produce consistent ratings with little fluctuation in the viewership. The consistency of ratings makes the programming attractive because of the predictability of audience size that the networks can promise advertisers. In comparison, when a television network launches a new prime-time entertainment show, there is no guarantee that it will be a hit with the audience; it may soon be cancelled. The rating of a sports event also occurs over a three-hour time period as opposed to a situation-comedy that might receive a high rating, but only for a thirty-minute time period.

There are many variables that impact the television rating of a sports event. One primary variable is the placement in the programming schedule; the day and time of the event. Rubin identifies two media-use orientations toward a medium and its content that are based on audience motives, attitudes, and behaviors: (1) ritualized media use and (2) instrumental media use.[62] Ritualized media use focuses on a particular medium, rather than on content. It indicates how people use their leisure time and which medium they attend to when all of these media options are available. In ritualized media use the tendency is to use the medium regardless of any specific content. Rubin explains that ritualized media use is about participating in a medium more out of habit to consume time, as it is the medium that the person enjoys. In ritualized media use people are turning on the television and randomly going through different channels during their leisure time attempting to find a program worthy of taking the time to view, as "watching" is the ritual activity.[63]

Instrumental media use focuses on purposive exposure to specific content and is more intentional and selective on the part of the individual audience member.[64] It is the content available through a particular medium at a particular time that is dictating the media use behavior. In an instrumental media use, people are purposely turning on their televisions and tuning into Fox on Saturday afternoon because they want to watch the baseball game. This instrumental mass media use can be a factor in a person's organizing his or her day so as to be done with any other activities and be available to participate in the mass media content at the time it is available. Television networks attempt to tap into both the ritualized and instrumental media use orientations by aligning certain programming with the leisure time of their desired audience.[65] Because of the desire to watch sports live there is not as much concern over the use of a DVR device, allowing the concepts of ritualized and instrumental media use to still apply, an outcome that is not applicable to other types of programming. The desire to watch sports live is especially attractive for advertisers that will have their commercials seen at the desired time.

The signing of a broadcast contract creates a partnership between a sports league and a television network in which both now have a vested interest in increasing the audience watching the games. In addition to being an essential revenue source, television networks provide sports leagues with their greatest source of exposure.[66] Exposure is ascertained through the league's placement in the television programming schedule, referring to the ritualized viewing motivation. In addition to game placement, determining which teams will play in these nationally televised games is very much a part of a league's exposure strategy, an attempt to create an instrumental viewing motivation. The selection of which teams will appear on nationally televised games is, in fact, the first step in setting up the entire schedule of games for some leagues. The general objective is to provide the audience with games involving the best teams and players at the best placement within the programming schedule. Offering the games with the best teams and players at the best placement in the programming schedule provides the best opportunity for higher viewership.[67]

One example of how the television networks and Major League Baseball have partnered to increase the television ratings has been the adjustment to the World Series schedule. In 1985, for the first time, all World Series games were played at night with the Series beginning on Saturday and Game Two on Sunday. After a travel day on Monday, games Three, Four, and Five were played in the different ballpark on Tuesday, Wednesday, and Thursday. After another travel day on Friday, the Series shifted back to the ballpark of the team with home field advantage for Game Six on Saturday and Game Seven on Sunday. Because two games were played on Saturday night, generally the night of the lowest television viewership, in 2007 Major League Baseball adjusted its World Series schedule so that only one game was played on Saturday. The World Series begins on Wednesday with Game Two on Thursday. After a travel day on Friday, games Three, Four, and Five are played on Saturday, Sunday, and Monday. After another travel day on Tuesday, the Series shifts back to the ballpark of the team with home field advantage for Game Six on Wednesday and Game Seven on Thursday (see table 3.2).

TABLE 3.2
2013 Major League Baseball Television Playoff Schedule
Wild Card Round

Cincinnati Reds v. Pittsburgh Pirates				Tampa Bay Rays v. Cleveland Indians			
Game	*Day/Date*	*Time*	*Network*	*Game*	*Day/Date*	*Time*	*Network*
1	Tues 10/1	8:00	TBS	1	Weds 10/2	8:00	TBS

Divisional Round

Tampa Bay Rays v. Boston Red Sox				Oakland Athletics v. Detroit Tigers			
Game	*Day/Date*	*Time*	*Network*	*Game*	*Day/Date*	*Time*	*Network*
1	Fri 10/4	3:00	TBS	1	Fri 10/4	9:30	TBS
2	Sat 10/5	5:30	TBS	2	Sat 10/5	9:00	TBS
3	Mon 10/7	6:00	TBS	3	Mon 10/7	1:00	MLB
4	Tues 10/8	8:30	TBS	4	Tues 10/8	5:00	TBS
				5	Thurs 10/10	8:00	TBS

Atlanta Braves v. Los Angeles Dodgers				Pittsburgh Pirates v. St. Louis Cardinals			
Game	*Day/Date*	*Time*	*Network*	*Game*	*Day/Date*	*Time*	*Network*
1	Thurs 10/3	8:30	TBS	1	Thurs 10/3	5:00	TBS
2	Fri 10/4	6:00	TBS	2	Fri 10/4	1:00	MLB
3	Sun 10/6	8:00	TBS	3	Sun 10/6	4:30	TBS
4	Mon 10/7	9:30	TBS	4	Mon 10/7	3:00	TBS
5	Weds 10/9	8:90	TBS				

League Championship Series

Boston Red Sox v. Detroit Tigers				St. Louis Cardinals v. Los Angeles Dodgers			
Game	*Day/Date*	*Time*	*Network*	*Game*	*Day/Date*	*Time*	*Network*
1	Sat 10/12	8:00	Fox	1	Fri 10/11	8:30	TBS
2	Sun 10/13	8:00	Fox	2	Sat 10/12	4:00	TBS
3	Tues 10/15	4:00	Fox	3	Mon 10/14	8:00	TBS
4	Weds 10/16	8:00	Fox	4	Tues 10/15	8:00	TBS
5	Thurs 10/17	8:00	Fox	5	Weds 10/16	4:00	TBS
6	Sat 10/19	8:00	Fox	6	Fri 10/18	8:30	TBS

World Series

St. Louis Cardinals v. Boston Red Sox			
Game	*Day/Date*	*Time*	*Network*
1	Weds 10/23	8:07	Fox
2	Thurs 10/24	8:07	Fox
3	Sat 10/26	8:07	Fox
4	Sun 10/27	8:15	Fox
5	Mon 10/28	8:07	Fox
6	Weds 10/30	8:07	Fox

Another variable affecting the World Series and other playoff television ratings is the length of the series. The overall rating for a playoff series can be skewed if the series only goes four or five games, as it is the series-determining sixth and seventh games that draw a higher audience, particularly attracting the casual fan (see table 3.3). For example, the New York Yankees against the

Arizona Diamondbacks in Game Seven of the World Series in 2001 produced a television rating of 23.5, the Anaheim Angels against the San Francisco Giants in Game Seven in 2002 produced a television rating of 17.9, and the St. Louis Cardinals against the Texas Rangers in 2012 produced a television rating of 14.7.

TABLE 3.3
World Series Ratings 2000–2012[68]

Year	Teams	No. of Games	Rating
2000	New York Yankees v. New York Mets	5	12.4
2001	Arizona Diamondbacks v. New York Yankees	7	15.7
2002	Anaheim Angels v. San Francisco Giants	7	11.9
2003	Florida Marlins v. New York Yankees	6	12.8
2004	Boston Red Sox v. St. Louis Cardinals	4	15.8
2005	Chicago White Sox v. Houston Astros	4	11.1
2006	St. Louis Cardinals v. Detroit Tigers	5	10.1
2007	Boston Red Sox v. Colorado Rockies	4	10.6
2008	Philadelphia Phillies v. Tampa Bay Rays	5	8.4
2009	New York Yankees v. Philadelphia Phillies	6	11.7
2010	San Francisco Giants v. Texas Rangers	6	8.4
2011	St. Louis Cardinals v. Texas Rangers	7	10.0
2012	San Francisco Giants v. Detroit Tigers	4	7.6
2013	Boston Red Sox v. St. Louis Cardinals	6	8.9

Another example of the league and television network trying to boost the ratings is that the All-Star Game is now being played with the winning league earning home field advantage in the World Series. After the 2002 All-Star Game ended in a tie when both teams ran out of pitchers, it was determined that in 2003 the winning league of the All-Star Game would receive home field advantage in the World Series (see table 3.4).

TABLE 3.4
All-Star Game Ratings[69]

Year	Rating
2001	11.0
2002	9.5
2003	9.5
2004	8.8
2005	8.1
2006	9.3
2007	8.4
2008	9.3
2009	8.9
2010	7.5
2011	6.9
2012	6.8
2013	6.9

Television ratings are also obtained on a local level for each team by measuring the viewership of their games on their local channels in comparison to all television households in that city. In 2013, the Detroit Tigers for the second year in a row had the highest average television rating for their games with a 9.6, a more than 40 percent increase from 2011. With the ratings being a percentage measurement, a city with a larger population having more television households and more diverse interests would understandably have lower ratings. For example, in 2013, the Los Angeles Angels, 1.15, and Chicago White Sox, 1.14, were both in the bottom five of teams' local television ratings. In terms of overall viewership, however, the larger cities obviously have more viewers. In 2013, the New York Yankees on the YES Network averaged 194,000 households for their games, drawing the most viewers of any team.[70]

As for the television rating of individual games, one important variable is if the game is competitive. Much as the competitiveness of the overall playoff series influences television ratings, the game's being competitive is a crucial ratings variable, as a blowout will cause the casual fans to immediately change the channel, and even ardent fans of the teams playing, particularly the losing team, might turn the game off. Wenner and Gantz claim the number one motivation for watching sports concerns winning; once the outcome of the game is no longer in doubt, fans lose the major motivation for watching.[71] The best scenario is that there are good teams playing in the game and the score remains close, with the outcome not decided until the end.

The business relationship between sports leagues is summarized as one where television networks, and advertisers act together in which "the proper exposure and positioning in the program schedule and offering the best product to viewers in the form of teams, players, and matchups are essential to achieve the best television rating, and subsequently to earn the greatest advertising revenue, which would initially benefit the network—and eventually the league—when negotiating its next broadcast rights contract."[72]

In addition to attracting a difficult-to-reach audience demographic that is desired by advertisers, television networks attain valuable promotion possibilities through broadcasting sports programming.[73] Sports programming offers easy opportunities to promote other programming that is on the network during the actual game or event, not having to only use commercial time for promotion when viewers might be changing channels or are away from their televisions. It is not uncommon for an announcer during a break in the action of a game to indicate what will be appearing next or what will be upcoming at a later date on the network. Lever and Wheeler point out, "Astronomical costs (rights fees) can be justified by giving valuable exposure to new series and entertainment specials through promotional spots."[74]

Turner prominently uses its broadcasting of the baseball playoffs to promote its late night talk show starring Conan O'Brien. In 2010 when *Conan* debuted on Turner, the promotion featured commercials and a blimp that flew over Yankee Stadium for the playoff games in New York that was orange and simply displayed the word "Conan." When overhead shots of the stadium were shown, the blimp was referred to by the Turner announcers at several points during the broadcasts. During the 2013 World Series Fox promoted its Sunday afternoon NFL coverage, its Web site, and even showed stars from its prime-time entertainment shows in attendance at the games. Conversely, Fox used its Sunday afternoon NFL coverage to promote the World Series broadcasts as well. Game Four of the World Series in 2013 had an NFL game between the Denver Broncos, featuring Peyton Manning, and the Washington Redskins as a lead-in show.

Just as the network is using game broadcasts to promote its other content, so too are sports leagues using the vehicle of game broadcasts to promote other aspects of their business. Leagues and teams obviously promote their Web sites during televised games. For Major League Baseball the World Series does more than establish the baseball champion for that year; it is its greatest promotional communication opportunity. Merchandise can be promoted, such as by teams wearing hats with a special World Series logo. The same style t-shirts worn during championship celebrations are also immediately available for fans.

During the World Series, Major League Baseball also promotes its charitable endeavors. For the fifth consecutive year, in 2013 each World Series game had a primary charitable theme. In 2013, Game One of the World Series honored military veterans and their families. Game Two featured Major League Baseball's involvement with of the Boys and Girls Club of America and Habitat for Humanity. Game Three featured Major League Baseball's Reviving Baseball in Inner Cities (RBI) program, an outreach program to the African American community that provides youth in disadvantaged areas an opportunity to learn and enjoy the game of baseball. Game Four was tied to Major League Baseball's Stand Up to Cancer campaign, its biggest philanthropic effort. Fox's telecast of the World Series featured in-game announcements about each of these endeavors.

Similar to the advantageous characteristic of the network promoting other network shows or the league promoting other aspects of its business during the actual game telecast, sports programming offers the opportunity for a television network to generate advertising revenue within the framework of the program content itself by selling sponsored elements of the game's broadcast. As audiences are provided with a multitude of communication vehicles to experience media content, advertisers simply need to be in the locations where their brands will be noticed by their desired target audiences. Bellamy and Traudt explain the necessity of brand exposure: "The fundamental concept is that a recognizable brand will more easily attract and retain customers than an unrecognizable one."[75] Because of its brand exposure possibilities, sponsorship of sports properties has become an important promotional communication strategy.

Unlike sports television, most other programming, including prime-time dramas, movies, news magazine shows, and situation comedies, can only offer commercial time to advertisers. The sports format allows for companies to have their brand name in the title of the sports event (e.g., State Farm Home Run Derby, Tostitos Fiesta Bowl); to have signage at a prominent location on the field, such as the rotating signs behind home plate for a baseball game, and advertiser billboards; to show still shots of a company logo when coming out of commercial with a voice-over announcing the company name and slogan against the backdrop of the live event; to have sponsored elements where the announcers repeatedly give the name of the corporation, such as an in-game box score (e.g., Geico Box Score); and other sponsored items such as pre-game or post-game shows, scoreboards, starting lineups, and players of the game. All of these serve as extra forms of advertising revenue. People might change channels during commercials, but it can be logically concluded that if they tuned in to watch a game, during the playing of that game they cannot generally escape the brand exposure. During the five games of the 2010 World Series, Chevrolet had 41 minutes and 41 seconds of on-screen brand exposure, worth an estimated $19.8 million.[76]

The benefits to the sports property or the broadcast network upon entering into sponsorship agreements are obvious as they add another major revenue stream to their business. There are also many benefits to the sponsoring brand that complement the needed branded exposure. What makes sponsorship such an attractive strategy for many corporations is that all of the parameters of the deal are negotiable and bound only by what the sponsor and the sponsored property can agree to.[77] Although a sponsorship can take on many different forms, and therefore is difficult to define, researchers have identified the core components of a sponsorship agreement as an investment by the corporate sponsor in exchange for the exploitable commercial potential associated with the event or property.[78]

One of the negotiated components of a sponsorship agreement is the characteristic of exclusivity for the sponsoring corporation within its particular product category. Sports leagues and their teams sell exclusivity in a variety of product categories (e.g., airlines, automobiles, financial services). Exclusivity simply eliminates any competition that one company might receive from a rival within that product category at the sponsored event or location.[79] Miyazaki and Morgan explain, "The ability to be an exclusive sponsor in one's product category presumably aids in avoiding the competitive interference that typically is experienced in other media contexts."[80] For some industries, such as beer, soda, and credit cards, the characteristic of exclusivity provides them not only with brand exposure, but the additional advantage of stadium point-of-purchase sales of their brand products to an audience without competition.

In addition to brand exposure and exclusivity, many authors indicate that developing and communicating a brand association between the sponsoring brand and the sponsored property is an objective that can be achieved through a sponsorship.[81] Dean explains, "For the payment of a fee (or other value) to the sponsee, the sponsor receives the right to associate itself with the sponsee or event." He adds, "By associating itself with the sponsee, the sponsoring firm/brand shares in the image of the sponsee."[82] Stipp and Schiavone point out that the sponsorship goals assume that the target audience for the sponsorship will transfer their loyalty from the sponsored property or event to the sponsor itself.[83] To help achieve this transfer the sponsorship agreement allows the advertisers to communicate their association to the sports property by granting the sponsors rights to use content (e.g., footage of that sport), and logos that they could use on their product packaging or in their advertisements. For example, because Pepsi is a sponsor of Major League Baseball and the New York Mets, their logos can appear on a case or even an individual can or bottle of Pepsi.

Sponsorship associations can be an effective way of differentiating one brand from its competition.[84] And, perhaps, most importantly, several researchers have even indicated that achieving a brand association transfer through sponsorship strategies could potentially influence an increase in purchasing the products of the sponsoring brand.[85] Harvey summarizes it thus: "Sponsorship changes the consumer's perception of a specific sponsor—which can rub off positively on brands that sponsor in terms of willingness to purchase those brands."[86]

The sponsorship can be activated in a manner that highlights a brand association or brand theme. Activation can simply be thought of as consisting of the methods used by sponsors to communicate and better associate and connect their brand to the property and to consumers. Cornwell, Weeks, and Roy formally define activation as "collateral communication of a brand's relationship with a property."[87] The activation program can be flexible and customized to better achieve the branding goals of the sponsor and can entail opportunities for better brand exposure and recall, consumer experiences or contests, and product usage.[88] Researchers report that the activation programs developed are a major factor in the success of a sponsorship. Meenaghan states, "The success of the sponsorship program will be dependent to a large extent of how it is implemented."[89] Cornwell et al. claim "Both the weight and the nature of leveraging activities are central to the communication effects achieved in sponsorship."[90]

Media Providing Baseball News and Information

Beyond presenting the actual live games, the mass media play an essential role in providing news and information surrounding the games, the teams, and the players. Fans desire to learn the latest team and player news, learn of trades or free agency developments, hear commentary from managers and players, read editorials or player features in newspapers, magazines, or on Internet blogs, and listen to commentary on sports radio. Fans even look for media opportunities to express their own opinions of the sport through talk radio, Facebook, Twitter, and a variety of Web sites. Even when games are not being played, there is no off-season for baseball news and information, as the "Hot Stove" following player free agency and trades garners significant interest from baseball fans. Buttny and Jensen point out, "Daily storylines on players in the print and electronic media provide a ready resource for the discursive aspects of the game."[91] They summarize, "If baseball is the national pastime, then talking about baseball is one of our most enduring social rituals."[92]

Immediately surrounding the game, teams have extensive pre-game and post-game shows featuring highlights, interviews, and game storyline updates. Post-game shows often feature live interviews with the manager and the key players from that night's game. National television programs focusing on baseball, such as ESPN's *Baseball Tonight*, show highlights from all of that day's games. Beyond that immediate coverage it is more than simply facts and highlights that people are interested in; they seek out analysis of events. When a game is played or a story about a team or a player occurs, the audience searches the media to explain the importance of the event. It is the many sports reporters around the country who interact with the team and analyze events by selecting certain highlights and quotes from athletes and coaches to write the stories that help place events into some meaningful context. Jamieson and Waldman explain the general role of the journalist, stating:

> Journalists help mold public understanding and opinion by deciding what is important and what may be ignored, what is subject to debate and what is beyond question, and what is true and false. In order to make those judgments, they have to navigate an often confusing thicket of information and assertions. "Facts" can be difficult to discern and relate to the public, particularly in a context in which the news is driven by politicians and other interested parties who selectively offer some pieces of information while suppressing others.[93]

In speaking specifically about sports journalism, Bob Ryan, columnist for the *Boston Globe*, explained that the obligation of the reporter is to serve the reader. The reporter has the ability to "gain access to circumstances the fan does not have," and provides the audience with "information that is filtered through your perspective."[94] Christine Brennan, noted sports writer for *USA Today*, commented on the job of a newspaper columnist, stating it is "to examine the larger picture."[95]

Wenner summarizes:

> The sports journalist is servant to many. Professional ethics call on the sports journalist to report the news accurately and fairly to the audience. At the same time, the sports journalist often reports for a media organization that may make stylistic or substantive demands on that reporting. And finally, the sports journalist must remain on good terms with sports organizations their teams, players, coaches, and other personnel, for without access to these sources, there is no access to the "inside story" that is so valued by the mediated sports audience.[96]

As the role of the broadcast announcer is significant to the relationship of baseball and the fan, so is the role of the baseball writer. All Major League Baseball teams have newspaper beat writers who travel with and are assigned to cover the team on a daily basis. (It should be noted that some sports-talk radio stations, too, have beat reporters that are covering the team on a daily basis. For example, WFAN in New York has a beat reporter assigned for both the Yankees and the Mets.) There are also writers for national print publications and Internet blogs who cover baseball and will travel to the location that provides the most intriguing story. The technology creating more media vehicles has simply created more media need for access to players and managers to write their stories.

Peter Gammons, Hall of Fame writer and former columnist for the *Boston Globe* and *Sports Illustrated*, commented, "Publishers and news editors have no clue. They have no understanding that the baseball beat is the toughest beat in the newspaper business. It means severe personal sacrifices." He added,

> The baseball beat today is much tougher now than when I was traveling with the Red Sox for the *Globe*. There is far less access. Ten times the bodies in the clubhouse. The Internet, radio, television have broadened the baseball information universe. And yet our business, I am proud to say, keeps producing generation after generation of young reporters who are tireless, good, and fair. Throughout my career I have tried to be guided by one principle, that because I am human I have the right to like people. But because I am professional, I have no right to dislike any one.[97]

In terms of access to the players and managers Castle explains that Major League Baseball is far superior in what is permissible in comparison to football and basketball, which have stricter media access policies.[98] In Major League Baseball, teams' clubhouses open three hours and thirty minutes before and close one hour before the game's first pitch. The members of the media are permitted inside the clubhouse during that time, but the players are not required to speak with the media. Some may be receiving medical treatment, others may be taking extra batting or fielding practice, and others may simply choose not to talk to the media prior to games. The clubhouse reopens ten minutes after the final out of the game. There is no exact time that the reporters have to leave the clubhouse after the game, although many are on deadline to file their stories. After the game the manager of the team has to speak with the media. Again, although the reporters are in the clubhouse after the game, the players are not obligated to speak with them. In the playoffs there are more demands and obligations for players to speak with the media. For example, the day before each playoff game the starting pitchers of that game hold a press conference with the media.

In 2009 Major League Baseball began having a media day for all players from both teams playing in the World Series. Each player would sit at a table and be available to all media for 45 minutes. Major League Baseball has used a similar media strategy for its All-Star Game players since 1999. The hope is that with the players being easily accessible, more media outlets would cover the World Series. Patrick Courtney, Major League Baseball vice president of public relations, stated, "With the success we've had with our All-Star media day, we thought it would be great if we replicated it at the World Series. We talked to all of the clubs at the end of the year and asked them to plan a spot at their ballpark." He added, "The more availability allows for more coverage, and more coverage leads to more promotion of the World Series."[99]

The prominent role of the baseball reporter is most evident through the responsibilities of the Baseball Writers Association of America, a professional association of journalists writing for newspapers, magazines, and qualifying Web sites. Founded in 1908 with the simple goal of improving working conditions for sportswriters, the association continues to work with Major League Baseball and its teams to facilitate clubhouse and press box access. Perhaps the most recognizable duty of the association is voting for admission into the Baseball Hall of Fame. Writers with ten years of membership can cast a vote for a player's candidacy for the Hall of Fame. The association also votes for the following annual awards: Cy Young, Most Valuable Player, Rookie of the Year, and Manager of the Year. In 1931 the association appointed two committees and first elected Most Valuable Players in each league, with Lefty Grove winning the American League MVP and Frankie Frisch winning the National League award.

Recognizing "meritorious contributions to baseball writing," the J.G. Taylor Spink Award is the highest award given by the Baseball Writers Association of America. Named for J.G. Taylor Spink, publisher of the *Sporting News* from

1914 to 1962, it is the oldest award given by the Hall of Fame. Spink himself was the first recipient, in 1962. Winners receive the award but are not elected to the Hall of Fame. Recipients are, however, often referred to as Hall of Famers and recognized with a plaque in the Hall of Fame library. Spink Award winners are invited to give a speech at the Hall of Fame induction ceremony.

Following a sport is also done through various social media platforms. In a survey of 516 Major League Baseball fans conducted in April 2010 by Catalyst Public Relations, 61 percent of fans consider themselves a bigger fan since they started following their favorite teams on Facebook, Twitter, and other social media platforms. More than half of Major League Baseball fans, 51 percent, reported that they spend more time watching and following the league now than they did prior to their social media usage. Fans are more likely to use social media sites to keep up with scores and player news than for any other reason. The survey reported that half of Major League Baseball fans would rather follow a player on Facebook than wait for that player to be interviewed on television. One-third of fans surveyed considered Facebook and one-quarter of fans surveyed considered Twitter to be "very credible" sources of information. Three-fourths of fans want athletes to engage with them directly through social media, although only 13 percent of Major League Baseball fans follow specific players. Finally, half of game day-related social media interactions occur once the game is over, with 19 percent of interactions among Major League Baseball fans occurring pre-game, and 30 percent of interactions occurring during the game.[100] On the day of Game Two of the 2010 World Series, C.J. Wilson, former Texas Rangers starting pitcher, did not speak with the media, but he did post a message on Twitter. Beginning in 2012, when players were finished playing in the All-Star Game they could visit social media rooms and interact with fans from computer stations set up near the team's clubhouse. Fifteen All-Star players visited the social media rooms in 2013.

The people responsible for coordinating the daily interaction among players, managers, and the media are the league and individual team public relations directors. As the liaisons between the team and the media, public relations directors are responsible for providing the media with any biographical and statistical information that they need to competently report on the game and the team. This includes creating a media guide prior to the season and developing game notes for every game with updated statistical information from the current season. Public relations directors will also field special media requests for interviews with the players or manager and make recommendations to them as to whether they should fulfill the request.

In trying to obtain media coverage, public relations practitioners function in a role of advocacy on behalf of the organizations they represent.[101] These public relations professionals are entrusted with the responsibility to present the organization they represent in the most positive manner to its various stakeholders. The idea of advocacy emanates from a larger philosophy that the actions of the organization and the communication of these actions done through public relations can encourage media coverage and ultimately positively influence public opinion.[102] The public relations department is using the media to promote the team and the league by getting stories about players consistently placed in many media locations. The sports public relations professional is trying to exploit access and not limit coverage, while trying to balance the time demands on the team's players and coaches.[103] Major League Baseball hands out its post-season awards over a several-day period, with each day having a winner of one of its different awards announced (e.g., Monday, Cy Young Awards; Tuesday, MVP Awards) so as to having a continuing presence in the news media. Hopwood claims, "For a sports organization, public relations can, if handled professionally, become its most cost-effective communications mechanism."[104]

Because of the importance of interactions with the media, several major league team public relations departments have begun extensive media training for their players, managers, and front office personnel who might be interviewed by the press. The Chicago White Sox have been conducting media training since 1997. White Sox Vice President Scott Reifert explained, "We did it in January before SoxFest (the White Sox annual fan convention). We'd bring in media trainers in English and Spanish. We'd do mock interviews and have the players interview each other. Some guys learned it and enjoyed it, but some guys were never comfortable with it. At least they were exposed to it."[105] The Cleveland Indians focus their media training on the team's top prospects, holding sessions in the winter. Bart Swain, media relations director, explained, "We get them acclimated to the city and the media. We work with them once a week on different techniques. We have actual media sessions and do mock interviews. The big thing about this business is trust."[106]

League-Produced Content

Public relations efforts, however, do not guarantee that your league or team will receive media coverage or that the specific perspective that is desired will be the predominant angle of the coverage. The personnel of the mass media organization (reporters, editors, producers) still perform the gatekeeping function of selecting which stories they will cover and which quotes or perspectives will appear in their coverage. To circumvent the gatekeeping process from media members who are not a part of the league, communications vehicles and original content have been developed by sports leagues themselves.

The most prominent area where content is produced by the league and does not have to go through the filter of the media is the Major League Baseball official Web site. MLB.com is a one-stop location for all of the relevant information about the league, including scores, standings, schedules, latest league and team news, video highlights, tickets, and merchandise.

Fans can register on mlb.com, where they provide their demographic information and elect to receive e-mails from the league that feature weekly or daily headlines, merchandise discounts, ticket offers, or fantasy news. Of the MLB.com registrants, 73 percent are male, 70 percent are between the ages of 19 and 45, 78 percent have individual incomes greater than $40,000, 91 percent have graduated from high school, and 88 percent return to the MLB.com Web site within three days of their last visit.[107]

From the mlb.com Web site, fans can also access each team's Web site. All team Web sites are coordinated by Major League Baseball Advanced Media to provide consistency in style and content. The front page of all team sites has the following subheadings: (1) News, featuring all the latest team headlines, official press releases, game notes, and links to the team's minor league affiliates; (2) Video, including team's season highlights; (3) Scoreboard, showing the day's scores; (4) Stats, containing the season's team and player statistics as well as the team's historical statistics; (5) Schedule, the team's game schedule, including the stadium's promotional dates; (6) Roster, having biographies of team and front office personnel; (7) Community, showing all of the team's charitable fundraising, corporate social responsibility, and outreach programs; (8) Fans, including a feature where a fan can sign up to receive free e-mails from the team with the latest team news and special ticket offers, and a special link to a section specifically designed for kids; (9) Stadium, providing all information (e.g., directions, parking, panoramic views) about the team's home ballpark; (10) Rewards, where fans can register and connect their Twitter accounts to receive points and earn team-related rewards when Tweeting using the team hashtag (e.g., #orioles); (11) Tickets, discussing all options such as season tickets, multi-game packages, and individual game tickets; (12) Mobile, containing information about Major League Baseball's mobile offerings; (13) Shop, where fans can purchase team merchandise; (14) MLB.TV, which quickly links fans to the MLB.TV main page; and (15) Fantasy, which provides links to the mlb.com fantasy games. There is also a pull-down menu quickly linking the visitor to all Major League Baseball teams' Web sites.

The MLB.com Web site allows several interactive opportunities for fans. One of these interactive components is the voting for the All-Star Game. In addition to voting at the ballpark, fans can vote online for a player for the All-Star Game. Teams have used All-Star voting to market themselves and spur ticket sales. In order to vote online fans have to register for a team's e-newsletter.

In the past, for example, the Texas Rangers offered two free game tickets to fans who voted at least twenty times with the Rangers marked as their favorite team. In another example, the Los Angeles Dodgers have had images of their players at the top of their Web site encouraging fans to vote while also promoting ticket discount offers. Josh Rawitch, the Dodgers' vice president of communications, stated, "Any time you're talking about players potentially being All-Stars for the Dodgers, it ratchets up interest in the team."[108]

For the final roster spot in the All-Star Game since 2002, fans have selected the player for the National League and American League teams exclusively through online voting. Fans can now cast votes through Twitter and text messaging. A record 79.2 million votes were cast in 2013, passing the previous high by more than 10 million votes.[109] Steve Delabar of the Toronto Blue Jays earned 9.6 million votes and Freddie Freeman of the Atlanta Braves earned 19.7 million votes to win their respective leagues' fan vote.

Leagues have long created and produced their own television programming. MLB Productions is the video production division of Major League Baseball. With unparalleled access to the game and its players, MLB Productions creates original programming, DVDs, video games, and commercials to support and promote the sport. MLB Productions possesses more than 100,000 hours of historic footage.[110]

Among its content, MLB Productions is the producer of *This Week in Baseball*. Debuting in 1977 and narrated by Mel Allen until his death in 1996, *This Week in Baseball* is the longest-running sports anthology series in American television broadcast history. *This Week in Baseball* appears on Fox before its Saturday afternoon game-of-the-week telecast. MLB Productions produces the official World Series DVD, for which potentially more than 100 hours of game highlights and all-access footage have to be cut down to a one-hour film. The DVD is released quickly after the conclusion of the World Series, making it available for the holiday shopping season.[111] MLB Productions also creates video games that try to simulate a player's true game-playing abilities using official major league scouting reports.

The MLB Network provides a media vehicle for league-owned and -produced content. As for its original programming, during the regular season the signature show of the network is *MLB Tonight*, a live nightly studio show that begins at 6:00 p.m. and airs until the final out of all of that day's Major League Baseball games is recorded. *MLB Tonight* is televised from Studio 3, named in honor of Babe Ruth, and features live glimpses of games in progress, game highlights, interviews with players after their games are completed, and analysis from former major league players, managers, and prominent baseball reporters. To capture the day's game action, MLB Network produces *Quick Pitch*, a daily highlight program that airs after all Major League Baseball games on that day have ended. The show re-airs the following morning, allowing multiple opportunities for fans to see the highlights of the previous day's games. The *Plays of the Week* program highlights the best Major League Baseball action during that period.

The MLB Network provides baseball with a channel that allows for more extensive coverage of events, such as the Major League Baseball draft or the trade deadline, that would receive less coverage in other media venues. The draft is televised live and the MLB Network has all-day coverage of the trade deadline, providing breaking news and analysis of all of the deals.

During the off-season, *Hot Stove Live* is a nightly program that discusses the latest trade and free agent news. Prior to the season MLB Network produces its *30 Clubs in 30 Days* series, a one-hour preview of each Major League Baseball team featuring player and manager interviews as well as analysis from network commentators.

MLB Network has produced reality-based programming, such as *The Pen*, which provided an exclusive behind-the-scenes examination of the season from the perspective of the Philadelphia Phillies' relief pitchers. *The Club* featured an in-depth look at the front office dealings of the Chicago White Sox with behind-the-scenes footage and interviews with Jerry Reinsdorf, chairman, Kenny Williams, general manager, and Ozzie Guillen, former manager.

Several programs on the MLB Network celebrate the history of the game. *Prime 9* is a program that counts down and debates the top nine within a given category, such as the top nine All-Star Game moments or the top nine catchers. *Baseball Seasons* chronicles the pertinent stories and shows the important plays from an entire Major League Baseball season. The MLB Network also rebroadcasts classic games in their entirety.

Diamond Demos has the network's analysts demonstrate how to execute various baseball plays. *Diamond Demos* is filmed in Studio 42, named for Jackie Robinson. Studio 42 is designed as a replica of a baseball field with a half-scale infield made of field turf measuring 45 feet from base to base and 30 feet from home plate to the pitcher's mound. The Studio 42 field has a replica outfield wall with padding and brick designs and an out-of-town scoreboard, modeled after the one at Citizens Bank Park in Philadelphia, which is updated in real time.

Because the MLB Network is a league production, questions can be raised as to its journalistic integrity in covering the controversial stories about the league. However, the MLB Network received positive comments for its coverage of the breaking news that Alex Rodriguez, Yankees third baseman, three-time MVP, and perennial All-Star, had tested positive for performance enhancing drugs. Tim Lemke, from the *Washington Times*, commented, "The MLB Network went a long way toward establishing itself as a credible source of news over the weekend by responding quickly and thoroughly to reports that Yankees third baseman Alex Rodriguez tested positive for steroids in 2003." By bringing in its top analysts and baseball reporters, having Bob Costas interview *Sports Illustrated*'s Selena Roberts, the journalist who broke the story, and securing interviews with Rodriguez's former teammates, Lemke wrote, the network "served fans well by providing hours of analysis with no evident bias. A lesser network might have downplayed the story as unsurprising, old or not meaningful. Instead, the network's hosts and analysts showed little regard for how the news would reflect on the league."[112] Diane Pucin of the *Los Angeles Times* offered similar praise of the MLB Network's reporting on the Rodriguez story. She wrote, "The most compelling coverage of the A-Rod steroid scandal has been in the most unexpected place: the new cable channel MLB Network." Pucin added, "The channel owned by Major League Baseball has not ducked the story, even though it tarnishes the sport and its best player."[113]

In evaluating the coverage of the Rodriguez story by the MLB Network, Bob Costas stated, "For the baseball network to have this happen so soon and then do such a good job, it showed the network is willing to tackle an important issue straight up. When you look back at the start of this network, I think these few days will be very, very noteworthy."[114] Major League Baseball spokesman Matt Bourne added, "For the network to be credible, they need to cover any issue. This was obviously a major issue that impacted Major League Baseball, and they covered it appropriately."[115]

Ultimately, what the MLB Network provides is a guaranteed place on television where the subject is always going to be baseball. While baseball competes with other sports for attention on ESPN's *SportsCenter*, and *Baseball Tonight* might be shifted in the programming schedule or not broadcast at all due to other ESPN programming commitments; or the sport competes for attention in print publications such as *Sports Illustrated* or *USA Today*, the topic is a certainty on the MLB Network, and the baseball fan always has a place to go to learn about and enjoy his or her favorite sport.

Local cable stations also feature support programming about the teams in their respective markets, such as *Detroit Tigers Weekly* on Fox Sports Detroit, *Indians Roundtable* on Fox Sports Ohio, and *Inside the Marlins* on Fox Sports Florida. Other programming includes manager shows, such as the *Joe Girardi Show*, or programming geared to kids, such as the Yes Network's *Yankees on Deck*. Several cable stations broadcast "hot stove" shows during the off-season. They also break into programming if important team news occurs, such as broadcasting the press conference of a player that recently signed with that team or reporting that a manager is fired. For example, SportsNet New York (SNY), cable television home of the New York Mets, preempted programming to carry news that the general manager, Omar Minaya, and the manager, Jerry Manuel, were not going to return to the Mets after the 2010 season. The SNY coverage included a live press conference with Mets owners Fred and Jeff Wilpon. SNY featured live coverage of its press conference on October 29, 2010, announcing the hiring of new general manager, Sandy Alderson. The Alderson press conference was also streamed live on Mets.com.

Support programming extends to radio as well; many managers have weekly appearances on their local sports talk radio stations. In 2013, WFAN in New York had weekly appearances by both Joe Girardi, Yankees manager, and Terry Collins, Mets manager.

All of this media content is necessary because of the many desires of the sports audience. While the term "sports fans" generally connotes a group of people with similar characteristics in their needs, desires, and experiences of sports-related content and products and there is a clear common interest centered on games and events, "sports fans" are not a monolithic group in their behavior. Different audience members have different needs and desires and experience sports-related content and products in a variety of ways. Satisfying all of these "sports fans" represents a challenge to any sports organization, but also creates an opportunity for a league and its teams to communicate and connect with all of its fans in a manner that they desire. Unique league-branded products and different promotional communication strategies can be developed to facilitate all fans' experiencing the league brand.

Sports teams and leagues very much think of themselves as brands.[116] Shank explains, "The broad purpose of branding a product is to allow an organization to distinguish and differentiate itself from all others in the marketplace."[117] He contends that the outcome of building the sports brand is to "ultimately affect consumer behaviors, such as increasing attendance, merchandising sales, or participation in sports." Companies, including sports leagues, can also grow their business by developing their own brand extensions, leveraging their established brand name to introduce new products or enter a new product area.[118] Brand extensions are powerful because the new product or service comes with instant credibility, as the brand has already been accepted and proven in the marketplace.[119] Keller summarizes that brand extensions can help an organization strengthen its brand image, broaden its customer base, and contribute to its long-term viability.[120]

James, et al., point out that for sports organizations, "financial success is predicated, in large part, on the creation of an adequate income stream. This necessitates that sport teams attract, develop, and maintain a relationship with a substantial number of sports consumers."[121] Major League Baseball understands that its audience is not monolithic and that there are multiple ranges of support needed to reach the entire Major League Baseball fan base. In addition to the games televised by their broadcast partners, Major League Baseball has created a form of content designed to reach a certain target audience. From the child who is playing the video game and wearing the Derek Jeter or Albert Pujols jersey to the person who has behind-the-plate season tickets, all of these people are customers of some form of the league's product. Leagues have to cater to different types of fans with different types of media uses and behaviors, but all of the different media vehicles available help provide a different league-branded product for each type of fan. It leaves Major League Baseball with at least some form of its product geared to almost every audience demographic—no group is left out.[122]

Fantasy Baseball

Since box scores were first printed in the newspaper, statistics have been a prominent part of the baseball dialogue. It is baseball's magical statistics that resonate so deeply with fans. Seasonal performance measures such as 20 wins or 100 RBIs have been distinguished markings of a player's successful season. In 2012, Miguel Cabrera, the Tigers third baseman, achieved the triple crown of leading the league in home runs, RBIs, and batting average, the first time a player had accomplished this since 1967. Historical performance standards of 3,000 hits, 500 home runs, and 300 wins have been accomplishments that have been determinants in getting into the Hall of Fame (although the era of performance-enhancing drugs has altered the evaluation of players with these statistical achievements).

One baseball game provides multiple statistics that can be used to compare players from the game's current group of major leaguers as well as to compare of players from different generations. In his speech when receiving the Ford Frick Award at the Hall of Fame induction ceremony in 1981, Ernie Harwell said, "Baseball is a spirited race of man against man, reflex against reflex, a game of inches. Every skill is measured. Every heroic, every failing is seen and cheered, or booed. And then it becomes a statistic."[123] Strate comments, "In most games the players keep score, and in many they tally a variety of figures, but no game rivals baseball in its diversity of mathematical calculations and manipulations."[124] Recognizing the importance of statistics, Major League Baseball has hired the Elias Sports Bureau to be its official statistician. The Elias Sports Bureau has provided historical and statistical services for professional sports leagues since 1913.[125]

The multitude of statistics that are produced during a baseball game have created another reason for people to pay attention to baseball: fantasy baseball. With statistics as the basis for the game and because technology makes it easy to compile and distribute statistics and to follow players' performances, fantasy baseball has become an additional reason that Major League Baseball is so popular with fans. Networks, Web sites, and magazines have all capitalized on this opportunity and tailored their coverage of baseball specifically to fantasy baseball players. Baerg contends that because fantasy sports are an increasingly important part of the sports culture, traditional media outlets are devoting more attention to fantasy sports.[126] In-game statistics have always been updated, such as displaying a player's season hitting statistics when he comes to bat for the first time in the game, and in subsequent at-bats seeing what he has done in that particular game; but now perhaps the complete in-game box score is provided more frequently.

The fantasy game competition is easy to follow not only through the traditional medium of watching baseball games on television, but also through the Internet, with Web sites updating real-time statistics. Roy and Goss point out that participating in fantasy sports is made easy through Web sites; that the sites are often free or of little expense contributes to the number of fantasy players.[127]

Academic research about the phenomenon of fantasy sports is continuing to develop. Several articles chronicle the history, participant demographic profile, economic impact, and cultural impact of fantasy sports.[128] One prominent area in the study of fantasy sports focuses on the motivations of fantasy sports participants.[129] Roy and Goss contend that fantasy sports participation is motivated by both internal psychological variables and external social variables. They explain that the internal psychological variables are the ability to: (1) exert control as the owner of a team through such activities as creating a team name and logo, selecting the players, making trades, and putting together a starting lineup, (2) to escape reality in getting away from daily routines and stress; and (3) to acquire the feeling of achievement obtained from defeating the competition in a fantasy matchup.[130]

Other scholars have elaborated on these internal motivating factors for fantasy participation. Davis and Duncan identify the fan's ability to demonstrate his or her sports knowledge in drafting players.[131] Farquhar and Meeds stress that the ability to gather information and statistics about the actual sport and its players, and the fantasy sports participants' desire for victory, motivated them to join a fantasy league.[132] Bernhard and Eade claim that the gambling involved could serve as a motivating factor for fantasy participants.[133]

In documenting the external variables, Roy and Goss explain that being a part of a community with shared interests and the opportunity to socialize with family, friends, and colleagues are motivating factors for fantasy sports participation.[134] Bernhard and Eade stress that the Internet assists with the socialization aspect of playing fantasy sports since participants are permitted to post comments on league message boards.[135] Because of all of these variables, Davis and Duncan provide some evidence from fantasy players who state that their motivation for watching a game is largely due to having a player participating in the real game on their fantasy team.[136] In fact, interest in seeing how fantasy players perform can serve as the most influential factor in a fan's watching a game.[137]

The Major League Baseball Web site includes a series of fantasy games for fans. In addition to the more traditional fantasy baseball game that relies on players' statistical performances, unique games have been created. One such game is mlb.com's "Beat the Streak" contest, in which the object is for the fan to pick one player every day that he or she believes will get a hit. If that major league player does get a hit, the fan's streak continues. If the major league player does not get a hit, the fan's streak ends. The first contestant to reach 57 games, surpassing the actual major league record of Joe Dimaggio's hitting in 56 consecutive games, will win a prize that in 2013 was $5.6 million. These fantasy games provide consistent visitors to the mlb.com Web site.

Media and the International Audience

In his 2006 book *Growing the Game: The Globalization of Major League Baseball*, Alan Klein contends, "Major League Baseball's efforts at globalization are not only provident for the future of the sport but also critical to its prosperity. The ability of the game to rely upon its domestic base of fans and players has receded to the point where globalizing is imperative."[138] In realizing the opportunities to grow the game of baseball and the Major League Baseball brand, several communication and media initiatives have been implemented to reach people outside of the United States.

Major League Baseball International has been created with the mission statement that it "focuses on the worldwide growth of baseball and the promotion of Major League Baseball and Major League Baseball Club Trademarks and Copyrights through special events, broadcasting, market development, licensing and sponsorship initiatives. Major League Baseball International is committed to showcasing the world's best baseball talent through international events around the globe."[139] Major League Baseball International supports its mission with a presence in Beijing, London, Sydney, and Tokyo. Its initiatives include providing equipment and instruction about the game of baseball in different parts of the world. The Major League Baseball Web site is available in Spanish, Japanese, and Korean. Additionally, on several occasions Major League Baseball has begun its regular season with games in Japan. Exhibition games have even been played in China.

In terms of media, Major League Baseball broadcasts games in 233 countries and territories and game telecasts are re-transmitted in 17 different languages.[140] Major League Baseball has partnered with ESPN International since 1994 to distribute games. As part of the broadcast rights agreement negotiated with Major League Baseball in 2012 that extends until 2021, ESPN International will transmit more than 125 regular season games, the All-Star Game, playoff games, and the World Series, to fans in 40 countries in Europe, Latin America, the Caribbean, the Middle East, Africa, Israel, Australia, New Zealand, the Pacific islands, and cruise ships.[141] In Canada, Major League Baseball International has an agreement with Rogers Sportsnet that runs through 2013 and brings at least 250 regular season games to fans throughout Canada. In Taiwan, Formosa Television has been a broadcast partner since 2007 and has a contract that runs through 2012. Major League Baseball is the most popular sports programming on Formosa Television. In 2009, Major League Baseball International entered into agreements with three broadcasters in China, which bring regional coverage of the World Series to more than 250 million viewers.[142] In Japan, fueled by the popularity of Japanese stars Ichiro Suzuki and Hideki Matsui, the firm Dentsu, Inc., a leading global sports marketing company, has an agreement with Major League Baseball International to be the television and radio partner in Japan through 2015.[143] In 2011, YouTube began broadcasting all Major League Baseball games on its Web site in Japan. Games are available 36 hours after they air. YouTube in Japan also provided highlight reels for every game from 2009 and 2010.[144]

Major League Baseball International produces a completely independent world feed for the All-Star Game, the playoffs, and the World Series to distribute to its television partners around the world. The world feed "allows Major League Baseball International and international announcers to focus more on international players and provide information that is especially interesting to a worldwide audience." It also means that broadcasters around the world receive a feed that is clean of in-game promotions and branding from other networks.[145] This "clean feed" provides the opportunity for virtual advertising displays, such as behind home plate, to be included in multiple broadcasts for specific audiences.

To further the global reach of baseball, the World Baseball Classic was created and sanctioned by Major League Baseball and the International Baseball Federation. Even South Africa fielded a team with the hope of raising the profile of baseball in the country.[146] The tournament, featuring teams from sixteen countries was first played in 2006. The second tournament was held in 2009. Japan, led by Boston Red Sox pitcher and two-time World Baseball Classic MVP Daisuke Matsuzaka, won the first two tournaments with the Dominican Republic winning in 2013. Beginning in 2013 the World Baseball

Classic will be played every four years. The tournament has expanded to twenty-eight countries qualifying for the sixteen-team tournament. The MLB Network will broadcast all games for the 2013 and 2017 tournaments.

Summary

The role that the mass media play in experiencing and enjoying the game of baseball is undoubtedly significant. While technology has changed both the way mass media content is distributed and the way it is used, the necessity to use some form of media to experience baseball remains. Major League Baseball and its audience have made adjustments in their behavior. New media vehicles do not necessarily replace older forms of media; rather, these new media vehicles simply provide another opportunity to experience baseball-related content. Fans still watch the World Series on television, but if that option is not available to them they can now watch it online. Fans have more options to read and learn about the games and players through Internet blogs, while still having the opportunity to read traditional newspaper or magazine stories.

As for its impact on the business of Major League Baseball, the media, both national and local television and radio, continue to be a vital source of revenue, although discrepancies about how to equitably share that revenue do exist. The media have not had a negative impact on stadium attendance; more than 73 million fans have visited ballparks every year since 2004. The media have largely helped grow the Major League Baseball business by developing content offerings that provide revenue, such as the MLB Network or content explicitly for online and handheld devices. In recognizing that its fan base is very diverse in how it experiences the sport, Major League Baseball has developed media initiatives to reach multiple audiences. The media have also been the vehicle that helps promote the Major League Baseball brand internationally.

The relationship between baseball and the media is almost certain to change because technology will continue to advance the possibilities. Which television network will fans be watching the World Series on in future years? Which ancillary communication vehicles will be available for fans to experience Major League Baseball games and other league content? These are simply unknown. What is known is that as long as baseball fans desire to experience the game and don't have a ticket, the mass media in some form will be their option. And, after the game ends, fans will want to hear from the players and managers involved, seek analysis from journalists they respect, and use the media to offer their own opinions.

Notes

1. Ernie Harwell, "Hall of Fame Induction Speech," August 2, 1981, http://www.baseball-almanac-com/hof/Ernie_Harwell_HOF_Induction.shtml.

2. Gary Gumpert and Susan J. Drucker, eds., *Take Me Out to the Ballgame: Communicating Baseball* (Cresskill, NJ: Hampton, 2002), 4.

3. Jack Barwind, "Baseball Is a Storied Game," in *Take Me Out to the Ballgame: Communicating Baseball*, eds. Gary Gumpert and Susan J. Drucker (Cresskill, NJ: Hampton, 2002), 23.

4. Lloyd R. Sloan, "The Motives of Sports Fans," in *Sports, Games, and Play: Social and Psychological Viewpoints*, ed. Jeffrey H. Goldstein (Hillside, NJ: Erlbaum, 1989), 176–77.

5. Thomas A. Tutko, "Personality Change in the American Sport Scene," in *Sports, Games, and Play: Social and Psychological Viewpoints*, ed. Jeffrey H. Goldstein (Hillside, NJ: Erlbaum, 1989), 113.

6. Daniel L. Wann, Michael P. Schrader, and Anthony M. Wilson, "Sport Fan Motivation: Questionnaire Validation, Comparisons by Sport, and Relationship to Athletic Motivation," *Journal of Sport Behavior* 22 (1999): 114–139.

7. Lawrence A. Wenner and Walter Gantz, "The Audience Experience with Sports on Television," in *Media, Sports, and Society*, ed. Lawrence A. Wenner (Newbury Park, CA: Sage, 1989), 241–269; Adam C. Earnheardt, Paul M. Haridakis, and Barbara S. Hugenberg, *Sports Fans, Identity, and Socialization: Exploring the Fandemonium* (Lanham, MD: Lexington, 2012).

8. William Sutton, Mark A. McDonald, George R. Milne, and John Cimperman, "Creating and Fostering Fan Identification in Professional Sports," *Sports Marketing Quarterly* 6 (1997): 15–22.

9. Nick Trujillo and Bob Krizek, "Emotionality in the Stands and in the Field: Expressing Self Through Baseball," *Journal of Sport and Social Issues* 18 (1994): 306.

10. Michael A. Hogg and Dominic Abrams, *Social Identifications: A Social Psychology of Intergroup Relations and Group Processes* (London: Routledge, 1988), 128.

11. Michael Lewis, "Franchise Relocation and Fan Allegiance," *Journal of Sport and Social Issues* 25 (2001): 8.

12. Lawrence A. Wenner and Walter Gantz, "Watching Sports on Television: Audience Experience, Gender, Fanship, and Marriage," in *Mediasport*, ed. Lawrence A. Wenner (London: Routledge, 1998), 236.

13. Daniel L. Wann, Michael P. Schrader, and Anthony M. Wilson, "Sport Fan Motivation: Questionnaire Validation, Comparisons by Sport, and Relationship to Athletic Motivation," *Journal of Sport Behavior* 22 (1999).

14. Lawrence A. Wenner and Walter Gantz, "Watching Sports on Television"; Dolf Zillmann, Jennings Bryant, and Barry S. Sapolsky, "Enjoyment from Sports Spectatorship," in *Sports, Games, and Play: Social and Psychological Viewpoints*, ed. Jeffrey H. Goldstein (Hillside, NJ: Erlbaum, 1989), 241–278.

15. Wenner and Gantz, "Watching Sports on Television," 238.

16. Zillmann, Bryant, and Sapolsky, "Enjoyment from Sports Spectatorship," 256.

17. John A. Fortunato, "The Rival Concept: An Analysis of the 2002 Monday Night Football Season," *Journal of Sport Management* 18 (2004): 383–97.

18. Zillmann, Bryant, and Sapolsky, "Enjoyment from Sports Spectatorship," 256.

19. Bernie Mullin, Stephen Hardy, and William Sutton, *Sport Marketing*, 3rd ed. (Champaign, IL: Human Kinetics, 2007).

20. Daniel Funk and Jeff James, "The Psychological Continuum Model: A Conceptual Framework for Understanding an Individual's Psychological Connection to Sport," *Sport Management Review* 4 (2001): 119–50.

21. Sandra J. Ball-Rokeach and Melvin L. DeFleur, "The Interdependence of the Media and Other Social Systems," in *Inter/Media: Interpersonal Communication in a Media World*, ed. Gary Gumpert and Robert Cathcart (New York: Oxford University Press, 1986), 81–96.

22. Pablo Halpern, "Media Dependency and Political Perceptions in an Authoritarian Political System," *Journal of Communication* 44 (1994): 39–52.

23. Eric Fisher, "Finish Gives Selig Hope: Commish Thinks MLB's Late Rebound at Gate Signals Healthy '14'," *Street and Smith's Sports Business Journal* 16 (October 7–13, 2013): 4. For a listing of the year-by-year attendance totals for Major League Baseball, including each team, see: http://espn.go.com/mlb/attendance.

24. Brien R. Williams, "The Structure of Televised Football," *Journal of Communication* 27 (1977): 135.

25. Janet Lever and Stanton Wheeler, "Mass Media and the Experience of Sport," *Communication Research* 20 (1993): 125–143; Lawrence A. Wenner, *Media, Sports, and Society* (Newbury Park, CA: Sage, 1989).

26. History, "First Televised Major League Baseball Game," http://www.history.com/this-day-in-history/first-televised-major-league-baseball-game.

27. Geoffrey C. Ward and Ken Burns, *Baseball: An Illustrated Story* (New York: Knopf, 1994).

28. Cited by Ward and Burns, *Baseball*, 331.

29. John Ourand, "Fox, Turner Contribute to $12B Rights Haul for MLB," *Street and Smith's Sports Business Journal* 15 (September 24–30, 2012): 1, 6; Sports Media Watch, "Fox Cuts Back on Regular Season Baseball; Blackouts for Regional Games to Be Lifted," October 2, 2012, http://www.sportsmediawatch.com/2012/10/fox-cuts-back-on-regular-season-baseball-blackouts-for-regional-games-to-be-lifted/.

30. Ourand, "Fox, Turner Contribute."

31. John Ourand and Michael Smith, "NCAA's Money-Making Matchup: How CBS, Turner Made the Numbers Work in $10.8 Billion Deal," *Street and Smith's Sports Business Journal* 13 (April 26–May 2, 2010): 1, 27.

32. Ourand, "Fox, Turner Contribute."

33. For several historical dates, see Gumpert and Drucker, *Take Me Out to the Ballgame*; David Nemec, *The 20th Century Baseball Chronicle: A Year-by-Year History of Major League Baseball* (Montreal: Tormont, 1992).

34. John Ourand, "No MLB Yet for Sirius Subscribers," *Street and Smith's Sports Business Journal* 11 (March 9, 2009): 1.

35. Nemec, *20th Century Baseball Chronicle*.

36. F. Scott Regan, "The Baseball Announcer: America's 'Groit,'" in *Cooperstown Symposium on Baseball and the American Culture*, ed. Alvin L. Hall (Westport, CT: Meckler, 1990), 213.

37. Ibid., 215.

38. Curt Smith, *The Storytellers: From Mel Allen to Bob Costas: Sixty Years of Baseball Tales from the Broadcast Booth* (New York: Macmillan, 1995), 1.

39. Seattle Mariners, "Hall of Fame Broadcaster Dave Niehaus Passes Away. Voice of the Mariners Called Every Season in Mariners History," press release, Wednesday November 10, 2010, http://www.mariners.com.

40. Steve Kelley, "Words Can't Describe Impact of This Loss," *Seattle Times*, http://seattletimes.nwsource.com/html/stevekelley/2013400903_kelley11.html.

41. Nemec, *20th Century Baseball Chronicle*.

42. Donald E. Parente, "The Interdependence of Sports and Television," *Journal of Communication* 27 (1977): 128.

43. Nemec, *20th Century Baseball Chronicle*.

44. Robert V. Bellamy, Jr., "Professional Sports Organizations: Media Strategies," in *Media, Sports, and Society*, ed. Lawrence A. Wenner (Newbury Park, CA: Sage, 1989), 120.

45. John A. Fortunato, *The Ultimate Assist: The Relationship and Broadcast Strategies of the NBA and Television Networks* (Cresskill, NJ: Hampton, 2001).

46. Ourand, "Fox, Turner Contribute."

47. Richard Deitsch, "A Shot at the Champ: Fox Promises to Come Out Swinging with a New 24/7 Channel, but Can FS1 Really Challenge ESPN?" *Sports Illustrated*, March 18, 2013, 16.

48. Fortunato, *The Ultimate Assist*, 157.

49. Andrew Zimbalist, *The Bottom Line: Observations and Arguments on the Sports Business* (Philadelphia: Temple University Press, 2006), 1.

50. John A. Fortunato, "Pete Rozelle: Developing and Communicating the Sports Brand," *International Journal of Sport Communication* 1 (2008): 361–77.

51. Jayson Stark, "How the New CBS Changes Baseball," ESPN.com, November 22, 2012, http://www.espn.go.com/mlb/story/_/id/7270203/baseball-new-labor-deal-truly-historic-one.

52. Bob Nightengale, "Yankees to Pay Record $29 Million Luxury Tax," *USA Today*, September 11, 2013, 4C.

53. John Ourand, "Deal with Dodgers Shifts Attention to Local Team Rights," *Street and Smith's Sports Business Journal* 15 (February 11–17, 2013): 12.

54. "2013 MLB Team Salaries," USAToday.com, http://www.usatoday.com/sports/mlb/salaries/2013/team/all/.

55. Eric Fisher, "He Set the Standard," *Street and Smith's Sports Business Journal* 13 (July 19–25, 2010): 1, 32–34.

56. John A. Fortunato, "The Advertising Ramifications of the YES Network/Cablevision Lawsuit," *Rutgers Law Record* 27 (2003), http://www.lawrecord.com/archive/vol27.html.

57. Richard Sandomir, "Regional Sports Networks Show the Money," *New York Times*, August 20, 2011, D1.

58. John Ourand, "Broader Reach: Youth Sports See Broadband as a Winning Model for Boosting Exposure," *Street and Smith's Sports Business Journal* 12 (August 17–23, 2009): 15–16, 22.

59. Wenner, *Media, Sports, and Society*, 14.

60. Robert V. Bellamy, Jr., "The Evolving Television Sports Marketplace," in *Mediasport*, ed. Wenner, 73.

61. James G. Webster and Lawrence W. Lichty, *Ratings Analysis: Theory and Practice* (Hillside, NJ: Erlbaum, 1991), p. 3.

62. Alan M. Rubin, "Ritualized and Instrumental Television Viewing," *Journal of Communication* 34 (1984): 67–77.

63. Alan M. Rubin, "The Uses-and-Gratifications Perspective of Media Effects," in *Media Effects: Advances in Theory and Research*, 2nd ed., ed. Jennings Bryant and Dolf Zillmann (Mahwah, NJ: Hampton, 2002), 525–548.

64. Rubin, "Ritualized and Instrumental Television Viewing"; Alan M. Rubin and Elizabeth M. Perse, "Audience Activity and Television News Gratifications," *Communication Research* 14 (1987): 58–84.

65. Fortunato, *The Ultimate Assist.*

66. Ibid., 11.

67. Ibid., 70; John A. Fortunato, "The NFL Programming Schedule: A Study of Agenda-Setting," *Journal of Sports Media* 3 (2008): 27–49.

68. "Tale of the Tape: NBA vs. MLB, Part II," October 30, 2013, http://www.sportsmediawatch.com/2012/10/tale-of-the-tape-nba-vs-mlb-part-ii/.

69. "All-Star Game Television Ratings," Baseball-almanac.com, http://www.baseball-almanac.com/asgbox/asgtv.shtml; "MLB All-Star Ratings: Despite N. Y. Factor, ASG Ties Second-Lowest Overnight," July 17, 2013, http://www.sportsmediawatch.com/2013/07/mlb-all-star-ratings-despite-n-y-factor-asg-ties-second-lowest-overnight/.

70. John Ourand and David Broughton, "Smallest Markets Show Ratings Boost," *Street and Smith's Sports Business Journal* 16 (September 30–October 6, 2013): 4.

71. Wenner and Gantz, "Watching Sports on Television."

72. Fortunato, *The Ultimate Assist*, 73.

73. Susan T. Eastman, *Research in Media Promotion* (Mahwah, NJ: Lawrence Erlbaum, 2000); John A. Fortunato, "CBS Promotion of Future Programming During the 2011 NCAA Tournament," *Journal of Promotion Management* 18 (2012): 474–88.

74. Lever and Wheeler, "Mass Media and the Experience of Sport," 135.

75. Robert B. Bellamy, Jr., and Paul J. Traudt, "Television Branding as Promotion," in *Research in Media Promotion*, ed. Susan T. Eastman (Mahwah, NJ: Lawrence Erlbaum, 2000), 127.

76. David Broughton, "A-B, Gatorade Keep Leads but See Numbers Fall," November 10, 2010, Sportsbusinessjournal.com, http://www.sportsbusinessdaily.com/Journal/Issues/2010/11/20101115/This-Weeks-Issue/A-B-Gatorade-Keep-Leads-But-See-Numbers-Fall.aspx.

77. John A. Fortunato, *Sports Sponsorship: Principles and Practices* (Jefferson, NC: McFarland, 2013).

78. Tony Meenaghan, "The Role of Sponsorship in the Marketing Communications Mix," *International Journal of Advertising* 10 (1991): 35–47; Mullin et al., *Sport Marketing.*

79. Fortunato, *Sports Sponsorship.*

80. Anthony D. Miyazaki and Angela Morgan, "Assessing Market Value of Event Sponsoring: Corporate Olympic Sponsorship," *Journal of Advertising Research*, 41 (2001): 10.

81. T. Bettina Cornwell and Isabelle Maignan, "An International Review of Sponsorship Research," *Journal of Advertising* 27 (1998): 1–21; Kevin P. Gwinner and John Eaton, "Building Brand Image Through Event Sponsorship: The Role of Image Transfer," *Journal of Advertising* 28 (1999): 47–58.

82. Dwane H. Dean, "Associating the Corporation with a Charitable Event Through Sponsorship: Measuring the Effects on Corporate Community Relations," *Journal of Advertising* 31 (2002): 78.

83. Horst Stipp and Nicholas P. Schiavone, "Modeling the Impact of Olympic Sponsorship on Corporate Image," *Journal of Advertising Research* 34 (1996): 22–28.

84. Fortunato, *Sports Sponsorship*; Gwinner and Eaton, "Building Brand Image Through Event Sponsorship"; Stipp and Schiavone, "Modeling the Impact of Olympic Sponsorship."

85. Cornwell and Maignan, "International Review of Sponsorship Research"; Dean, "Associating the Corporation with a Charitable Event"; Miyazaki and Morgan, "Assessing Market Value of Event Sponsoring."

86. Bill Harvey, "Measuring the Effects of Sponsorship," *Journal of Advertising Research* 41 (2001): 64.

87. T. Bettina Cornwell, C.S. Weeks, and Donald P. Roy, "Sponsorship-Linked Marketing: Opening the Black Box," *Journal of Advertising* 34 (2005): 36.

88. Fortunato, *Sports Sponsorship*.

89. Meenaghan, "Role of Sponsorship," 43.

90. Cornwell et al., "Sponsorship-Linked Marketing," 36.

91. Richard Buttny and Arthur D. Jensen, "Hot-Stove League Talk," in *Take Me Out to the Ballgame: Communicating Baseball*, ed. Gary Gumpert and Susan J. Drucker (Cresskill, NJ: Hampton, 2002), 73.

92. Buttny and Jensen, "Hot-Stove League Talk," 72.

93. Kathleen Hall Jamieson and Paul Waldman, *The Press Effect: Politicians, Journalists, and the Stories That Shape the Political World* (New York: Oxford University Press, 2003), xiii.

94. Cited in Fortunato, *The Ultimate Assist*, 116.

95. Christine Brennan, "Annika Accomplished More with Her Achievement than She Realizes," *USA Today*, May 27, 2003, 13c.

96. Wenner, *Media, Sports, and Society*, 38.

97. Peter Gammons, Hall of Fame Induction Speech, August 1, 2005, http://sports.espn.go.com/mlb/news/story?id=2121535.

98. George Castle, *Baseball and the Media: How Fans Lose in Today's Coverage of the Game* (Lincoln: University of Nebraska Press, 2006).

99. Bob Nightengale, "Series Gets Super-Sized Interview Day," *USA Today*, October 27, 2009, 3C.

100. David Broughton, "Survey: Social-Media Use Builds Fan Avidity," *Street and Smith's Sports Business Journal* 13 (July 26–August 1, 2010): 9.

101. William A. Benoit, *Accounts, Excuses, and Apologies: A Theory of Image Restoration Strategies* (Albany: State University of New York Press, 1995); Edward Bernays, *The Engineering of Consent* (Norman: University of Oklahoma Press, 1955); Michael Phau and Hua-Hsin Wan, "Persuasion: An Intrinsic Function of Public Relations," in *Public Relations Theory II*, ed. Carl H. Botan and Vincent Hazelton (Mahwah, NJ: Lawrence Erlbaum, 2006), 101–36.

102. Benoit, *Accounts, Excuses, and Apologies*; Maxwell E. McCombs, Donald L. Shaw, and David Weaver, *Communication and Democracy: Exploring the Intellectual Frontiers in Agenda-Setting Theory* (Mahwah, NJ: Lawrence Erlbaum, 1997).

103. John A. Fortunato, "Public Relations Strategies for Creating Mass Media

Content: A Case Study of the National Basketball Association," *Public Relations Review* 26 (2000): 481–97.

104. Maria Hopwood, "Sports Public Relations," in *Marketing of Sport*, ed. Simon Chadwick and John Beech (Upper Saddle River, NJ: Prentice Hall, 2007): 293.

105. Cited by Castle, *Baseball and the Media*, 259.

106. Castle, *Baseball and the Media*, 259.

107. MLB, "About Us," http://mlb.mlb.com/sponsorship/mediakit/about_us.jsp.

108. Laura Myers, "New Pieces in Baseball's Electoral College: Online Voting and Social Media Become Game Changers in Fans' All-Star Balloting," *Los Angeles Times*, June 27, 2010, C1.

109. Major League Baseball Press Release, "Freeman, Delabar Win Record-Breaking Final Vote," July 11, 2013, http://www.mlb.com.

110. MLB, "MLB Productions," http://mlb.mlb.com/mlb/video/mlb_productions/feature.jsp?content=overview.

111. Eric Fisher, "Giants Want to Become an Economic Force," *Street and Smith's Sports Business Journal* 13 (November 8–14, 2010): 5.

112. Tim Lemke, "MLB Network Passes Test," *The Washington Times*, February 12, 2009, C2.

113. Diane Pucin, "MLB Network Steps Up to the Plate on A-Rod Story," *Los Angeles Times*, February 10, 2009, D4.

114. Quoted in Pucin, "MLB Network Steps Up."

115. Quoted in Lemke, "MLB Network Passes Test."

116. Mullin, et al., *Sport Marketing*; Matthew D. Shank, *Sports Marketing: A Strategic Perspective*, 3rd ed. (Upper Saddle River, NJ: Pearson, 2005).

117. Shank, *Sports Marketing*, 228.

118. Thomas O'Guinn, Chris T. Allen, and Richard J. Semenik, *Advertising and Integrated Brand Promotion*, 4th ed. (Mason, OH: Thomson, 2006); Artemsia Apostolopoulou, "Brand Extensions by U.S. Professional Sports Teams: Motivations and Keys to Success," *Sport Marketing Quarterly* 11 (2002): 205–14.

119. Bellamy and Traudt, "Television Branding as Promotion"; Scott Davis, *Brand Asset Management: Driving Profitable Growth Through Your Brands* (San Francisco, CA: Jossey-Bass, 2002).

120. Kevin L. Keller, *Strategic Brand Management: Building, Measuring, and Managing Brand Equity* (Upper Saddle River, NJ: Prentice Hall, 1998).

121. Jeffrey D. James, Richard H. Kolbe, and Galen T. Trail, "Psychological Connection to a New Sport Team: Building or Maintaining the Consumer Base?" *Sport Marketing Quarterly* 11 (2002): 215.

122. John A. Fortunato, "The Many Faces of 'Fans': How the NBA Reaches Out to Its Different Audience Segments," in *Sports Fans, Identity and Socialization: Exploring the Fandemonium*, ed. Adam C. Earnheardt, Paul M. Haridikis, and Barbara Hugenberg (Lanham, MD: Lexington, 2012): 165–176.

123. Ernie Harwell, Hall of Fame Induction Speech, August 2, 1981, http://www.baseball-almanac-com/hof/Ernie_Harwell_HOF_Induction.shtml.

124. Lance Strate, "The Medium of Baseball," in *Take Me Out to the Ballgame: Communicating Baseball*, ed. Gary Gumpert and Susan J. Drucker (Cresskill, NJ: Hampton, 2002), 64.

125. The Elias Sports Bureau, http://www.esb.com.

126. Andrew Baerg, "Just a Fantasy? Exploring Fantasy Sports," *Electronic Journal of Communication* 19 (2009), http://www.cios.org/www/ejc/v19n34toc.htm.

127. Donald P. Roy and Benjamin D. Goss, "A Conceptual Framework of Influences on Fantasy Sports Consumption," *Marketing Management Journal* 17 (2007): 96–108.

128. Baerg, "Just a Fantasy?"; Nickolas W. Davis and Margaret C. Duncan, "Sports Knowledge Is Power: Reinforcing Masculine Privilege Through Fantasy Sport League Participation," *Journal of Sport and Social Issues* 30 (2006): 244–64; Roy and Goss, "A Conceptual Framework."

129. Bo J. Bernhard and Vincent H. Eade, "Gambling in a Fantasy World: An Exploratory Study of Rotisserie Baseball Games," *UNLV Gaming Research and Review Journal* 9 (2005): 29–42; Davis and Duncan, "Sports Knowledge Is Power"; Roy and Goss, "A Conceptual Framework."

130. Roy and Goss, "A Conceptual Framework."

131. Davis and Duncan, "Sports Knowledge Is Power."

132. Lee Farquhar and Robert T. Meeds, "Types of Fantasy Sports Users and Their Motivations," *Journal of Computer-Mediated Communication* 12 (2007): 1208–28.

133. Bernhard and Eade, "Gambling in a Fantasy World."

134. Roy and Goss, "A Conceptual Framework."

135. Bernhard and Eade, "Gambling in a Fantasy World."

136. Davis and Duncan, "Sports Knowledge Is Power."

137. John A. Fortunato, "The Influence of Fantasy Football on NFL Television Ratings," *Journal of Sports Administration & Supervision* 3 (2011): 74–90.

138. Alan M. Klein, *Growing the Game: The Globalization of Major League Baseball* (New Haven, CT: Yale University Press, 2006).

139. MLB, "MLB International," http://mlb.mlb.com/mlb/international/sections.jsp?feature=mlbi.

140. Ibid.

141. "ESPN, MLB Reach Eight-Year Multiplatform Rights Extension; More MLB for the Caribbean and Latin America," *ESPN Media Zone*, August 28, 2012, http://espnmediazone3.com/wmpu/blog/category/espn.international/page2/.

142. MLB, "MLB International," http://mlb.mlb.com/mlb/international/sections.jsp?feature=mlbi.

143. MLB, "MLB International," http://mlb.mlb.com/mlb/international/sections.jsp?feature=mlbi_broadcasting.

144. *Street and Smith's Sports Business Journal* 12 (September 6–12, 2010): 10.

145. MLB, "MLB International," http://mlb.mlb.com/mlb/international/sections.jsp?feature=mlbi_broadcasting.

146. Kevin Baxter, "Baseball's Not Quite Cricket in South Africa," *Los Angeles Times*, August 19, 2010, http://articles.latimes.com/2010/aug/19/sports/la-sp-south-africa-baseball-20100820.

Suggested Readings

Castle, George (2007). *Baseball and the Media: How Fans Lose in Today's Coverage of the Game.* Lincoln: University of Nebraska Press, Bison Books.

Fortunato, John A. (2013). *Sports Sponsorship: Principles and Practices*. Jefferson, NC: McFarland.

Fortunato, John A. (2013). Television Broadcast Rights: Still the Golden Goose. In P.M. Pedersen (Ed.). *Routledge Handbook of Sport Communication* (pp. 188–196). New York: Routledge.

L'Etang, Jacquie (2013). *Sports Public Relations*. Thousand Oaks, CA: Sage.

Zimbalist, Andrew (2004). *May the Best Team Win: Baseball Economics and Public Policy*. Washington, DC: Brookings Institution Press.

Zimbalist, Andrew (2013). *In the Best Interests of Baseball? Governing the National Pastime*. Lincoln: University of Nebraska Press.

4

Law

MITCHELL NATHANSON

Introduction

The intermingling of baseball and the law has historically been complicated and confusing, for while America's game has been officially exempted from the law in some areas, it is subject to the law in a myriad of others. As an unfortunate result, both the nature of baseball's famous (or infamous, depending upon one's perspective) antitrust exemption as well as the applicability of a whole host of other laws to it remain frustratingly murky. What exactly is baseball's antitrust exemption? How was it created? Why was it created? What does the exemption mean for practical purposes? On all of these points, few can agree. Likewise, confusion reigns when it comes to a discussion of all of those laws that do indeed apply, at least in theory, to Major League Baseball; many wonder why it seems that baseball, or at least those who run it, so often get a pass from the judiciary in the absence of similar exemptions. In this chapter, we'll attempt to make sense of this.

Much of the relationship between baseball and the law can be understood through two distinct trilogies of cases (one focusing on baseball's antitrust exemption, another focusing on the nature of judicial deference to the authority granted to baseball's office of the commissioner) along with a more recent decision that seemingly ties the theories underlying the two trilogies together and uses them to point the way toward a new and different way this relationship will be defined during the 21st century. Baseball, by virtue of its historic status as our National Pastime, has always held a special place in our nation's, and therefore quite naturally our federal judiciary's, heart; and for this reason many of the decisions involving the game seem, and at times are, incongruous with the law as we understand it. This, if the past is any guide, will most likely continue into the foreseeable future. The form of such judicial deference and rule-bending may look very different going forward, however, if this most recent case is a harbinger of things to come.

The Antitrust Trilogy

THE CREATION OF THE EXEMPTION

In a perfect world, we would discuss the scope of baseball's antitrust exemption before delving into its history and development. However, because its scope is unclear and because so much of the debate over the scope appears to hinge upon the historical development of the exemption, it is therefore necessary to tackle this first.[1] The Sherman Act (the act from which baseball was subsequently exempted) is a federal statute enacted in 1890 in response to a growing popular outcry against the proliferation of large trusts throughout the country in the latter half of the nineteenth century. The statute itself, as originally enacted, was brief in length but broad in scope, stating flatly in its first section, "Every contract, combination in the form of trust or otherwise, or conspiracy, in restraint of trade or commerce among the several States, or with foreign nations, is declared to be illegal." In its second section, the act stipulated that "every person who shall monopolize, or attempt to monopolize, or combine or conspire with any other person or persons, to monopolize any part of the trade or commerce among the several States, or with foreign nations, shall be deemed guilty of a felony." At first glance, the Sherman Act appears to be a relatively simple, straightforward piece of legislation. In practice it became something else altogether. This became particularly evident when the United States Supreme Court was faced with adjudging the actions of Major League Baseball within this context.

By way of background, Major League Baseball found itself before the Justices as a result of its battle with an upstart and rival major league, the Federal League. Prior to the birth of the Federal League, Major League Baseball consisted of two major leagues: the National, formed in 1876, and the American, formed out of the ashes of the old Western League and proclaimed (by its president Ban Johnson) in 1901 as an upstart and rival major league itself. After a brief war over players, the Nationals begrudgingly accepted the Americans in 1903 through the signing of a peace agreement known as the National Agreement, wherein each league agreed to recognize the other as an equal, recognize and honor each others' contracts and, most importantly, recognize and observe the reserve clause—a unilaterally imposed term inserted in all player contracts that bound each player to his team indefinitely. Through the reserve clause, Major League Baseball, through the National and American leagues, was able to control the contracts, and therefore the players themselves, for eternity, thereby impeding the ability of potential rival leagues to attract top talent away from the more established National and American leagues.

In 1913 a rival league, the Federal League, emerged, although initially it claimed to be nothing of the sort. A year later, however, it expanded and, seemingly flush with capital, declared itself a third major league, a putative equal of the National and American.[2] It sought fans as well as talent from its more established rivals and refused to honor the reserve clause, using as its strategy the lure of larger salaries to entice National and American League players to abandon their contracts and jump to the upstart Federal League. The result was inevitable: despite the presence of the reserve clause, major league player salaries increased rapidly as the established owners attempted to ward off the threat. By the close of the 1915 season, the by-now clearly underfunded Federal League was buckling under the weight of the salary war it had started. By December 1915, the Federal League was all but defunct: several of the Federal League owners had sued Major League Baseball and had accepted buyouts, while others were permitted to buy major league franchises. The Baltimore Federal League club, however, opted out of the settlement (or was not invited to the settlement meeting; the record is not clear). The other Federal League owners subsequently attempted to settle with Baltimore but Baltimore refused, choosing instead to sue Major League Baseball (among others) in federal court.

Technically, the Baltimore club filed suit under Section 4 of the Clayton Act, which was enacted in 1914 as a supplement to the Sherman Act. In its pleadings, Baltimore alleged that the defendants violated the act by monopolizing talent and restraining trade. At the trial level, Baltimore emerged victorious when the judge instructed the jury that the defendants did indeed engage in interstate commerce and that, through the reserve clause and National Agreement, a monopoly was created. Because of this, the only question for the jury was one focusing on damages. The jury found that the Baltimore franchise suffered damages in the amount of $80,000 which, when trebled pursuant to Section 4 of the Clayton Act, amounted to a verdict of $240,000 in favor of the Baltimore club, plus counsel fees. Major League Baseball appealed the verdict to the District of Columbia Circuit, which reversed the trial court's decision and set up the showdown at the Supreme Court. In essence, the D.C. Circuit court held that Major League Baseball did not engage in interstate commerce (a ruling we will return to in greater depth shortly) and, therefore, its actions could not be regulated by way of either the Sherman or Clayton acts. This time, it was Baltimore's turn to appeal, which it did; this appeal led to the first of the three cases within baseball's antitrust trilogy: *Federal Baseball Club of Baltimore v. National League of Professional Baseball Clubs.*[3]

In *Federal Baseball*, the Supreme Court, in an opinion authored by Oliver Wendell Holmes, solidified the exemption in 1922 that the D.C. Circuit court created a year earlier. In all of one paragraph, Justice Holmes dismissed the business of Major League Baseball as "purely state affairs" (an opinion that we will likewise return to in greater detail later). Although acknowledging that state lines are crossed in the giving of "exhibitions of base ball" and that money changes hands pursuant to these exhibitions, Justice Holmes nevertheless held that "transport is a mere incident, not the essential thing." Thus, baseball could not be considered interstate commerce and, as a result, could not be subject to federal antitrust law, which applies only to "commerce among the [several] states."

In 1953, the Supreme Court revisited its 1922 opinion in the second of the trilogy, *Toolson v. New York Yankees, Inc.*[4] That case involved a suit brought under §1 of the Sherman Act. Eschewing the opportunity to clarify the scope of the judicially created exemption, the Supreme Court issued a one-paragraph per curium order holding once again that the Sherman Act did not apply to Major League Baseball. The Court rested its holding on its 1922 decision and further stated that congressional inaction during the previous thirty-one had years served to cement the exemption and that it was up to Congress, not the Court, to destroy it.

Finally, in 1972, the Supreme Court revisited the issue for the final time to date in the third legal decision of the trilogy, *Flood v. Kuhn*.[5] Without delving into more detail than is necessary for our purposes here, this case involved an attempt by star St. Louis Cardinals outfielder Curt Flood to refuse a trade to the Phillies. In essence, his argument, like the ones in *Federal Baseball* and *Toolson* beforehand, focused on the anticompetitive nature of baseball's reserve clause. Flood argued that the clause violated the Sherman Act and, as such, was illegal. This time, in a much more lengthy opinion, the court waxed nostalgic about the history of baseball and reviewed the relationship between the antitrust laws and other major sports before concluding (in a departure from the Court's decision in *Federal Baseball*) that although baseball was in fact engaged in interstate commerce, its holdings in *Federal Baseball* and *Toolson* were nevertheless "aberration[s] confined to baseball."[6] In upholding the exemption for the third time, the Court one more time focused on Congress's "positive inaction" in justifying the continued existence of the exemption.

As this brief overview of the antitrust trilogy demonstrates, nowhere within these three decisions is there a discussion of the scope of the exemption. Rather, this issue has been repeatedly brushed aside and the entire issue lain on the doorstep of Congress to either abolish it or further define it. With the exception of the Curt Flood Act of 1998[7] (which only further muddied the waters by stating, on the one hand, that "major league baseball players are covered under the antitrust laws," and, on the other, that irrespective of this statement, the overwhelming majority of the exemptions to the antitrust acts that existed prior to the Curt Flood Act remained intact), Congress has chosen to remain silent, causing confusion as to what the exemption covers and what, if anything, is outside of its scope.

What most observers seem to be in agreement on, however, is that regardless of the scope of the exemption, the mere acts of creating and upholding it are examples of baseball's unique treatment under the law. Indeed, even the Justices themselves admit as much; Justice Blackmun's opinion in *Flood* went beyond merely identifying the exemption as the above-noted "aberration"; he announced within the opinion that "with its reserve system enjoying exemption from the federal antitrust laws, baseball is, in a very distinct sense, an exception and an anomaly." Further, he stated, "Even though others might regard this as 'unrealistic, inconsistent, or illogical' ... the aberration is an established one, and one that has been recognized not only in *Federal Baseball* and *Toolson*, but in ... a total of five consecutive cases in this Court. It is an aberration that has been with us now for half a century, one heretofore deemed fully entitled to the benefit of stare decisis, and one that has survived the Court's expanding concept of interstate commerce. It rests on a recognition and an acceptance of baseball's unique characteristics and needs." Finally, and forcefully, he concluded, "Other professional sports operating interstate— football, boxing, basketball, and, presumably, hockey and golf are not so exempt."[8] Popular opinion, judicial and otherwise, has likewise treated baseball's antitrust exemption as an aberration, and an ill-conceived and unjustifiable one at that. In a 1970 opinion, the Second Circuit "freely acknowledge[d] our belief that *Federal Baseball* was not one of Mr. Justice Holmes' happiest days,"[9] while John Helyar, in his authoritative treatise on baseball's labor issues, *Lords of the Realm*, summarized both his and the received wisdom that Holmes's decision "was a piece of fiction, one that would grow sillier with each passing year."[10]

But was it? From a modern perspective, it certainly seems to be; the rationale employed by the *Federal Baseball* court clearly does not hold up when analyzed alongside other, more modern antitrust decisions. This much was acknowledged by the *Flood* Court when it reversed Justice Holmes's ruling (although not the overall decision itself) that baseball was not engaged in interstate commerce. And the mere fact that both *Toolson* and *Flood* have been allowed to stand, undisturbed, despite this acknowledgement is testament that baseball, being baseball, has been accorded special treatment in this area, at least to an extent. But what about the *Federal Baseball* opinion itself—was it really a piece of fiction? When viewed within the context of its era, the surprising answer is that perhaps it was not.

In many respects, *Federal Baseball* was very much a product of its time, although the national reverence for baseball also seems to have played at least a supporting role in the outcome of the case at both the Circuit and Supreme Court levels. Despite national fervor over the ominous presence of large trusts in the latter half of the nineteenth century, the Sherman Act itself was initially considered little more than a ceremonial concession to this growing national unease. Something had to be done on the political level to respond, at least superficially, to the outcry and so the Sherman Act was passed, although few governmental officials viewed it as a legitimate or even necessary check. Despite his reputation as a "trust buster," Teddy Roosevelt held a rather generous view of most of them, considering all but the most obviously insidious a necessary function of a modern economy. "The man who advocates destroying the trusts by measures which would paralyze the industries of the country is at least a quack and at worst an enemy to the Republic," he remarked early in his presidency.[11] He, not unlike many within positions of power during the era, was not looking for excuses to bring down trusts or break up monopolies. Instead, he made, or at least attempted to make, distinctions between what he considered "good" and "bad" trusts. As he believed that trusts and monopolies themselves were not "bad" by definition, he limited the staffing of the Antitrust Division of the Department of Justice to a mere five attorneys with an annual budget of $100,000. In the words of historian Richard Hofstadter: "By definition, since only a handful of suits could be undertaken each year, there could hardly be very many 'bad' businesses. Such was the situation as T. R. left it during his presidency."[12] In sum, pursuant to Roosevelt's logic, because the modern American economy could not be inherently "bad," neither could there be many inherently "bad" trusts. Enforcement against the few bad apples pursuant to the Sherman Act would be the exception rather than the rule, his trust-busting reputation notwithstanding.

By the second decade of the twentieth century and into the era encapsulating the *Federal Baseball* decision, the White House's view of trusts had not evolved very much. President Woodrow Wilson exchanged Roosevelt's rudimentary definitions of "good" and "bad" trusts for the only slightly less rudimentary concepts of "free" and "illicit" competition, with "free" competition resulting in increased "efficiencies" and "illicit" competition resulting in unwanted inefficiencies. Like Roosevelt, Wilson believed in the necessity and inevitability of modern trusts, saying, "The elaboration of business upon a great co-operative scale is characteristic of our time and has come about by the natural operation of modern civilization.... We shall never return to the old order of individual competition."[13] As for what distinguished an efficient from an inefficient trust, no one knew for sure. In practice, it seemed as if, nomenclature aside, Wilson was still operating on the level of Roosevelt's playing field of "good" and "bad" trusts. And within such a framework, many trusts and monopolies would be left unchecked by the Sherman Act.

Not surprisingly within this environment, by the early 1920s a majority of the Supreme Court (whose members are, after all, nominated by the president) felt similarly, although they expressed their beliefs in more technical language. Of course, each Justice had his own view on the matter and some Justices were more wary of trusts than others, but as a whole, the Court was hesitant to check them. Justice Holmes, the author of the *Federal Baseball* decision, viewed the Sherman Act with condescension, once remarking privately that it was "a humbug based on economic ignorance and incompetence."[14] While his fellow Justices may not have shared the extremity of his disdain, the test the Court fashioned during this era was one that resulted in many trusts and monopolies being held to be outside the scope of the federal antitrust laws. Unless the trust had a significant impact on interstate commerce, it would be allowed to stand; a mere incidental impact would not be sufficient.[15] This was consistent with the Court's more fundamental position that Congress's power to legislate pursuant to the Constitution's Commerce Clause was rather limited—a view that evolved significantly in later years.[16] This test was perhaps rooted in the basic belief at the time that, as a general principle, trusts and monopolies were only "bad" (to use Roosevelt's term) when they significantly impacted local autonomy.[17] If they had only an incidental or indirect affect on it, they were not inherently odious and were as such beyond Congress's grasp.

Within this political and legal setting, *Federal Baseball* fits in neatly. Major League Baseball's trust (which resulted in this instance in the reserve clause that was at the center of the dispute between the parties) clearly met Roosevelt's rudimentary test as, even in the wake of the Black Sox scandal involving the fix of the 1919 World Series, baseball—our National Pastime—could be nothing other than a "good" trust (popular sentiment at the time blamed the players and/or outside gambling influences rather than White Sox owner Charles Comiskey for the fix). And it most likely would pass muster under Wilson's "efficiency" test as well, as the Circuit Court found persuasive the owners' argument that without the reserve clause, competitive balance within Major League Baseball would be ruined.[18] Likewise, as the owners argued and the Circuit and Supreme Court agreed, the baseball trust not only did not threaten local autonomy, it complimented and contributed to it. As the Circuit Court noted, the game of Major League Baseball "is local in its beginning and in its end."[19] Without the trust, so the theory went, the local presentations of "exhibitions of baseball" (to use the court's terminology) would be impossible. The choice of language by first the Circuit and later the Supreme Court was most likely not accidental: by repeatedly referring to the subject of the litigation as "exhibitions" of baseball, rather than the "business" or "industry" of baseball, both courts were quite clearly signaling that such events—mere exhibitions—could have nothing more than an incidental affect on interstate commerce. Certainly, the cultural significance of baseball played an important role in the courts' rulings. However, once the issue before the judges and Justices was framed through the lens of baseball as a game rather than as a business (a choice that likewise owed much to the game's societal standing), the resulting decisions were far from aberrations. The Supreme Court's subsequent decisions in *Toolson* and *Flood*, however, rendered in more modern eras when Congress's sweeping power under the Commerce Clause was already clear and recognized, are much more difficult to justify. In many respects, it is these decisions, rather than *Federal Baseball*, that were aberrant and that, to paraphrase Helyar, grew sillier with each passing year.

THE SCOPE OF THE EXEMPTION

With the development of baseball's antitrust exemption as a guide, we can now turn to the more pressing issues going forward: what, after all, is exempted as a result of *Federal Baseball* and its progeny, and what does this mean from a practical perspective? As stated in the introduction to this chapter, neither of these questions leads to a clear, easily definable answer. Technically, if the antitrust trilogy is taken as a literal template, the exemption appears to cover only matters involving baseball's reserve clause. Each of the three cases involved challenges to Major League Baseball's system of retaining players in perpetuity, regardless of their contract status. In fact, the lower court opinion in *Federal Baseball* focused specifically on this system and baseball's resultant monopoly on the talent pool, and its ability to quash rival leagues.[20] The lower court assumed consideration (although never explicitly stating what such consideration consisted of) in exchange for the players' acceptance of the clause in their contracts and, for the reasons discussed above, held the issue to be outside of the scope of the Sherman Act.[21] The plaintiffs in *Toolson* and *Flood* likewise focused singularly on the reserve clause as the basis for their antitrust challenges.[22]

Drawing on the trilogy, lower courts have taken differing views on the scope of the exemption. In 1993, the Eastern District of Pennsylvania in *Piazza v. Major League Baseball* held that, consistent with the trilogy, the exemption extends no further than the reserve clauses in players contracts.[23] Other lower courts, however, have taken a broader view, holding that the exemption applies to the entire business of baseball. The Federal Western District of Washington in *McCoy v. Major League Baseball* in essence threw up its hands over the issue and held that, until Congress or the Supreme Court "see[s] fit to alter the rule," baseball in its entirety is blanketed by the exemption.[24] As the Supreme Court has not taken it upon itself to resolve this disagreement (and probably won't in the future, due to the presence of the Curt Flood Act of 1998 that purports to resolve everything but in fact resolves very little), we need to look elsewhere to discover the true impact of the exemption in practice if not in theory. And the first question we need to ask is perhaps the most obvious one: did the exemption protect the reserve clause from legal challenge?

There are perhaps as many assumptions concerning the theoretical nexus between the reserve clause and the exemption as there are stitches on a baseball. Some commentators have gone so far as to conclude that the reserve clause actually is a *product* of the exemption.[25] However, Major League Baseball's "reserve system" (which resulted in the reserve clause's being incorporated into every professional baseball player's contract soon thereafter) predates *Federal Baseball* and the granting of baseball's antitrust exemption by almost half a century and, instead, has its roots in the creation of the National League in 1876. As such, its origins are wholly separate from that of the exemption and, as history demonstrated in the dismantling of the unilaterally imposed reserve clause in 1975, its workings were always irrelevant to it. Thus, to answer our first question, the simple answer is: No. However, a fuller understanding of this answer requires a more complete explanation of the series of events that led up to the fateful 1975 arbitration decision that answered this question once and for all.

In many ways, baseball's owners have been misguided in their approach to player relations, but one thing they could not be accused of was being stupid. They, if not the general public, understood quite clearly for decades prior to the 1975 decision the failings of the reserve clause and recognized its Achilles' Heel. While some of them surely knew earlier, by 1946, they all were made aware of the fact that above all else, the reserve clause could not be permitted to be adjudicated.[26] As they would learn, by way of a secret report of their Major League Steering Committee, while their antitrust exemption might bar rival leagues from mounting challenges to the clause (such as the Federal League in *Federal Baseball*), it would not prevent the players themselves from doing so. And once the players had taken this step, the reserve clause was as good as dead. This report, presented to the owners at their meeting in Chicago on August 27, 1946, undertook, in part, the task of examining the reserve clause and predicting its ability to withstand legal scrutiny should the dreaded litigation occur.[27] Its conclusions were clear and dire: "In the well-considered opinion of counsel for both Major Leagues, the present reserve clause could not be enforced in an equity court in a suit for specific performance, nor as the basis for a restraining order to prevent a player from playing elsewhere, or to prevent outsiders from inducing a player to breach his contract."[28]

The report supported its conclusions by focusing on the failings of the reserve clause under contract law: its terms of renewal were indefinite, it lacked consideration, it was not freely bargained for, and its insertion into player contracts was the result of an inequality of bargaining power. In short, it failed to meet several of the requirements outlined in any first-year course in contract law. More importantly, the committee realized that MLB's antitrust exemption could not save it from these failings.

In order to remedy these contractual ills, the committee proposed (and the owners eventually adopted) a revised reserve clause. The revised clause would solve the indefiniteness problem by expressly limiting the owners' renewal option to one year and by placing a floor of 25 percent (or $5,000, whichever was greater) on the amount that a player's contract could be unilaterally reduced through the reserve clause. The committee concluded that these contractual modifications would increase the likelihood of the reserve clause withstanding judicial scrutiny because they rendered the clause "less harsh" than its predecessor. In addition, the owners threw what they believed at the time to be a harmless bone to the players: the creation of a Major-Minor League Executive Council. Among its roles, the council would allow for the airing of grievances by player representatives on contract matters as well as other aspects of player-team relations. Little did they know it at the time, but this would eventually result in the litigation they had worked so hard to avoid.

At first the system worked just as intended from the owners' perspective. Council hearings were one-sided affairs that merely offered the players an opportunity to air their gripes to management. The owners would listen to the grievances and either take action or not, for they were not required to do anything in response. The players were satisfied that they now had a mechanism in place to vent and did not appear to be too concerned with the fact that the mechanism did not increase their bargaining leverage one iota. The illusion of communication was in place and, from both sides, this appeared to be the most important thing.

In 1954, the players created the Major League Baseball Players Association (MLBPA) in an effort to streamline the system and to create a conduit of information to the council. The dynamics of the system, however, remained unchanged. What *had* changed was that now, with the creation of both the council and the MLBPA, all of the tools were in place for the systematic dismantling of the reserve clause through contract law. All that was need was someone on the players' side to see beyond the red herring of the antitrust exemption and recognize how easily penetrable the clause was. That person was Marvin Miller.

Miller was hired as director of the MLBPA in 1966 and by 1969, had dealt the first major blow to the reserve clause by obtaining a ruling from the

National Labor Relations Board that professional baseball was, contrary to the Supreme Court's ruling in *Federal Baseball*, indeed part of interstate commerce and as such was subject to the provisions of the National Labor Relations Act (NLRA). With the MLBPA now protected under the NLRA, it was entitled to basic labor relations rights, including the right to bargain collectively. The MLBPA would, in the following six years, use these rights to expose the reserve clause's weaknesses under contract law.

Ironically, the recognition of the MLBPA as a legitimate bargaining unit under the NLRA most likely shored up many of the reserve clause's contractual weaknesses identified by the steering committee back in 1946 and, as such, bolstered the legality of the clause, at least temporarily. For now, it could no longer be said that any future incarnation of the reserve clause was the product of inequality at the bargaining table. Consideration would also be more likely to be found, given the equality of bargaining power between the owners and the MLBPA. However, the NLRB's 1969 decision opened the door to additional attacks on the reserve clause based on contract law—attacks that focused not on relative bargaining power but on the specific language of the clause. As an additional ironic twist, the specific language that would ultimately doom the reserve clause would be the "one year renewal option" language—the very language inserted into the clause by the owners back in 1946 in an effort to solve the indefiniteness problem. Little did they know at the time that they had merely replaced one contractual failing with another.

Before that could be accomplished, however, the MLBPA needed a mechanism by which to test this language. It got it in the 1970 collective bargaining agreement when the owners agreed to an arbitration provision—something the 1946 steering committee report explicitly counseled against.[29] In the fall of 1975, the historic arbitration hearing of Dodgers pitcher Andy Messersmith and Expos pitcher Dave McNally commenced. At issue was paragraph 10A of the Uniform Players Contract, which had remained effectively unchanged since the 1946 modifications. In relevant part, the paragraph read: "The Club shall have the right to renew this contract for the period of one year on the same terms." Messersmith and McNally failed to sign contracts for the 1975 season.[30] Pursuant to this reserve clause, their teams (the Dodgers and Expos, respectively) renewed their contracts unilaterally. At the end of the 1975 season, because neither agreed to terms during the 1975 season, Messersmith and McNally declared themselves free agents, arguing that the phrase meant that their team might renew their contract for one season but no more. The owners, not surprisingly, argued that the clause protected their right to renew their contract indefinitely. In short, the issue before independent arbitrator Peter Seitz was one of basic contract interpretation—the Achilles' Heel of the reserve clause.

During the arbitration, the owners were faced with what they had always been loath to do: argue the merits of the reserve clause under basic contract law. Knowing that their antitrust exemption would not save them, they attempted to divert attention from the obvious with a wide-ranging argument that basically contended that it wasn't really paragraph 10A that was at issue. Instead, it was the entire foundation of Major League Baseball.[31] It was an intricate maze of interwoven rules and regulations that together formed the backbone of our National Pastime. All of this reached back to the 19th century and had served baseball—players, owners and fans—well. A ruling against them, they contended, could very well lead to the collapse of the entire industry.

It was a valiant effort but, before Seitz, an attorney with a background in labor issues and conversant in the intricacies of contract law, they realistically had little chance of success. Despite the force of their argument, they knew that ultimately, Seitz would see the case as the MLBPA urged him to: as a simple case of contract interpretation, separate and apart from both the complicated history of the game and its antitrust exemption. Thus they were not surprised when, on December 23, 1975, Seitz issued his ruling. As expected, he ruled that paragraph 10A meant what it said: that the owners' reserve rights extended no further than one year. Upon completion of the delivery of his opinion, a representative of the owners literally handed Seitz his already-prepared and fully executed walking papers, firing him on the spot as umpire of future grievance cases.[32] No matter; the damage had already been done. The reserve clause was done in, much as the owners had feared for decades, through a simple matter of contract interpretation. The antitrust exemption had proven as irrelevant to its demise as it was to its creation.

Technically, the reserve clause did not die that day. It survived, badly tattered and devoid of much of its power per Seitz's ruling, until it was written out of the 1976 collective bargaining agreement which granted all players free agent status after their sixth year of major league service, subject of course to their right to contract out of this privilege.[33] That the antitrust exemption remained fully intact, and that the *Federal Baseball, Toolson* and *Flood* rulings remaining untouched in any way despite the collapse of the system it was alleged to have protected for over half a century, is perhaps the most damning evidence that it never bore any relationship to the reserve clause at all. In the end, as the owners had understood for decades, the exemption was irrelevant to the reserve clause, and it was the most fundamental principles of contract law that would doom it forever. If anything, the exemption proved to be little more than an obstacle to the means of attack rather than the roadblock many had assumed it to be.

So, if the exemption had no bearing on the reserve clause, the next question that arises is whether it impacts the business of baseball in other ways.

Here again, many people have argued that it does, and they have pointed their fingers at the issues of franchise relocation and expansion. It is in these areas, they contend, that the antitrust exemption separates baseball from its sporting brethren, most notably the NFL, which does not have a similar exemption.[34] As the issues of relocation and expansion are somewhat different, we'll address each in turn, beginning with franchise relocation.

In order to better appreciate this issue, we first need to understand how the professional sports franchise relocation issue plays out when it is officially subject to the Sherman Act. We can then compare this with how franchise relocation is resolved within Major League Baseball. Once we do so, it becomes clear that when it comes to franchise relocation, Major League Baseball's antitrust exemption represents merely a difference without a distinction.

First, a brief discussion of franchise relocation pursuant to the Sherman Act. In the beginning of the 1980 NFL season, the Los Angeles Rams decided to play their home games in Anaheim, leaving their former home, the Los Angeles Coliseum, without a tenant for the season. In order to fill the void, the coliseum courted the Oakland Raiders until eventually, the Raiders decided to abandon Oakland for Los Angeles and the coliseum, setting off a flurry of litigation. At issue was NFL Rule 4.3, which initially provided that unanimous approval was needed for a franchise to relocate into the home territory of another NFL franchise. After the suit was initially dismissed and the NFL revised Rule 4.3 to require merely three-fourths approval, the coliseum renewed its suit when the Raiders formally announced their intention to relocate and the NFL voted 22–0 to prevent them.

Because the NFL is subject to the Sherman Act, the appellate court, in this instance the 9th Circuit, analyzed Rule 4.3 under its "rule of reason" approach. Under this approach, a balancing test is used in which the procompetitive effects of the restraint are weighed against the anticompetitive effects with the goal of determining the reasonableness of the restraint. Although various factors are analyzed (such as facts peculiar to the industry, the nature of the market, and the reasons for the restraint), the hallmark of the "rule of reason" approach is the absence of a set of fixed rules for determining a violation of §1 of the Sherman Act. This is in contrast to the "per se" approach, which simply concludes that the restraint is violative of §1 on its face. Not surprisingly, courts are hesitant to apply the "per se" approach because they at least are receptive to entertaining arguments regarding the procompetitive effects of most restraints. Under its "rule of reason" approach, the 9th Circuit upheld the jury verdict below that found that Rule 4.3 violated the Sherman Act. As a result of this decision (commonly referred to as "*Raiders I*"), the NFL was powerless to prevent the Raiders from moving to Los Angeles and into the Coliseum.[35]

Raiders I provides a helpful baseline for analysis of Major League Baseball's ability to restrict franchise relocation pursuant to its antitrust exemption because Major League Baseball's rules for relocation are strikingly similar to the NFL's revised Rule 4.3, which was struck down by the 9th Circuit. For example, in order for an existing major league franchise to move into an unoccupied territory with a population under 2.4 million, three-fourths approval of other teams is required.[36] While it appears that no approval is needed for movement to an unoccupied city with a population exceeding 2.4 million, it should be noted that currently, no such city exists in the United States. Further, a franchise can move into a city occupied by a team in another league (an American League team into a city currently occupied by a National League team, for example) only if its ballpark is at least five miles away from the preexisting team's ballpark and if three-fourths of the other teams approve.

Thus, it appears that without the exemption, Major League Baseball would be subject to the same "rule of reason" analysis that was applied by the 9th Circuit in *Raiders I*. It would also appear that without the exemption, the owners would likely be adjudicated powerless to stop franchise movement, much as NFL owners have been subsequent to the 9th Circuit's decision. Indeed, after *Raiders I*, the NFL's Colts (Baltimore to Indianapolis), Browns (Cleveland to Baltimore), Rams (Los Angeles to St. Louis), Cardinals (St. Louis to Phoenix), Oilers (Houston to Nashville) and Raiders again (Los Angeles back to Oakland) all shifted cities, with the league unable to quell the turmoil. However, in practice, MLB owners are just as powerless to prevent franchise relocation despite the window dressing of the exemption. Accordingly, it is of little matter that Major League Baseball enjoys an exemption whereas other sports such as the NFL do not. In the end, when it comes to franchise relocation, everyone is, in fact, playing under the same rules.

Without delving into the specifics of various relocation attempts through baseball history (which would require a chapter unto itself),[37] it is apparent that the exemption has had little or no practical effect, simply due to the fact that baseball clearly has not benefited from its purported ability to prevent franchise relocation. In his testimony before the Antitrust Subcommittee of the Senate Judiciary Committee in 1992, then-interim-commissioner Bud Selig testified that after the 9th Circuit's *Raiders I* decision, only Major League Baseball had the ability "to stop a franchise from abandoning its local community."[38] Further, he stated that it was the Sherman Act that "has been the cause of many problems, including franchise instability, that exist in the other professional sports today."[39] The "chaos and inefficiency" caused by the application of antitrust laws to the issue of franchise relocation had resulted, in Selig's opinion, in the inability of other leagues such as the NFL to protect local communities against maverick team owners' bolting for greener pastures in search of greater profits.[40]

If only this were true. In reality, the volume of relocations of Major League Baseball franchises actually exceeds that of the NFL since 1950. Prior to the NFL's aforementioned wave of relocation after *Raiders I* in the 1980s and early 1990s, only the relocation of the Chicago Cardinals to St. Louis took place during this period, for a total of eight out-of-market franchise relocations during the past fifty-five years.[41] By contrast, Major League Baseball has seen eleven such relocations during this time: the Braves (Boston to Milwaukee in 1953 and then Milwaukee to Atlanta in 1966); the Browns (St. Louis to Baltimore in 1954); the Athletics (Philadelphia to Kansas City in 1955 and then Kansas City to Oakland in 1968); the Dodgers (Brooklyn to Los Angeles in 1958); the Giants (New York to San Francisco in 1958); the Senators (Washington to Minnesota in 1961); the expansion Senators (Washington to Texas in 1972); the Pilots (Seattle to Milwaukee in 1970) and the Expos (Montreal to Washington in 2005). If the antitrust exemption was designed to give Major League Baseball the ability to protect local communities against maverick owners, it certainly has not worked out that way. If anything, there has been more instability in Major League Baseball than the NFL given the fact that some MLB franchises have relocated multiple times and that cities such as Milwaukee, Seattle and Washington have seen teams arrive, leave and then arrive again during this time period. In the NFL, other than the renegade Raiders and hapless Cardinals, franchises have tended to stay put once they have relocated.

While some of the above-noted major league baseball relocations clearly had the blessing of a majority (or even a supermajority) of fellow owners, others did not. In the end, however, league opposition has never proven to be an insurmountable hurdle for those owners seeking greener pastures. Despite the presence of their antitrust exemption, MLB owners have historically been reluctant to press their alleged advantage in this area. Some of their hesitancy surely stems from their unwillingness to stand against their fellow owners, whom they may need on their side should they decide to relocate in the future. But some of it also stems from a fear of litigating this issue under the exemption and discovering that their exemption buys them much less than what many have historically boasted. In the end, they have simply preferred to stand back and do nothing rather than stand up and find out that they're not as different from their sporting brethren as they'd like to believe.

The issue of expansion is somewhat different than the issue of relocation in that it involves a different aspect of Major League Baseball's antitrust exemption. Relocation focuses on the issues outlined in *Raiders I* where the exemption theoretically (although as shown above, not in practice) allows Major League Baseball, as opposed to its brethren in the NFL and other professional sports leagues, to collectively restrain trade in additional markets that otherwise could support a franchise. The exemption's purported effect on expansion is somewhat different in that it theoretically permits Major League Baseball to maintain a monopoly over qualified professional baseball players through its reserve clause such that rival leagues are unable to compete due to the lack of competent personnel. Thus, it harkens back to *Federal Baseball* and its shield against rival leagues challenging the legality of the reserve clause through the Sherman Act. However, as the following demonstrates, because there were at least two ways to circumvent this limitation (through either congressional repeal of *Federal Baseball* or judicial review of the reserve clause based on contract law), the exemption provided no protection to the owners when the issue of expansion through a proposed third major league reared its head in the late 1950s and early 1960s.

If the five franchise relocations that occurred in rapid order during the 1950s demonstrated to the owners that their antitrust exemption was not as ironclad as the Supreme Court in *Federal Baseball* had made it appear to be, the events leading up to the first-ever expansion in the history of the game demonstrated a complete capitulation by the owners to the tenets of the Sherman Act in practice if not officially. As we will see, the owners were adamantly opposed to expansion and indeed fought it for as long as they could. However, in the end, political pressure placed on them by Congress to act *reasonably* in matters pertaining to expansion—even though their exemption permitted them to act otherwise—left them with no choice but to give in. As a result, along with even more franchise relocation, four new teams were added against their will in 1961 and 1962.

Prior to the 1958 season, the Brooklyn Dodgers and New York Giants relocated to Los Angeles and San Francisco, respectively. This may have placated West Coast baseball fans and Congress (which had been applying increasing amounts of pressure on MLB to expand westward or suffer the consequences through the dismantling of their antitrust exemption) temporarily, but the moves created an entirely new web of legal problems for Major League Baseball and the questionable power of its antitrust exemption. As a result of these relocations, New York was left with only one team and with no presence in the National League, whereas previously it comprised twenty-five percent of the senior circuit. Almost immediately after the departure of the Dodgers and Giants, a push was made to reestablish a National League presence in New York.

Specifically, New York mayor Robert Wagner formed a "Mayor's Baseball Committee" and appointed the politically well-connected William Shea to head it. Eventually, Shea organized a coalition of potential owners from relatively large cities (New York, Atlanta, Dallas–Fort Worth, Houston, Denver, Minneapolis–St. Paul, Toronto and Buffalo) with the stated mission of seeking major league status together as the Continental League—a third major league. Initially, Major League Baseball did as its exemption permitted it to do: simply ignore the upstart challenger. Shea and his Continental League cohorts, however, were well aware of the power of congressional threats and actively played this card in their effort to force Major League Baseball to comply with the Sherman Act and permit expansion against their will. Fortunately for Shea, the head of House Judiciary Committee was Emanuel Celler of Brooklyn, whose district had recently lost its Dodgers and who pined for another team. He, along with Estes Kefauver, his counterpart in the Senate, quickly became willing allies in Shea's attempt to limit the effect of Major League Baseball's antitrust exemption.

In October of 1959, Celler publicly criticized the treatment of the Continental League by the MLB owners and announced that he planned to take up the suggestion of the Supreme Court in *Toolson* and introduce legislation reversing *Federal Baseball* in the upcoming legislative session. Three months later, in January of 1960, Senator Kefauver, chair of the Senate's Antimonopoly Subcommittee, likewise expressed dismay over the treatment of the Continental League and announced that baseball would be put on their agenda in its next session as well. Shea did his part to stoke the flames even further when he stated that he was keeping Congress informed of every step of the Continental League's progress and issued an ultimatum to the MLB owners: "Help us or suffer the consequences." If Major League Baseball was going to continue to lean on its exemption as a crutch to prevent the formation of the Continental League, Shea was going to see to it that Congress kicked this crutch out from under it.

In essence, Shea had two options available to him: he could either continue to press the issue with Congress and compel it to reverse *Federal Baseball* (which would therefore permit rival leagues such as the Continental to then challenge the reserve clause as violative of the Sherman Act) or he could simply raid the rosters of major and minor league teams and force the owners to initiate a suit that would eventually focus on the legality of their reserve clause. By forcing Major League Baseball to file suit, rather than doing it himself, he would avoid the hurdle of arguing the merits of the reserve clause under antitrust law and compel Major League Baseball to instead argue that those players jumping to the Continental League were in breach of the reserve clause. This would necessitate an analysis of the reserve clause's legality under contract law rather than its relation with the antitrust laws. By so focusing the issue, Shea was confident of a ruling in his favor—a ruling that would, in effect, render practically every major and minor league player a free agent and permit the Continental League to thereafter legally raid the rosters of Organized Baseball despite the exemption. This was precisely what the owners had feared ever since 1946 (and which would eventually doom the reserve clause in 1975) and had thereafter worked furiously to prevent. Shea was well aware of the MLB owners' aversion to litigation over the issue and even said so publicly: "I don't believe they'd dare sue us if we raided them for players. They know they wouldn't have a leg to stand on."[42] By playing on these fears, Shea eventually was able to force Major League Baseball to do precisely what its exemption permitted it to avoid.

Shea and the Continental League continued to hammer away on both fronts. In May 1960, hearings commenced over a bill introduced by Senator Kefauver that would limit the scope of Major League Baseball's control over players. If it passed, the expanse of the reserve clause would be severely curtailed because the MLB owners would be limited to control over a total of just 100 players at the major and minor league level and of these, all but 40 would be subject to an annual unlimited draft by all interested clubs, including those in the Continental League. Because Major League Baseball would lose control over the vast majority of potential players, its ability to prevent unwanted expansion through its exemption would be diminished.

Despite the owners' worries over the hearings (indeed, all sixteen of them met in a special summit meeting just two days prior), they concluded with the owners dodging, at least on the surface, yet another bullet. The Kefauver bill was sent back to committee on June 28, 1960, virtually killing the possibility that it could be passed in the immediate future. It was subject to reconsideration, however, pending the veracity of Major League Baseball's pledge of cooperation with the Continental League. Thus, in stalling the bill, Congress was able to extract a promise from the MLB owners that they would act in ways contrary to their rights under *Federal Baseball*, thus calling into question the effectiveness of that ruling in the practical, day-to-day operations of Major League Baseball.

With the two-headed dragon of the judicial and legislative branches looming over them, the MLB owners knew that they would have to give ground. Their reserve clause was going to be challenged, either through antitrust or contract law, and likely defeated if they continued to resist the pressure to expand. On July 18, 1960, less than three weeks after the Pyrrhic victory that was the return of the Kefauver bill to committee, Major League Baseball announced that, for the first time in its history, it would indeed expand. Initially, the National League announced its expansion plans, accepting a start-up team in New York and promising more teams to come. A few weeks later, Major League Baseball struck a deal with the Continental League by announcing that in exchange for the extinction of the rival league, four of its proposed clubs would be admitted to the American and National leagues.[43] By October, the National League agreed to add Houston as an additional team and announced that the New York and Houston clubs would begin play in 1962. Soon thereafter, the American League followed suit and announced that Minneapolis–St. Paul would receive the relocated Washington Senators franchise and that expansion franchises would be placed in Washington, D.C., and Los Angeles. Although the American League backtracked from its earlier commitment to add teams from the Continental League ownership group, the Continental League reported "no hard feelings."[44]

By the end of this flurry of activity, Major League Baseball had expanded by twenty percent despite its vigilant opposition. Theoretically, it should have been able to rely on *Federal Baseball* and its protection of the reserve clause to maintain its monopoly over qualified professional baseball players and prevent unwanted expansion of any sort. In reality, however, it was forced to admit that its antitrust exemption offered it no such power. Although it was technically able to fend off a rival league, it was only able to do so after agreeing to admit half of its teams into the major leagues. If this can be considered a victory for Major League Baseball and affirmation of its exemption, it should be noted that in its zeal to protect its exemption and reserve clause, it bargained away much of the power these tools supposedly gave it.

Baseball's antitrust exemption is not completely without practical effect, however, and the sequence of events that ultimately led to the expansion of Major League Baseball into the Tampa–St. Petersburg market perhaps illustrates the major practical effect of baseball's antitrust exemption. To some degree, Major League Baseball *was* able to dictate the nature of expansion into Tampa more so than leagues not protected through an antitrust exemption. However, once again, and just as in those other leagues, it was not able to prevent unwanted expansion despite its unique legal protection. Whether the procedural advantages available to Major League Baseball through its exemption result in significant practical advantages relative to leagues not so protected is open to debate.

In August 1992, San Francisco Giants owner Bob Lurie announced that he had sold his Giants to a group of investors known as the Tampa Bay Partnership for $115 million. The Tampa Bay Partnership intended to move the Giants to Florida. In its effort to keep the Giants in San Francisco, Major League Baseball then began to undercut the sale and seek an alternative buyer who would not relocate the team. Eventually, Major League Baseball located a group of local San Francisco investors who offered to buy the team for $100 million. In the meantime, it announced that two members of the Tampa Bay Partnership, Vincent Piazza and Vincent Tirendi, had failed its background check. Piazza and Tirendi subsequently filed suit against Major League Baseball.[45] On November 10, 1992, the owners rejected the offer of a revamped Tampa Bay Partnership (this one not including Piazza or Tirendi). Eleven days later, Lurie sold the Giants to the group of San Francisco investors for $100 million and the team remained in San Francisco.

If Major League Baseball's antitrust exemption had real teeth, this would mark the end of the story. However, because it does not, the Giants' relocation story embarked on its second act. Once again, politics played a role in Major League Baseball's affairs as its attempt to make practical use of its exemption caught the eye of Congress. The Antitrust Subcommittee of the Senate Judiciary Committee subsequently scheduled hearings to consider anew the possibility of overturning *Federal Baseball* and revoking the exemption.[46] Among those called to testify was then-interim commissioner Bud Selig, who pleaded with the subcommittee not to do so on the grounds that the Giants situation "certainly cannot be said to be evidence that MLB has abused its antitrust exemption."[47]

Selig's comment could not have been more illustrative of the practical impact of Major League Baseball's antitrust exemption, for what is the purpose of an exemption from a system of laws that compels those subject to them to act reasonably but gives a license to act *unreasonably*? Theoretically, because Major League Baseball is exempt from the antitrust laws, it should be able to abuse them. That it understands that it does not have license to do so throws grave doubt over the value of the exemption as a practical tool. Selig's statement revealed much about MLB's actual relationship with its exemption because what he was saying, in essence, was that the reason MLB was not abusing its exemption was because, in actuality, it was (and always had been) attempting de facto compliance with the Sherman Act in MLB's continuing effort to keep Congress from stepping in and compelling MLB to comply with the Sherman Act as a matter of law.

The flurry of activity that followed Selig's testimony is further validation of the veracity of this statement. Major League Baseball, although technically empowered to let the matter drop and leave the Tampa Bay Partnership group on the outside looking in, nevertheless took action to demonstrate its reasonableness to Congress in its effort to appease it and prevent it from stripping MLB of its exemption. In September of 1994, Major League Baseball settled its lawsuit with Piazza and Tirendi. Although the terms of the settlement were confidential, Piazza shortly thereafter told a member of the St. Petersburg media that the Tampa–St. Petersburg area would be getting a major league franchise soon. Six months later, Piazza was proved prescient, as the owners unanimously granted Tampa an expansion franchise.

In the end, the owners understood that, ultimately, their exemption was meaningless when it came to issues of franchise relocation and expansion. Therefore, they had no choice but to see to it that Tampa received either an expansion or relocated franchise. For nearly half a century, history had demonstrated that, despite their exemption, they are not free to deny legitimate cities, such as Milwaukee and Baltimore in the early 1950s or Tampa in the 1990s, with major league facilities already in place and with the population necessary to support a Major League baseball franchise. Rather than risk yet another round of congressional hearings, the owners acted swiftly to do what they knew Congress would ultimately force them to do anyway—award Tampa a major league franchise.

After all, they would be in violation of the Sherman Act if they did not.

The "Powers of the Commissioner" Trilogy

THE DEVELOPMENT OF THE TRILOGY

The antitrust trilogy represents an explicit judicial acknowledgement of the extra-legal status of Major League Baseball, at least in theory although not, as we've seen, in practice. However, there is also a murky, implicit judicial acknowledgement of MLB's extra-legal status that exists this time in practice although not in theory. This makes itself apparent through an examination of a trilogy of federal cases that focus on the powers of the Office of the Commissioner of Baseball. Given the wide swath of power granted by the owners to their first commissioner, Kenesaw Mountain Landis, the issue emerged of just how sweeping these powers were and when (or even if) they were subject to judicial oversight. The conclusion that can be reached upon examination of these cases is that, in practice, MLB is accorded significant deference given its status as our National Pastime. In fact, as this trilogy indicates, federal courts have been very willing to defer to MLB in a myriad of ways, treating it over and over differently from other businesses and even unlike other professional sports leagues.[48]

This becomes apparent when we examine the first case within our trilogy, *Milwaukee American Association v. Landis*.[49] Here, in 1931, the Northern District of Illinois put its stamp of approval on the unique and powerful authority inherent in Judge Landis's commissioner's office. When asked to consider the legality of Landis's autocratic control over MLB pursuant to the 1921 Major League Agreement (which, among other things, created the Office of the Commissioner of Baseball), the federal court did not hesitate to grant to MLB what it most likely would have considered an impermissible concentration of power in almost any other circumstance. The facts of that case were somewhat convoluted and involved the repeated reassignment and optioning of a player who at one point was under contract to the St. Louis Cardinals but whose contractual status was now in doubt, given that each team he was assigned to was either owned or controlled by the Cardinals. In short, Commissioner Landis ruled that St. Louis's option of the player to Milwaukee of the minor league American Association was void and that the player must either be returned to St. Louis, transferred to another club not controlled or owned by St. Louis (unlike Milwaukee), or released unconditionally. Landis, who was vociferously opposed to the "farm system" as pioneered by Branch Rickey's Cardinals, wherein one club owned or controlled several minor league clubs and shuffled players throughout, took a strong stand against such joint ownership, ruling that, in this case, such shuffling was contrary to the "best interests" of the game, pursuant to the power granted him under the 1921 Major League Agreement.

By way of background, the 1921 Major League Agreement bestowed significant power in the hands of the newly created Commissioner of Baseball: he (Landis) was to be the final arbiter of disputes between leagues, clubs and players, the determinant of punishment for any conduct he deemed to be contrary to the best interests of the game, and the arbiter of disagreements over proposed amendments to league rules. In a catch-all provision Landis would invoke numerous times throughout his tenure, and that would seemingly provide authority for virtually any action he wished to take, the agreement permitted him "to take other steps as he might deem necessary and proper in the interest and morale of the players and the honor of the game."[50] And perhaps most importantly, the owners expressly waived any rights to challenge Landis's rulings in court, "no matter what would be the severity of the new Commissioner's discipline."[51] Taken together, the agreement anointed Landis with "autocratic power over everyone in baseball, from the humblest bat boy to a major league president."[52] At issue before the District Court of the Northern District of Illinois was whether this was in fact the case; whether Landis's "best interests" power held any legal weight when challenged in a court of law.

At the outset of the opinion, the court made clear that in fact it did. The court took notice of the broad swath of power granted to the commissioner by the owners in an effort to "preserve discipline and a high standard of morale," concluding that this "disclose[s] a clear intent upon the part of the parties to endow the commissioner with all the attributes of a benevolent but absolute despot and all the disciplinary powers of the proverbial pater familias." As such, the court was quite willing to defer to MLB in its efforts to preserve a code of conduct above and beyond that required by the legal system. This, by itself, was not unusual or improper. However, the court then went further when, despite acknowledging the reality that the Major League Agreement permitted Landis the authority of an "absolute despot," failed to likewise acknowledge that this was at least potentially dangerous. Instead, it gave its blessing to this seemingly boundless grant of power, refusing to even consider the possibility that such unchecked authority could be abused, choosing instead to be comforted by the notion that the individual so armed would wield it wisely:

> The provisions are so unlimited in character that we can conclude only that the parties did not intend so to limit the meaning of conduct detrimental to baseball, but intended to vest in the commissioner jurisdiction to prevent any conduct destructive to the aim of the code.... So great was the parties' confidence in the man selected for the position and so great the trust placed in him that certain of the agreements were to continue only so long as he should remain commissioner.

A further indication of the extent to which the court was willing to defer to the authority of Commissioner Landis was its response to the argument that the provision of the Major League Agreement wherein the club owners expressly waived their right of access to the courts was in violation of public policy in that it deprived the court of its jurisdiction. Once again, the court appeared to be untroubled by this unchecked grant of absolute power to one man. While acknowledging that most such provisions are "commonly held void," here, the court held that submission of a dispute to Commissioner Landis as arbiter was not, provided that his decision was not unsupported by the evidence or "unless the decision is upon some basis without legal foundation or beyond legal recognition." What was left unsaid was how these determinations were to be made if all access to the courts was barred. In a roundabout fashion, the court soothed itself by concluding that the rulings of the commissioner of baseball could never be considered arbitrary or improper because they were necessarily made in furtherance of his pursuit "to keep the game of baseball clean." In a case that, on its face, would seem to raise red flags, and which the court plainly acknowledged the presence of absolute, unchecked, despotic power, the court curiously chose these qualities as justification for deferring to a private body rather than stepping in and acting as a judicial check.

After Landis's death in 1944, MLB did in fact revise the Major League Agreement, removing the prohibition of access to judicial review and reining in future commissioners' power by requiring that only conduct in violation of a specific league rule could run afoul of the "best interests" clause. However, these limitations lasted only twenty years; in 1964 outgoing commissioner Ford Frick convinced club owners to strike these changes and return to the office of the commissioner the broad array of unchecked powers enjoyed by Judge Landis. And once again, the federal judiciary (in the second and third cases within this trilogy) confirmed both that these powers had been restored in full and that it would defer to MLB just as it had under Commissioner Landis.

Only twelve years after the restitution of the commissioner's full powers, they were once again the subject of a legal challenge. In June of 1976, Oakland A's owner Charles O. Finley sold some of his star players to the Boston Red Sox and New York Yankees rather than risk losing them to free agency at the end of the season. Commissioner Bowie Kuhn nullified the sales, asserting that because they would debilitate the A's and upset the competitive balance of the American League, they were in violation of the "best interests" clause. Finley challenged Kuhn's ruling in federal court, and the case, *Finley v. Kuhn*,[53] (the second within the trilogy) eventually reached the Seventh Circuit Court of Appeals in 1978. In upholding Kuhn's actions, the court recalled and reiterated Justice Blackmun's refrain in *Flood* that "baseball cannot be analogized to any other business or even to any other sport or entertainment." Likewise, the court noted that baseball's commissioner was similarly unique in that in no other sport or business was there a comparable position; one designed to protect and promote the "morale of the players and the honor of the game." "While it is true," the court announced, "that professional baseball selected as its first Commissioner a federal judge, it intended only him and not the judiciary as a whole to be its umpire and governor." Moreover, the court tacitly embraced the unique role of baseball in American society when it noted that in 1957, the Supreme Court held that, unlike baseball, the antitrust laws do in fact apply to professional football. This, the court reasoned, was a "substantive pronouncement" with regard to the nexus between baseball and the legal system in that it indicated that baseball was something special and should be treated differently by the legal system than other professional sports.

The court then expanded upon the holding in *Landis* by ruling that the actions of the commissioner can even be arbitrary and in direct contradiction of his previous rulings without running afoul of either the Major League Agreement or the law. A's owner Finley contended that, at a minimum, the commissioner's actions must be consistent with "prior baseball tradition" and that his power was limited to ruling only on those violations that were either immoral or unethical or which were in contradiction to posted league rules. The court rejected these claims and thereby rejected any limitations placed upon the power of the commissioner to act, unchecked, pursuant to the "best interests" clause. From the language of the court's opinion in *Landis*, it does not appear that that even that court was willing to go to this extreme, citing as it did the requirement that the commissioner's actions be consistent with "legal foundation." The *Finley* court's recognition of the power of the commissioner to act in an arbitrary fashion apparently rejected this most basic limitation.

The *Finley* court did, however, establish a two-pronged test to determine when it would be justifiable for the judiciary to intercede in baseball's affairs; however, this test was couched in an excess of language so deferential to the autonomy of MLB that it was unclear precisely when a court could intervene under cloak of this authority. Specifically, the court held that MLB must "follow the basic rudiments of due process of law." In addition, MLB must follow its own rules and regulations. Failure to adhere to either of these parameters would constitute exceptions to the judicial nonreviewability clause. Absent these facts, the court was content to steer clear of the legal business of baseball, declaring, "Any other conclusion would involve the courts in not only interpreting often complex rules of baseball to determine if they were violated but also, as noted in the *Landis* case, the 'intent of the (baseball) code,' an even more complicated and subjective task." In myriad other circumstances, courts have been more than willing to intercede in the affairs of organizations with similarly confusing, Byzantine codes of conduct. But because those other organizations were not Major League Baseball, they were far less hesitant to do so than the Seventh Circuit was here.

As *Finley* was working its way through the federal judiciary, the final member of the trilogy, *Atlanta National League Baseball Club v. Kuhn*,[54] was filed—a case that demonstrated that when it came to judicial deference, *Finley* was hardly the last word. In that case, the Northern District of Georgia was presented with a squabble between Commissioner Kuhn and Braves owner Ted Turner that emanated from boasts made by Turner at an October 1976 cocktail party. At the party, Turner told San Francisco Giants owner Bob Lurie that he was willing to spend whatever it took to lure free agent Gary Matthews (who had just completed his option year with the Giants and who was soon to be a free agent) from the Giants to his Braves. The Braves had previously been fined for tampering with Matthews a month earlier and, as an additional punishment, Kuhn denied the Braves their selection in the first round of the January 1977 amateur draft. Lurie filed a complaint with Kuhn, and Kuhn held that Turner's comments were in violation of the "best interests" clause on several grounds. As a result, although Kuhn did not void the Braves' signing of Matthews (which occurred between the date of Turner's boast and the date of Kuhn's hearing on the matter), he did suspend Turner for one year and reaffirmed the stripping of the Braves' first-round draft choice in the 1977 amateur draft. Turner filed a complaint in federal court and, once again, the extent of the commissioner's "best interests" powers were examined by the judiciary. And once again, the judiciary read them to be remarkably broad.

Initially, the court seemed to push back against the extent of deference suggested by the *Finley* court when it rejected Kuhn's assertion that *Finley* held that the nonreviewabilty clause deprived the court of subject-matter jurisdiction. Instead, and seemingly in conflict with *Finley*, the court held that the actions of the commissioner could not be arbitrary and that the arbitrary nature of a commissioner's decision was one for the courts to decide. However, what it gave with one hand it then took with the other as, in exercising this judicial oversight function, the court demonstrated just how far it was willing to go in service to MLB; and how deferentially it was willing to treat MLB as compared to any other professional sports league. This became blatantly apparent when the *Atlanta* court tossed aside as irrelevant another case involving a professional sports league that was factually similar in many respects other than the most important one: namely, that it did not involve MLB. For reasons implied but unstated by the *Atlanta* court, this apparently made all the difference.

Three years earlier, the Western District of Texas was presented with *Professional Sports Ltd. v. The Virginia Squires Basketball Club, et al.*,[55] a case that involved the powers of the commissioner of the American Basketball Association, which, at the time, was a struggling rival of the established National Basketball Association. In that case, the plaintiffs, the San Antonio Spurs, purchased a player, George Gervin, from the Virginia Squires, for $225,000. Upon his review of the proposed purchase, the ABA's commissioner vetoed the sale, citing his authority under the ABA's by-laws, which permitted him to settle any and all disputes in which either a player or coach was a party. Similar to the Major League Agreement, the ABA's by-laws stated, "His decision[s] in such matters shall be final."[56] The Spurs challenged the commissioner's authority to intervene in this sale, and the court agreed that the commissioner had acted improperly. The court held that although the commissioner did have the power to act as an arbiter to settle disputes, he did not have such power when it was the commissioner himself who created the dispute. Here, as the court noted, both teams agreed upon the terms of the deal; only the commissioner objected to the arrangement. As such, the court held, "While the by-laws clearly contemplate arbitration by the commissioner of disputes between clubs when he is acting impartially, it would be unreasonable and unrealistic to believe that the club members ever intended to authorize him to settle disputes which he himself had instigated." Although the league's by-laws further empowered the commissioner to "cancel or terminate any contracts ... for violation of the provisions of the Certificate of Incorporation and By-Laws or for any action detrimental to the welfare of the League or professional basketball," the court held that this "best interests" clause would not save him in this case given that the commissioner's actions were taken without the required notice and hearing. The court held:

> The principles of fundamental fairness, as well as the by-laws themselves, contemplate a meaningful "notice and hearing" in actions taken under these sections, and since proceedings of this nature could have the effect of depriving a party of some property right, these terms should be construed to require at least the minimum essentials of "due process."

The *Atlanta* court acknowledged the holding in *Pro Sports Ltd.* but concluded that it was ultimately inapplicable to the issues before it. In dismissing Braves owner Ted Turner's argument that both *Pro Sports Ltd.* and *Atlanta* involved disputes initiated by the commissioner himself, the court held that here, Commissioner Kuhn was not acting pursuant to his power as an arbiter (which presumably would be improper in this instance, according to *Pro Sports Ltd.*) but rather, pursuant to his "best interests" power, which authorized him to investigate any act, either upon complaint or upon his own initiative, alleged or suspected to be in violation of the "best interests" of the game, and to determine the appropriate punishment, if any. The court, however, ignored the remainder of *Pro Sports Ltd.*, which contemplated the "best interests" clause of the ABA's by-laws by invoking the "principles of fundamental fairness" and by holding that any actions taken pursuant to this clause with the potential to affect a legal right must be accompanied by "at least the minimum essentials of due process." Unlike the *Pro Sports Ltd.* court, the *Atlanta* court ignored the bedrock principle of fundamental fairness by failing to take any steps to discern whether the Major League Agreement included any form of notice and hearing provisions in conjunction with the commissioner's "best interests" power, and if so, whether they were adhered to in this case at all, let alone in a "meaningful" way. Even the *Finley* court made passing mention of how "the basic rudiments of due process of law" must be followed; however, when put to the test, the *Atlanta* court was not prepared to hold MLB to this requirement.

The dichotomy between *Pro Sports Ltd.* and the MLB trilogy highlighted the differences in treatment by the federal judiciary toward professional sports leagues in general and MLB. According to *Pro Sports Ltd.*, leagues without the power and sway of MLB were subject to the rule of law and could not contract their way around their legal obligations through unfettered grants of authority that infringed upon the rights of others. Regardless of the vagaries of their by-laws or the power bestowed in their commissioners, players as well as others operating within these leagues were nonetheless afforded at least some level of judicially protected due process—certainly not Constitutional due process, but some level of fundamental fairness. The baseball cases indicated, however, that those operating under the MLB umbrella—players as well as noncompliant owners—did not enjoy this same right. Taken together, the *Landis, Finley* and *Atlanta* "best interests of baseball" trilogy stands for the proposition that MLB has the ability to waive the rudimentary due process rights of these individuals via the Major League Agreement regardless of any potential legal interests that may be at issue. In theory, there is no official, explicit exemption that would permit MLB such license. In practice, however, the judicial deference paid to MLB as evidenced through this trilogy appears to suggest otherwise.

Looking Ahead: A New Definition of "Deference" to Baseball

As we've seen to this point through the two trilogies, baseball has received special treatment by the federal judiciary, either in theory or in practice, in a myriad of ways. Because of its exalted status, federal courts at all levels have frequently done their best to consider the impact their rulings would have on our National Pastime, deferring time and again to those who run the game, perhaps out of fear for how their rulings could potentially impact this civic institution. "Baseball cannot be analogized to any other business or even to any other sport or entertainment," wrote the Seventh Circuit in *Finley*, and so more often than not it has not been. Instead, it has usually been treated as an exception—as an entity unique unto itself—as legal concepts such as due process, fundamental fairness, and the Sherman Act (at least in the *Toolson* and *Flood* decisions if not in *Federal Baseball*) have all taken turns being pushed to the side as the concept of baseball (i.e., the notion of baseball as America; the understanding that the game is our National Pastime) was protected above all else. As the Seventh Circuit likewise noted in 1978, the legal business of baseball was something best left to those who ran the game. As these cases seem to indicate, to the federal judiciary, baseball was, and is, different. Courts appear to be more willing to defer, to suspend the normal rules that would otherwise dictate the resolution of legal issues, in order to protect our national game. In the end, a sovereign nation of baseball emerged: an entity that grew to become either officially (as in the case of its antitrust exemption) or, more often, unofficially exempt from federal law on a whole host of issues due to its unique status within American society.

The Eastern District of Missouri's 2006 and Eighth Circuit's 2007 decisions in *C.B.C. Distribution and Marketing, Inc., v. Major League Baseball Advanced Media*[57] were, at first blush, little more than a continuation of this longstanding practice. In rulings that were much anticipated by fantasy baseball players everywhere, the courts once again justified the suspension of the normal rules of law that most likely would have otherwise dictated the outcome and held that baseball's elevated status necessitated a different result in the interest of protecting this national asset. However, this time there was a twist: despite the suspension of rules in order to pave the way toward a ruling that protected "baseball," both courts nevertheless held against the traditional protectors of the game, Major League Baseball. This holding, although certainly not the rationale that underpinned it, flew in the face of nearly a century of federal court decisions. For decades, as courts bent over backwards in deference to the game, there was an implicit assumption that a ruling for Major League Baseball was necessarily a ruling for "baseball" itself; after so many years of Major League Baseball holding itself out as the obvious and natural guardian of the game, Major League Baseball and the concept of "baseball" had become inexorably intertwined. With the two *C.B.C.* decisions, perhaps this nexus can no longer be so blithely assumed. Because of this, the *C.B.C.* decisions perhaps mark a turning point as well as an indication of how baseball cases will be handled from now on. Baseball, being our National Pastime, will most likely retain its special place within the heart of the federal judiciary and, as a result, can probably count on being treated with kid gloves from here on out. Major League Baseball, however, may very well be in for rougher judicial treatment than it has experienced in the past. That "baseball" and "Major League Baseball" are two distinct entities is something that the courts involved in the two baseball trilogies failed to even consider. If the *C.B.C.* ruling is any indication, however, the distinction between the two will become ever more apparent in the future. This distinction is of sufficient importance that the remainder of this chapter will be devoted to a discussion of the *C.B.C.* cases themselves along with their potential impact.[58]

As we will see, post–World War II societal changes, some directly impacting baseball and others with an indirect but no less forceful impact, have led to a societal, and therefore, judicial, separation of the traditional connection between Major League Baseball and the larger, more symbolic, concept of "baseball,"[59] all of which led up to the *C.B.C. Distribution* decisions that sought to protect the game but no longer entrusted Major League Baseball with this role. The rise of the Players Association, the diminishing status of club owners as a result of the corporate revolution of the 1960s, and the public demonization of both as a result of nearly four decades of labor unrest (including, most notably, the cancellation of the 1994 World Series), all combined to diminish the power of Major League Baseball as a cultural force even though the symbolic pull of the concept of baseball may be as strong as ever. As a result, although federal courts are just as likely now as they ever were to alter the legal rules of the game to protect baseball, the *C.B.C. Distribution* decisions perhaps signal a shift in judicial deference toward Major League Baseball, if not to the game itself.

The facts of the *C.B.C. Distribution* litigation were relatively straightforward. The litigants were Major League Baseball Advanced Media (MLB AM), an entity created by Major League Baseball to control the Internet and interactive media aspects of Major League Baseball, and C.B.C. Distribution and Marketing, Inc., a corporation that provided a variety of products, including the statistics, that facilitated fantasy baseball games over the Internet. MLB AM signed a five-year, $50 million deal with the Major League Baseball Players Association in 2005 in order to acquire what it believed to be the exclusive rights to the players' names and statistics for use in fantasy baseball as well as other forms of online content. In order to protect what it considered to be its property rights, MLB AM charged a licensing fee to online companies involved in fantasy baseball and issued cease-and-desist letters to those companies that refused to pay up. C.B.C. Distribution balked at the fee, contending that because the statistics were within the public domain—available to anyone who picked up a newspaper or any of the myriad baseball publications available on the newsstand—it had a First Amendment right to use the statistics. MLB AM disagreed, reiterating that it had purchased exclusive rights to them irrespective of the reality that they were otherwise publically available. As such, MLB AM contended that it was entitled to enforce those rights.

Several years earlier (and prior to the agreement between MLB AM and the Players Association), in 1995, C.B.C. had entered into licensing agreements with the Players Association that permitted C.B.C. to use the "logo, name, and symbol of the Players' Association, identified as the Trademarks, and the 'names, nicknames, likenesses, signatures, pictures, playing records and/or biographical data of each player,'" "for sale, advertising, promotion, and distribution of certain products," including, obviously, its online fantasy baseball games. These agreements expired on December 31, 2004. Interestingly, between 2001 and 2004, MLB AM itself offered fantasy baseball games on its Web site, MLB.com, without likewise obtaining a license or any other form of permission from the Players Association. In 2005, however, MLB AM and the Players Association reached the above-stated agreement, and on February 4, 2005, the joint venture approached C.B.C. Distribution, proposing that C.B.C. promote MLB AM's fantasy baseball games on C.B.C.'s Web site in exchange for a percentage of the resulting profits. C.B.C. then filed for declaratory relief, seeking a ruling that declared its First Amendment right to use the names and statistics of major league players without obtaining a licensing agreement. MLB AM counterclaimed, alleging that such use would violate the players' rights of publicity. Thus set the stage for the showdown between the First Amendment and the right of publicity within the context of online fantasy baseball games.

Ironically, MLB had been on the other side of this argument just a few years earlier when Al Gionfriddo, along with fellow 1930s and '40s major league players Pete Coscarart, Dolph Camilli, and Frankie Crosetti, sued it in California state court for using their likenesses without their consent in its All-Star Game and World Series programs as well as on its Web site.[60] There, the players alleged that their statutory and common law rights of publicity were violated, while Major League Baseball defended itself by invoking the First Amendment. With regard to the common law claim, after balancing the players' rights against "the public interest in the dissemination of news and information consistent with the democratic processes under the constitutional guarantees of free speech and of the press," the California Court of Appeal held that the balance tipped in favor of Major League Baseball and the First Amendment, noting that the public interest in baseball was significant. As the court stated, "Major league baseball is followed by millions of people across this country on a daily basis. Likewise, baseball fans have an abiding interest in the history of the game. The public has an enduring fascination in the records set by former players and in memorable moments from previous games." Thus, the court continued, "Balancing plaintiffs' negligible economic interests against the public's enduring fascination with baseball's past, we conclude that the public interest favoring free dissemination of information regarding baseball's history far outweighs any proprietary interests at stake." The court went even further with regard to Gionfriddo et al.'s statutory claim, holding that "baseball ... is, after all, 'the national pastime.' In view of baseball's pervasive influence on our culture, we conclude that the types of uses raised in the record before us are among the 'public affairs' uses exempt from consent [under the statute]." Once again, and consistent with the traditional treatment of the game by its brethren in the federal judiciary, the California appellate court held that baseball, being baseball, necessitated a different outcome than otherwise might have been the case.

The District Court in the *C.B.C. Distribution* case did not even need to engage in a balancing of interests, holding that the players did not meet their burden of proving that their rights of publicity under Missouri law had been violated. On appeal, the Eighth Circuit went even further in protecting the interest of "baseball" by disagreeing with the lower court in its ruling with regard to the players' rights of publicity. Here, the court held that the players did indeed meet all three prongs of Missouri's right of publicity test, but nevertheless held that this was irrelevant.[61] Even though the court held that C.B.C. used the players' names as symbols of its identity, without their consent, and with the intent of obtaining a commercial advantage, it was allowed to do so under the First Amendment given the national interest in baseball. Consistent with the *Gionfriddo* court, the *C.B.C.* court held that because the information at issue was already within the public domain, "it would be strange law that a person would not have a first amendment right to use information that is available to everyone." Further, the court rested its decision with regard to the balance between private and public interest by reciting the familiar litany of the national obsession with baseball: "Courts have also recognized the public value of information about the game of baseball and its players, referring to baseball as 'the national pastime.'"

Quoting *Gionfriddo*, the court concluded by noting that the "'recitation and discussion of factual data concerning the athletic performance of [players on Major League Baseball's Web site] command a substantial public interest, and, therefore, is a form of expression due substantial constitutional protection.' We find these views persuasive." Like the *Gionfriddo* court, here the Eighth Circuit ruled that regardless of the private rights at issue (perhaps insubstantial in the *Gionfriddo* case given, as the court noted, the limited instances in which these old-time ballplayers' likenesses were in fact used by Major League Baseball,[62] but certainly much more substantial in the *C.B.C.* litigation given that fantasy baseball is an industry that generates several hundred million dollars each year that could not exist without the players involved in that case), they would most likely never be significant enough to trump the public interest in protecting our National Pastime. Unlike *Gionfriddo*, however, here the decision was one that went against Major League Baseball. In a departure from historical precedent, the Eighth Circuit held that it was Major League Baseball that was impeding the public interest in baseball, not protecting it. Such a conclusion would have been unheard of just a generation or two earlier. For decades, Major League Baseball and the club owners who dominated the game prior to the ascension of the Players Association in the 1970s and '80s were larger-than-life figures who were not shy about promoting their role as guardians of our national game. And as we've seen through the two baseball trilogies, the judiciary more often than not compliantly deferred to them without question. In these cases, rulings in favor of Major League Baseball were unquestionably considered rulings in furtherance of the larger, overarching, concept of baseball as well. To the federal judiciary, the two were inseparable. The rulings in the *C.B.C.* cases separated the interests of baseball from the interests of those who ran its major league incarnation. The questions for us are the most basic ones: why, and why now? Some brief history is required to get to the root of all this.

Much of the rationale for the traditional judicial deference to Major League Baseball came from the judiciary's comfort in entrusting the thorny legal issues of baseball to the well-known stewards of the game. As stated earlier, the owners who ran the game up through the 1950s were household names who had, to many in the public, long demonstrated their baseball *bona fides*. There had always been some turnover in ownership ranks but the stalwarts—the O'Malleys, the Yawkeys, the Crosleys, the Carpenters, the Wrigleys, among others—had seemingly been "baseball men" forever and had accumulated a presupposed institutional knowledge of the business of baseball that many courts were hesitant to challenge. Just as importantly, although the owners bickered among themselves on more trivial issues, they often spoke with a unified voice on the bigger issues concerning the game. Because of this, in deferring to Major League Baseball, courts could be reassured that they were entrusting the resolution of significant questions to a well-known, learned body of baseball "experts."

Beginning in the 1960s, however, things began to change. Slowly at first but then more rapidly as the decades passed, owners began coming and going more frequently.[63] With the increase in turnover, they became increasingly anonymous. In addition, and partially as a result of the increase in turnover, the cohesiveness of the owners' "voice" began to dissipate as club owners disagreed on more fundamental questions concerning the game. By the 1980s and '90s, deferring to the owners increasingly led to more questions than answers: Who were the owners? What did they stand for? How would they protect the game of baseball? How *could* they protect the game of baseball given their increasingly disparate interests? By the time of the 2006 and 2007 *C.B.C.* decisions, deference to Major League Baseball was a far less reassuring prospect than it had ever been before. In short, the people at the ownership table by 2006 were far different in temperament and background than those sitting in those same chairs in 1960.

Mimicking the larger transformation of American society that was taking place in the wake of World War II, the (relatively) smaller "plantation" owners (as they were occasionally called) were being replaced by representatives of the corporate boardroom—men, and finally some women, in charge of multinational corporations. This would have profound effects on both the identity of the owners as a group and their ability to speak with a strong, unified voice. Corporate ownership and/or corporate influence was not a foreign concept to Major League Baseball prior to the 1960s, but as the decades wore on it saw more and more of it. As new owners arrived on the scene of the newly expanded National and American leagues (with four teams being added in 1961 and '62), they were, in one sense, far more powerful people than their predecessors: they were in most cases far richer and far more influential politically, given the realities of running a multi-national conglomerate (it's far easier to get the collective ear of Congress when your business operates in all fifty states rather than in one or two). But it was their individual power that brought the owners down collectively: having to answer to so many interests other than their baseball brethren simply made group cohesiveness impossible.

The corporate influx in Major League Baseball only grew more pronounced as the decades passed. Eventually, huge conglomerates such as Disney, Time Warner, the Tribune Company owned controlling interests in ball clubs. All of these investors had varied agendas, some baseball related, some not. Although the transition from plantation to boardroom ownership was completed by the 1990s, the new wave had begun disrupting and fraying the old guard from the moment it arrived several decades earlier.[64] With all of the varied interests now present at the owners' table, the ability of a powerful team such as the Yankees, to say nothing of the commissioner himself, to dictate an agenda or to speak on behalf of others, or for "baseball" for that matter, became increasingly difficult. How to persuade a conglomerate? There were simply too many layers of private agendas associated with each club to contend with; each one now had its own large, institutional problems to consider. Everyone was seemingly out for themselves with nobody left to look out for or speak on behalf of our National Pastime.

Starting in the '60s, the economics of baseball changed. A corporate revolution (in both baseball and American overall) amped-up the American economy and made everything bigger and more expensive, including major league baseball clubs. Significant debt service became an issue: clubs needed to consider it whenever making significant decisions. No longer could they simply fall blindly in line with one another; they had their creditors and shareholders to consider. Big money meant the arrival of big, powerful people and interests in the game, but people and interests with agendas that rarely considered the well being of their putative competitors. The old-guard plantation owners always considered themselves a powerful lot, but the source of their collective power was rooted in weakness rather than strength. When the individually powerful products of the corporate revolution infiltrated their ranks, the result was not enhanced power and prestige but, ironically, a dissipation of it. Their tight fraternity was finally cracked and once it was, the old guard's solidarity was irrevocably broken. They could no longer speak with one voice. Gone was their ability to speak for the concept of baseball, and so was the deference that came with that.

As the longtime stalwarts left the game, they were replaced with owners from the corporate boardroom who were more likely than their predecessors to enter and leave the scene quickly, seeking profit and then exiting either as soon as they had achieved it or found that it was not forthcoming in sufficient abundance. By 1963, either through expansion or recent transfers in ownership, six of ten AL owners were individuals who had not been members of the fraternity a mere three years earlier (in the NL it was four out of ten). Thus, at joint league meetings, half of the decision-makers were people new to one another. This dynamic added to the increasing difficulty of maintaining group cohesiveness.

The changes and turnover in ownership only increased throughout the next several years. In 1969, another round of expansion brought four more new faces to the table along with new owners in Cincinnati and Washington. By the 1970s, club owners were coming and going at an unprecedented rate. As stated earlier, though there had always been some turnover in ranks, ownership turnover was nothing like it was after the influx of the products of the corporate revolution. Something fundamentally changed in the nature of club owners; they simply were not staying in the game as long as they used to. Although the irony was most likely lost on most of the ownership group as it existed during the mid to late '70s, despite their charges of renegade behavior leveled at the players as a result of free agency, it was the owners who were carpet-bagging like never before. All of this had disastrous results for their once tight fraternity: in this atmosphere it was almost impossible for one owner to get to know another; before long they would be replaced by somebody else. Without fraternal allegiances everybody was out for themselves. Concepts such as vision and cohesiveness were a thing of the past. Without an institutional memory, owners meetings became pitched battles between self-serving owners interested only in what benefited them today; yesterday or tomorrow be damned.

The concurrent rise of the influence of the Players Association likewise took its toll on the owners' ability to speak for "baseball" and therefore protect its interests (as opposed to looking out only for their own). Now, with the increasingly more powerful and combative Players Association, there was no question that those who ran the game at the major league level did not speak with a unified voice. Eventually, it would be the players, rather than the owners, who would wield the real power within Major League Baseball. The shift in power within the game from the owners to the players did not result in a concurrent passing of the torch in terms of the role of spokesmen and protectors of the concept of baseball, however. While the owners faded into the background, the players, through their powerful Players Association, were never able to replace them as the conscience of the game. With repeated labor showdowns throughout the 1970s and '80s, and culminating in the 1994-95 strike that wiped out the 1994 World Series, public mistrust of the Players Association only grew more fervent. As a result, and because they were repeatedly vilified by the owners, the media, and consequently, the public, the players were unable to successfully become the voice for anything beyond their own self-interests. Eventually, it became fashionable to draw a line between Major League Baseball, comprising the increasingly anonymous owners and demonized Players Association on one side, and the purer, perhaps fictional, certainly larger, concept of baseball on the other. In the process, Major League Baseball, and all who resided within it, became divorced from the idea of baseball as our National Pastime. Inherent in this separation was the notion that the major leagues comprised only one aspect, and a less significant one at that, of the larger concept of baseball. By the time of the *C.B.C.* decisions, Major League Baseball (as well as the Players Association, who partnered with it through Major League Baseball Advanced Media), spoke only for itself and not more expansively for the game overall. All of this left the *C.B.C.* courts with the question of how to determine what was in the best interest of our national game, and who should decide. In a break with the past, the courts concluded that this time, they were the entity best qualified to speak on the game's behalf.

In their increasingly feverish battles with the Players Association, the owners set out to demonize their leader, Marvin Miller. This tactic proved unsuccessful, as the Players Association steamrolled over the weakened owners' cabal in showdown after showdown. On a grander scale, however, this tactic did however inflict lasting damage: the portrait of Miller and the Players Association they helped to create (and which Miller oftentimes did little to counteract) virtually assured that regardless of its power and sway within Major League Baseball, the Players Association would never be regarded as the stewards of the game the way the owners once were.

Whenever provided the opportunity, the owners, either through their mouthpiece, Commissioner Bowie Kuhn, or directly, would call into question Miller's patriotism. At one point, Kuhn stated that he believed Miller to harbor "a deep hatred and suspicion of the American right and American capitalism."[65] Sportswriters across the nation hammered away at the patriotism charge as well, labeling the leader of the Players Association "Comrade Miller" or "Marvin Millerinski."[66] Beyond the snarky communist-baiting monikers, critics disparaged Miller for having a "narrow mind," and in many ways they were correct: Miller refused to do what the owners had done for decades: to mythologize and romanticize the game; to make it a metaphor of idyllic American ideals. He refused to block out the negative and focus only on an idealized positive. He refused to use the rhetoric associated with the concept of baseball to justify the fundamental inequalities and subjugation that existed within Major League Baseball.

Quite simply, he had no interest in the larger concept of baseball. Instead, he was focused solely on the labor issues that confronted his clients and considered it his job to address them. In Miller's world, the game, as well as life, was cold, harsh, and unforgiving. He made it his job to point this out to both his players and the general public whenever possible. All of this doomed Miller and the Players Association in the court of public opinion, regardless of his strategic successes vis-à-vis the owners. Even if they could prevail at the bargaining table (as they overwhelmingly did), there would be little chance of their assuming the mantle of guardians of the game. For there was little chance that the well-being of our National Pastime would be entrusted to an entity headed by an alleged communist sympathizer who time and again focused the nation's attention on all that was wrong with the game rather than all that was right with it.

In retrospect, the *C.B.C.* decisions did not come out of the blue. Their seeds had been planted in Justice William O. Douglas's dissent in *Flood* 35 years earlier. In it, Douglas adopted Miller's worldview and, in so doing, focused on the absurdity of entrusting the owners with overseeing the public interest in baseball. In a direct rebuke of Justice Harry Blackmun (the author of the majority opinion) and those who held on to the traditional notion that the owners spoke for anyone other than themselves, Douglas remarked that the *Federal Baseball* decision was "a derelict in the stream of the law that we, its creator, should remove. Only a romantic view of a rather dismal business account over the last 50 years would keep that derelict in midstream."[67] Taking note of the modern realities of Major League Baseball (those realities ignored by the owners and hammered upon time and again by Miller), Douglas stated:

> Baseball is today big business that is packaged with beer, with broadcasting, and with other industries. The beneficiaries of the *Federal Baseball Club* decision are not the Babe Ruths, Ty Cobbs, and Lou Gehrigs. The owners, whose records many say reveal a proclivity for predatory practices, do not come to us with equities. The equities are with the victims of the reserve clause. I use the word "victims" in the Sherman Act sense, since a contract which forbids anyone to practice his calling is commonly called an unreasonable restraint of trade.[68]

Douglas's perspective received a measure of vindication in the *C.B.C.* decision when the Eighth Circuit balanced the competing interests and held that, contrary to Justice Blackmun's pronouncement, the public interest was contrary to, not inherent within, that of the owners. In essence, the Eighth Circuit held that the proprietors of the "dismal business" of baseball were incapable of looking beyond their personal pecuniary interests and acting in furtherance of the larger concept of baseball. The *C.B.C.* decision went even further, however, in that it did not merely hold against the owners; it held against the Players Association as well. That it did, as well as the fact that the owners and the Players Association were on the same side of the issue in this case, speaks volumes on how the image of Major League Baseball had changed in the thirty-five years between the *Flood* and *C.B.C.* decisions.

With each victory over the owners, the Players Association gained just a bit more stature within Major League Baseball. Within a remarkably short time, the players rose from inconsequential serfs to de facto partners with the owners in the running of the game. Although they were formally paired in ventures such as Major League Baseball Advanced Media, they were informally linked in a myriad of other ways as each successive collective bargaining agreement granted them an increasingly greater say over the business side of baseball. By the 1990s, the term "Major League Baseball" no longer implied merely the collection of owners along with the commissioner. Now, with the owners fading into the background (indeed, by this point most owners were unrecognizable even in their own cities—a far cry from the days of O'Malley, Yawkey, Wrigley, et al.), "Major League Baseball," at least in a business sense, implied the uneasy partnership between management and the Players Association. And since the labor waters had been so unsettled ever since the arrival of Marvin Miller and his emboldened union, many casual fans (along with many more hardcore fans as well) blamed the Players Association for the seemingly endless threatened work stoppages between 1972 (when the players first walked out in spring training, resulting in the shortening of the 1972 season) and 1994 (when baseball Armageddon arrived in the form of a canceled World Series). Led at first by the putative communist Miller, and later by the no less reviled Donald Fehr, there was little chance that the newly formed partnership at the helm of Major League Baseball would be able to speak persuasively on behalf of the larger concept of baseball. As a result, public respect and deference to the better judgment of the leaders of the modern game would most likely be less forthcoming than it had been in the game's master-servant plantation era. Ultimately, Marvin Miller achieved what he set out to do back when he assumed the position of executive director of the Players Association back in 1966; the era of the all-powerful plantation owner was over. But with its passing went Major League Baseball's authoritative voice as well.

It is interesting to speculate how federal courts in earlier eras would have ruled in the *C.B.C.* case. Given the lessons taught by the two baseball trilogies, they may very well have reached a different result, albeit in the interest in protecting the same concept—the notion of baseball as our National Pastime— that seemingly drove the Eighth Circuit in its decision. If it had existed,[69] these earlier courts would have most likely entrusted the industry of fantasy baseball to the seemingly benevolent owners, holding that because they had the public interest at heart, they would be better able to decide how to manage it so as to ensure that the national interest in both the game on the field, as well as the fantasy variation of it, would be protected and furthered. Instead, due to changes within the game, as well as larger societal shifts over the past half-century, the Eighth Circuit took the protection and promotion of the concept of baseball upon itself and substituted its own judgment for that of Major League Baseball's. It will be interesting to see just how many other federal courts will do the same.

Notes

1. For a more detailed examination of the impact of baseball's antitrust exemption, see Mitchell Nathanson, "The Irrelevance of Baseball's Antitrust Exemption: A Historical Review," *Rutgers L. Rev.* 1 (2005): 58, from which the discussion contained herein originated, in somewhat modified and expanded form.

2. There are a number of excellent sources for the details of the Federal League dispute and the emergence of the antitrust exemption. Supreme Court Justice Samuel Alito's account is particularly acute and concise. See, e.g.,, Samuel A. Alito, Jr., "The Origin of the Baseball Antitrust Exemption: *Federal Baseball Club of Baltimore, Inc. v. National League of Professional Baseball Players,*" *Baseball Research Journal* 86 (Fall 2009): 38.

3. 259 U.S. 200 (1922).

4. 346 U.S. 356 (1953) (per curiam).

5. 407 U.S. 258 (1972).

6. Ibid., 282.

7. 15 U.S.C. § 27a (Supp. IV 2000).

8. 407 U.S. at 282–83.

9. Salerno v. Am. League of Prof'l Baseball Clubs, 429 4.2d1003, 1005 (2d Cir. 1970).

10. John Helyar, *Lords of the Realm: The Real History of Baseball* (New York: Villard Books, 1994), 10.

11. Richard Hofstadter, *The Age of Reform: From Bryan to F.D.R.* (New York: Vintage Books, 1955), 246,

12. Ibid., 248.

13. Ibid., 249.

14. Letter from Oliver Wendell Holmes to Sir Frederick Pollock (Apr. 30, 1910), in *Holmes—Pollock Letters: The Correspondence of Mr. Justice Holmes and Sir Francis Pollock, 1874–1932*, vol. 1, at 163 (Mark DeWolfe Howe, ed., 1944) (quoted in Alito, "Origin of the Baseball Antitrust Exemption," 87).

15. Alito, "Origin of the Baseball Antitrust Exemption," 87.

16. Ibid., 92.

17. Robert H. Wiebe, *The Search for Order: 1877–1920* (New York: Hill and Wang, 1967), 52–53.

18. National League of Professional Baseball Clubs, et al., v. Federal Baseball Club of Baltimore, Inc., 269 F.681 (D.C. App., 1921), 687.

19. 269 F. at 685.

20. Nat'l League of Prof'l Baseball Clubs v. Fed. Baseball Club of Baltimore, Inc., 269 F. 681 (1920).

21. Ibid., 687. In fact, Major League Baseball took steps in 1914 specifically to create the illusion of consideration in the standard player contract that was subsequently reviewed in *Federal Baseball*. The revised standard contract stipulated a specified sum to be given to the player in exchange for the club's retaining of an option to re-sign the player the following season. This specified sum was intended by the owners to appear to be additional consideration paid to the player in exchange for the player's acceptance of the reserve clause in his contract. In reality, this sum was merely a portion of his overall salary and was, in practice, paid to the player regardless of whether the owner exercised the option. See Harold Seymour and Dorothy Seymour Mills, *Baseball: The Golden Age* (New York: Oxford University Press, 1989), 209.

22. See generally *Toolson*, 346 U.S. at 356; *Flood*, 407 U.S. at 258.

23. 831 F. Supp. 420 (E.D. Pa. 1993).

24. 911 F. Supp. 454, 458 (W.D. Wash. 1995).

25. See, e.g., Philip R. Bautista, Note, Congress Says "Yooou're Out!!!" to the Antitrust Exemption of Professional Baseball: A Discussion of the Current State of Player-Owner Collective Bargaining and the Impact of the Curt Flood Act of 1998, 15 Ohio St. J. On Disp. Resol. 445 supra note 4, at 452 (2000). ("The reserve system is a direct result of baseball's antitrust exemption, and, arising from the baseball trilogy, it is the most significant method by which the owners were able to restrain player movement in professional baseball.")

26. See Helyar, *Lords of the Realm*, at 36. Years later, in the 1960s, National League

counsel Lou Carroll of Wilkie, Farr and Gallagher was asked by the owners' chief negotiator and labor expert, John Gaherin, what he thought of the legality of baseball's reserve
clause. Carroll's response: "Don't ever let them try [it]" (ibid.).

27. See Joint Major League Committee, "Report of Major League Steering Committee for Submission to the National and American Leagues at Their Meetings in Chicago" (1946) (hereinafter "Joint Major League Committee"), available at http://www.
businessofbaseball.com/docs.thm#steering committee.

28. Ibid., 10.

29. The steering committee's report stated: "Your committee considered, and discarded as impracticable, suggestions that salary disputes be arbitrated.... In lieu of arbitration we requested counsel to revise the option clause so as to remove the grounds on
which the option could be attacked successfully" (ibid., 10).

30. Joseph Durso, Arbitrator Frees 2 Baseball Stars, New York Times, Dec. 24,
1975, 1.

31. For a more detailed accounting of the 1975 arbitration hearing, as well as the
events that preceded it, see Helyar, Lords of the Realm.

32. Red Smith, "Christmas Spirit," New York Times, Dec. 24, 1975, 15.

33. See Allen Lewis, "Ball Players, Owners, Reach Labor Accord," Philadelphia
Inquirer, July 13, 1976, 1C. Under terms of the 1976 collective bargaining agreement,
an agreed-upon reserve clause was implemented that tied players to their respective teams
for their first six years of major league service. Thereafter, they became free agents unless
they agreed to terms with their present club.

34. The Supreme Court expressly issued this ruling in Radovich v. National Football
League, 352 U.S. 445 (1957). The NFL does enjoy a limited statutorily created exemption
from the antitrust laws for the purposes of negotiating broadcast contracts (the Sports
Broadcasting Act of 1961), but that is beyond the scope of the discussion herein.

35. Los Angeles Memorial Coliseum Commission v. National Football League,
726 F.2d1381 (1984).

36. See "The Major League Constitution," art. V § 2(b) (2005) ("The vote of
three-fourths of the Major League Clubs shall be required for the approval of any of the
following: ... (3) The relocation of any Major League Club."

37. For further reading on this issue, see Nathanson, "The Irrelevance of Baseball's
Antitrust Exemption."

38. Allan Selig, "Major League Baseball and Its Antitrust Exemption," Seton Hall
J. Sport L. 4: 277, 281.

39. Ibid., 281–82.

40. Ibid., 281.

41. Local relocations such as the NFL's Giants and Jets from New York to New
Jersey, the Lions from Detroit to Pontiac, Mich., and back to Detroit again, and the
Redskins from Washington, D.C., to Landover, Maryland, have not been included
because these relocations did not affect the fan bases of these teams and did not result
in a franchise's abandoning its local community. In addition, the relocation of the Rams
from Cleveland to Los Angeles is not included, as this occurred after the 1945 season.

42. "War or Quit, Shea Says, If Kefauver Bill Fails," Washington Post, May 12, 1960,
C11.

43. See Joseph Sheenan, "Baseball to Add 4 Cities in Majors," New York Times,
Aug. 3, 1960, 1.

44. See John Drebinger, "American League, in '61, to Add Minneapolis and Los Angeles," *New York Times*, Oct. 27, 1960, 1, 46.

45. See *Piazza v. Major League Baseball*, 831 F. Supp. 420 (E.D. Pa. 1993).

46. See Selig, *Major League Baseball and Its Antitrust Exemption*, 278 (noting that the hearing before the Antitrust Subcommittee of the Senate Judiciary Committee was called for two reasons: (1) the National League's decision to not permit the relocation of the Giants to Tampa Bay; and (2) the recent resignation of baseball commissioner Francis "Fay" Vincent).

47. Ibid., 283.

48. For a more detailed examination of the impact of the baseball trilogy, see Mitchell Nathanson, "The Sovereign Nation of Baseball: Why Federal Law Does Not Apply to 'America's Game' and How It Got That Way," *Vill. Sports and Ent. L. J.* 49 (2009): 16, from which the discussion contained herein originated, in somewhat modified and expanded form. See also Mitchell Nathanson, *A People's History of Baseball* (Urbana: University of Illinois Press, 2012).

49. 49 F.2d 298 (E.D. Ill 1931).

50. Major League Agreement art. I §§ 2–4 (1921).

51. Ibid., at art. VII, § 2.

52. J. Spink, Judge Landis and Twenty-Five Years of Baseball (New York: Amereon, 1947), 76.

53. 569 F.2d 527 (7th Cir. 1978).

54. 432 F. Supp. 1213 (N.D. GA, 1977).

55. 373 F. Supp. 946 (W.D. TX, 1974).

56. Ibid. The relevant portion of the ABA's by-laws (Art. IV, § 5) stated: "The Commissioner shall hear and finally decide any dispute to which a player or a coach is a party. In all matters pertaining to the eligibility of players and all disputes arising between clubs relative to title to players' contracts, the Commissioner shall make such investigation, and call such witnesses and demand such papers as he deems necessary, and his decision in such matters shall be final."

57. 443 F.Supp. 2d 1077 (2006); 505 F.3d 818 (2007).

58. For a more detailed examination of the impact of the *C.B.C.* decision, see Mitchell Nathanson, "Truly Sovereign At Last: *C.B.C. Distribution v. MLB AM* and the Redefinition of the Concept of Baseball," *Oregon L. Rev.* 581 (2010): 89, from which the discussion contained herein originated, in somewhat modified and expanded form.

59. As used herein, the concept of baseball refers to the notion that baseball is not merely a game; instead it speaks to the American way of life and informs American values. This is sometimes referred to as the "baseball creed" (see Steven A. Riess, *Touching Base: Professional Baseball and American Culture in the Progressive Era* [Urbana: University of Illinois Press, 1992], 7–32); it posits that baseball stands in for America in name as well as in concept and is a valuable tool in the teaching and promotion of American values and ideals. In its most overt and cheerleading form (which was its earliest incarnation, in evidence from the late nineteenth century through the early decades of the twentieth), the hyperbole was particularly thick: baseball was promoted as "building manliness, character, and an ethic of success"; it molded youngsters, helping boys become better men not only through playing but also through simply watching the game; it contributed to the public health and was an agent for democratization (see ibid). All of this was neatly summed up by a journalist in 1907 who wrote, "A tonic, an exercise, a safety

valve, baseball is second only to death as a leveler. So long as it remains our national game, America will abide no monarchy, and anarchy will be slow" (ibid., 22). In later years, baseball events such as the integration of the game in 1947 were painted on a larger canvas as the concept of baseball was used to demonstrate American ideals with regard to the end of segregation (see Jules Tygiel, *Past Time: Baseball as History* [New York: Oxford University Press, 2000], 158). In fact, shortly after Jackie Robinson broke the color line in Major League Baseball, a group of promoters sought to send the Brooklyn Dodgers and Cleveland Indians—baseball's two most integrated teams—on a world tour to promote American ideals through the concept of baseball. One promoter stated that it was "most important that the Negro race be well represented, as living evidence of the opportunity to reach the top which America's No. 1 sport gives all participants regardless of race" (ibid.).

60. See Gionfriddo v. Major League Baseball, 94 Cal. App.4th 400 (2001).

61. *C.B.C. Distribution and Marketing, Inc., v. Major League Baseball Advanced Media, L.P.*, 505 F.3d 818, 822 (2007). ("In Missouri, 'the elements of a right of publicity action include: (1) That defendant used plaintiff's name as a symbol of his identity (2) without consent (3) and with the intent to obtain a commercial advantage" [quoting *Doe v. TCI Cablevision*, 110 S.W.3d 363, 369 (Mo. 2003)].)

62. See *Gionfriddo*, 94 Cal. App. at 414. The court noted that although the plaintiffs alleged that Major League Baseball affixed their names or images to merchandise such as T-shirts, lithographic prints, or other baseball souvenirs, "they were unable to present any evidence to the trial court of such uses by Baseball."

63. For a more in-depth analysis of this issue, see Leonard Koppett, *Koppett's Concise History of Major League Baseball* (New York: Carroll and Graf, 2004), 385, 399.

64. A detailed history of the rise of baseball's labor movement can be found in Charles P. Korr, *The End of Baseball as We Knew It: The Players Union, 1960–81* (Urbana: University of Illinois Press, 2002).

65. Bowie Kuhn, *Hardball: The Education of a Baseball Commissioner* (Lincoln: University of Nebraska Press, 1997), 77.

66. Korr, *The End of Baseball as We Knew It*, 43.

67. *Flood*, 407 U.S. at 286.

68. *Flood*, 407 U.S. at 287.

69. In fact, fantasy baseball, in one form or another, has been around for decades. Jack Kerouac played a rudimentary version of it as early as 1933. By 1938 he had developed a game that would be recognizable to modern fantasy baseball players in that he developed his own team names (he was fond of names based on automobiles, hence the "Boston Fords," "St. Louis LaSalles," etc.). He liked to imagine himself as a fantasy general manager and proposed "trades" for the purpose of stocking his own "fantasy" team." See Isaac Gerwitz, *Kerouac At Bat: Fantasy Sports and the King of the Beats* (New York: New York Public Library Books, 2009), 31. In 1960, the modern fantasy baseball game was born when sociologist William Gamson introduced his creation to a few of his colleagues at the Harvard School of Public Health. He called it the "Baseball Seminar" and explained that participants were to act as if they were general managers, bidding on the rights to actual major league players in an auction, and then playing games using these players' actual game statistics. See "Baseball Seminar: The First Fantasy Game?" in *Late Innings: A Documentary History of Baseball, 1945–1972*, ed. Dean A. Sullivan (Lincoln: University of Nebraska Press, 2002), 256–57. In 1979, an outgrowth of the Baseball

Seminar was created by writer and editor Daniel Okrent and friends at La Rotisserie Francaise restaurant in New York. They called it "Rotisserie Baseball" which eventually became known more generally as "fantasy baseball." See also Tygiel, *Past Time*, 199–200.

Suggested Readings

Alito, Samuel A., Jr. "The Origin of the Baseball Antitrust Exemption: *Federal Baseball Club of Baltimore, Inc. v. National League of Professional Baseball Players.*" *Baseball Research Journal* 86 (Fall 2009): 38.

Elias, Robert. *The Empire Strikes Out: How Baseball Sold U.S. Foreign Policy at Home and Promoted the American Way Abroad.* New York: New Press, 2010.

Helyar, John. *Lords of the Realm: The Real History of Baseball.* New York: Villard, 1994.

Koppett, Leonard. *Koppett's Concise History of Major League Baseball.* New York: Carroll and Graf, 2004.

Korr, Charles P. *The End of Baseball as We Knew It: The Players Union, 1960–81.* Urbana: University of Illinois Press, 2002.

Nathanson, Mitchell. *A People's History of Baseball.* Urbana: University of Illinois Press, 2012.

5

Fiction

TREY STRECKER

Introduction

What is a baseball novel? What can we learn from studying baseball fiction?

In the broadest terms, a novel is an extended fictional prose narrative, typically focused on "the representation of character ... either in a static condition or in the process of development as the result of events or actions" (Harmon and Holman 342).

In this context, deciding what makes a baseball novel a baseball novel appears to be a simple and straightforward issue. A baseball novel is "about" baseball, right? So what does it mean to say that a novel is about baseball? Is the protagonist a baseball player? Is the story focused on the game? How much baseball content is necessary to consider a book a baseball novel? American classics such as F. Scott Fitzgerald's *The Great Gatsby* and William Faulkner's *The Sound and the Fury* include some baseball content, yet no one would ever describe them as baseball novels.[1]

Literary critic Michael Oriard asserts that a baseball novel is not simply a novel about a current or former baseball player.[2] For Oriard, a baseball novel "is a novel that finds its vision of the individual and his condition in the basic meaning of the sport he plays, formerly played, or watches" (6). Baseball often serves as the environment in which the protagonist's story takes place. In this sense, "baseball's manifold subculture" (Candelaria 16) provides "a center in this vast and heterogeneous country—an ordered universe like Melville's *Pequod* or Twain's Mississippi River—that can comprehend all the varieties of American people and ideas" (Oriard 7).

It might seem counterintuitive, but baseball novels are rarely just *about* baseball; they are about people.[3] In fact, readers who look to baseball novels to learn how to play the game are likely to be as disappointed as young Henry Wiggen, the pitcher from Mark Harris's *The Southpaw*, who complains that some baseball stories, such as those of Ring Lardner, don't have enough baseball in them:

> Lardner did not seem to me to amount to much, half his stories containing women in them and the other half less about baseball then [*sic*] what was going on in the hotels and trains. He never seemed to care how the games come out [34].

On the most basic level, the focus of most serious baseball fiction is the individual, a character tested by his confrontation with a complex and challenging world. Baseball often provides a setting for the story, a challenge for the protagonist, or metaphorical resonance for the novel, but baseball novels are much more about the mythology of the sports hero, the performance of masculinity, the construction of identity, and the dynamics of innocence and disillusion, success and failure, youth and aging (and other universal themes) than they are about the game itself.

Baseball fiction exists as "a subgenre of the novel," like war novels or mysteries (Oriard 6). But calling the baseball novel is a subgenre does not mean it is sub-literary.[4] In fact, the best baseball novels can be as aesthetically sophisticated and formally complex as any literary fiction. In addition to reading these works for their literary qualities, we can also read them for their knowledge about the culture of baseball and baseball's role in American culture.

Many writers have observed that, as a game, baseball lends itself to telling stories. The game itself contains many different narratives—stories of an at-bat, an inning, a game, a season, or a career. Nevertheless, there is a relatively small canon of first-rate baseball fiction.[5] Here's a starting nine:

Lineup: The Baseball Canon
Ring Lardner's *You Know Me Al* (1916)
Bernard Malamud's *The Natural* (1952)
Mark Harris's *The Southpaw* (1953)
Eliot Asinof's *Man on Spikes* (1955)
Robert Coover's *The Universal Baseball Association* (1968)
William Brashler's *The Bing Long Traveling All-Stars and Motor Kings* (1973)
W.P. Kinsella's *Shoeless Joe* (1982)
Eric Rolfe Greenberg's *The Celebrant* (1983)
Darryl Brock's *If I Never Get Back* (1990)

This is not to suggest that these are the only baseball novels worth reading, but this list is a good starting point for any baseball fiction library.

This chapter will provide a general introduction to several significant baseball novels. Much as studying a line score cannot reveal the complexities of what happened in a particular game, this survey will not substitute for reading the fiction it discusses, but I hope it will serve to open some avenues of interpretation, discussion, and inquiry.

Early Baseball Fiction

The first novels about baseball were published shortly after the major leagues were established. Today, much of the value of studying the earliest baseball fiction is cultural or historical rather than literary. Novels such as *The Great Match, and Other Matches* and *Our Base Ball Club and How It Won the Pennant* depict the language, the rituals, and the cultural significance of baseball as it was played in small towns in the decades after the Civil War.

Mary Prudence Wells Smith's *The Great Match, and Other Matches* (1877) is the first novel devoted primarily to baseball.[6] *The Great Match* revolves around an intense rivalry between two small-town teams, Dornfield and Milltown, and follows the Dornfield community's preparation for the championship match. Scenes of the baseball team's practice and debates over the use of professional players are interwoven with social activities centered around baseball. Through the perspective of Molly Milton, the novel's protagonist, Smith pays close attention to the attitudes of female fans and their support of the local nine. As Molly's father observes, "This base-ball business ... unite[s] all the diverse interests in the village" (*The Great Match* 96).

In a similar way, Noah Brooks's *Our Base Ball Club and How It Won the Championship* (1884) also focuses on the baseball rivalry between neighboring towns. Tired of being bested by their rivals, two local clubs combine their best amateur baseball talent with a handful of professional players hired to strengthen the local aggregation. Both *The Great Match* and *Our Base Ball Club* highlight tensions between the country and the city. More importantly, they reveal the baseball team's central place in local communities and feature insight into nineteenth century baseball debates about participation versus competition, and amateurism versus professionalism.

Juvenile novels accounted for most baseball fiction published in the late nineteenth and early twentieth centuries. Baseball fiction generally, and baseball juveniles in particular, "exist in the tradition of success literature, in which a deserving young man achieves his deserved success in life" (Harris, "Horatio" 2). These novels—often a series of novels—follow the fortunes of their heroes from grade school sandlots to college fields, minor-league ballparks, and major-league diamonds. The ballplayer's struggles and successes are often reflected in the decline and rise of his team, his town, and his romantic life. With titles such as *Double-Curve Dan, The Pitcher Detective* (1888) and *Yale Murphy, the Great Short-stop, or The Little Midget of the Giants* (1892), the plots were often action-packed and formulaic, "relying on set situations of lowly beginnings, cruel reversals, overwhelming odds, industry, and success; of boy meets, loses, gets girl, money, victory; of evil which reigns supreme until goodness suddenly prevails..." (Coffin 137).

The best of the baseball juveniles were Burt L. Standish's Frank Merriwell novels and Lester Chadwick's Baseball Joe series, which "combined a boys'-adventure ... with unbelievable baseball action" (Partridge and Morris 22).[7] These early juvenile stories "did not even aspire to high art, but they did establish the tradition of American sports fiction within which and against which serious authors wrote" (Oriard 9).

Baseball Fiction Comes of Age

Baseball fiction came of age in the 1910s, as many baseball reporters, such as Ring Lardner, Charles Van Loan, Hugh Fullerton, and Heywood Broun brought "briskly written, formulaic sport fiction" to popular magazines (Partridge and Morris 23).[8] Reacting against the standardized plots of the idealistic dime novelists, Lardner's *You Know Me Al* and Broun's *The Sun Field* ventured beyond game action and dime-novel morality plays, offering more complex characters as well as "insights into man's life and the American scene" (Graber 1110). For Michael Oriard, "this period marks the beginning of a conscious sports fiction tradition of which Lardner was the most important early figure" (Oriard 16).

Lardner's fiction debunks the myth of the ballplayer-hero through the iconic character of Jack Keefe, the innocent and overconfident "busher" trying to break into the big leagues. An epistolary novel, Jack's story is told through his own semi-literate letters home to his friend Al. A rural rustic in the big city, Keefe's letters reveal the ballplayer's egotism and his naivete. He is talented, but unwilling to work or to hear criticism. Keefe disobeys training rules, second-guesses his coaches, ignores advice from more experienced teammates, and always has an alibi so that he can blame someone else for anything that goes wrong. Lardner lavishes attention on the human foibles of his ballplayers, but he reserves his scorn for those who do not take advantage of their natural talents.

Lardner populates his fictional world with real-life baseball characters, such as Ty Cobb, White Sox owner Charlie Comiskey, and spitball pitcher Ed Walsh. Lardner's fiction has an air of verisimilitude, yet readers quickly learn to question the reliability of Jack's first-person narration. Keefe is more complicated than many stock characters of pulp fiction; Keefe seems incapable of change, but modern critics have debated whether he is simply a conceited rube or his character flaws are more pathological.

Another important early baseball novel that examines the mythology of the ballplayer-hero is Heywood Broun's *The Sun Field* (1923). In Broun's novel, sportswriter George drags Judith Winthrop, a smart-talking feminist intellectual, to a baseball game, advising her to "turn out that electric light and come out and see the sun" (Broun 29–30), but she complains "not one of the whole thirty thousand [fans] is doing anything in his own right except eat[ing] a few peanuts. Those men down there on the grass are living, and the thirty thousand are just watching" (33). When the Yankee left fielder, Tiny Tyler, makes a spectacular catch to save the game, Judith responds to the beauty of the catch and the ballplayer—"You know, Apollo or whatever his name is" (37). She enthusiastically tells George, "The man who caught that ball created the most beautiful thing I ever saw in my life. No sculptor ever achieved anything like that arm and shoulder of his when he reached out for the ball" (43). George dismisses Judith's "ideas about the aesthetic aspects of baseball" and cautions that the superstar slugger "isn't a romantic symbol or anything like that" (42, 43).

George arranges to introduce Judith to the slugger as a roundabout romantic gesture. As Judith and Tiny fall in love—or "lust at first sight" (Broun 89)—she initially praises Tyler's strikeouts because he is "trying every minute for something supreme" (58). When George suggests Judith should admire the consistent singles hitting of little Whitey Witt, she scornfully replies that society is "smothered in safety," telling him that "those little pokes that your small rabbit-headed man is making may be safe enough but I don't find them particularly thrilling" (57).

In reality, of course, Tiny Tyler is not the Greek god Judith romanticizes him to be; "he is a competent, uneducated baseball player, a 'guess hitter,' ... [whose] attempts to cultivate himself are ludicrous and irritating to Judith" (Oriard 182, Broun 79). Tiny tries to appeal to Judith's intellectual side, buying a collection of "great books" and reading Schopenhauer and Shakespeare (Broun 106), but his ball playing suffers and they have a falling out.

After the World Series, Tiny goes on a barnstorming trip to Cuba, but customs officials refuse to let Judith travel as Judith Winthrop. Sticking to her feminist ideals, she refuses to go as Mrs. John Tyler, so she remains behind in New York (Broun 158). While traveling in Cuba, Tiny loses $10,000 at the horse track, drunkenly brawls with local thugs, and romances a well-known vaudeville actress.

As Tiny becomes "fat and out of condition," manager Miller Huggins invites Judith to spring training to "take charge of Tiny" and restore his lost heart (Broun 179). Judith is impressed that Hug appeals not to her wifely duty but to "the fidelity I owe to the New York American League Baseball Club" (Broun 179–180). Following several comic plot twists, including Tiny's unlikely congressional campaign, the novel ends happily with a marital reconciliation. The basis of their renewed relationship is neither romance nor heroics, but simply good, old-fashioned lust.

While Broun's novel takes a comically sophisticated stance toward the modern game, Lucy Kennedy takes a historical approach, looking back to the emergence of baseball in nineteenth century Brooklyn and New York. Lucy Kennedy's *The Sunlit Field* (1950) follows the fortunes of Po O'Reilly, a sixteen-year-old Irish orphan girl, and Larry Wainwright, a ballplayer, who become friends with Walt Whitman. Larry and Walt introduce Po to "a certain game of ball called—base," while the poet reminisces about the history of Brooklyn baseball and reports on games for the local newspapers (9). Set in 1857, Kennedy's novel celebrates the amateur game as it depicts a sport in transition, and the novel compresses several significant events from this period—the first rules convention, the first enclosed playing field, the first admission charge, the first all-star game, and the appearance of professional players—into a few seasons. For Whitman, and for Po O'Reilly, baseball provides an opportunity for workingmen "to enjoy life and improve their health while bonding in a spirit of fellowship." When Po witnesses her first baseball game and recalls "the thin gray men" like her father, "all the sap and color" drained from them by the mills, she is swept away by "the feeling of joy, of exuberance.... Of a people, running, shouting, raging, anxious, but caught-up, possessed by the delight of their own activity" (31).

In the novel, Po spies on the Atlantic club's practice and begins to understand why the artisan ballplayers are possessed by the game:

> With a sure flick of the wrist, you could catch the ball. A problem was solved. Out there, on the field, you were expert, equal to all occasions. Sometimes your foot slipped, or your hand or eye was not quite quick enough, and you didn't catch the bullet of lightning that was the ball. Sometimes someone else was faster than you. But usually you were out there battling with ease and speed and great skill. You were a great fellow. You could win! Sometimes you lost, but that simply put an edge of excitement on the battle. The big thing was—you *could* win. You often did. And it was a glorious feeling [Kennedy 148].

Before the opening game of the New York–Brooklyn all-star series, Po realizes that the opposing club has been stocked with "revolvers," mercenary players "who picked up money by coming on a team during some bitter neighborhood contest and winning it, no matter how, for the team with the most money" (242). For Po, the pastoral conceit of "the sunlit field" is revealed as an illusion, as professionalism and profits transform the game.

Baseball Myth and Baseball Reality

In the early 1950s, with the publication of Bernard Malamud's *The Natural* (1951) and Mark Harris's *The Southpaw* (1952), approaches to the literary baseball novel split "into the imaginative world of metafiction and magic realism and ... into the realistic world of adult problems and contemporary controversies..." (Peterson 90–91). Following the mythic, often postmodern approach are novels such as Robert Coover's *The Universal Baseball Association—J. Henry Waugh, Prop.*, Phillip Roth's *The Great American Novel*, and Jerome Charyn's *The Seventh Babe*. These postmodern baseball fictions focus less on the game itself or the sport's history and more on baseball's (and America's) mythologies and the process of hero creation—issues of storytelling and narrative. Following Harris in the realist vein are novels like Eric Rolfe Greenberg's *The Celebrant*, Eliot Asinof's *Man on Spikes*, William Brashler's *The Bingo Long Traveling All-Stars and Motor Kings*, and Darryl Brock's *Havana Heat*.

Told in the same semi-literate dialect as Ring Lardner's *You Know Me Al*, Mark Harris's *The Southpaw* is narrated from the perspective of Henry Wiggen, a young left-handed pitching ace for the New York Mammoths.[9] After he joins the Mammoths, Henry experiences an awakening when he realizes that his boyhood hero, Sad Sam Yale, "ain't all he is cracked up to be" in the biography Henry read as a boy (35). Fed up with "fairy tales" about baseball (306), Henry writes his own story, recounting his own turbulent interactions with team ownership, management, the press, and the fans. During his rookie season, Henry is seduced by Miss Patricia Moors, the Mammoths' wealthy owner, and by his willingness to do anything—even throw an illegal spitball—to win. With Holly, his hometown sweetheart, to serve as his moral compass, Henry learns to be his own man and matures in ways baseball statistics don't reveal (348). As a "southpaw," Holly tells Henry that he will always be an independent thinker, "Henry the Navigator," a lefthander in "a righthanded world" (347, 307).

Like Harris's Henry Wiggen, Malamud's Roy Hobbs is a supremely talented athlete, an artist who excels inside the foul lines but who struggles off the field. Both men desire to become "an immortal" (Harris 230), and both have women in their lives who urge them to put baseball in perspective as a part of their lives, not life itself.

In *The Natural*, Roy Hobbs is a promising pitching prospect on his way to a tryout with the Chicago Cubs when he is shot by a deranged fan.[10] Fifteen years later, Roy reappears, an aging rookie trying to break in with the woebegone New York Knights, a team their manager calls "a last place, dead-to-the-neck ball team" (43). After so many years away from baseball, Roy is on a mission "to be the greatest there ever was in the game" (122). After the Knights' left fielder is killed in a collision with the outfield wall, Roy takes his place, and "a new day dawn[s] on Knights Field" (97). With Roy in the lineup, the Knights begin to win, and Roy is torn between two women: the seductive Memo Paris and the matronly Iris Lemon, who wants Roy to learn from his past.

As the team enters the final weeks of the pennant chase fighting for first place, Roy becomes severely ill, and doctors warn him he should give up baseball. Suddenly faced with the end of his baseball career, Roy is visited in the hospital by Judge Banner, the Knights' owner, who offers him money to throw the game. When the Judge raises his offer to $80,000 and tells Roy that one of his teammates is already in on the fix, Roy succumbs to temptation and agrees to lose the game. At the end of the game, Roy changes his mind, but it is too late, and the aging slugger is struck out by Herman Youngberry, a rising young "phenom" like Roy once was. As the novel closes, newspaper headlines brand Roy a "sellout" and predict "he will be excluded from the game and all his records forever destroyed" (261–62).

Roy Hobbs is a talented baseball player, but Malamud casts his story as a hero's tale by weaving historical baseball lore with Arthurian legend and Fisher King mythology. Malamaud acknowledged that he felt he needed to add this mythic subtext for readers to take his baseball novel seriously. In any case, Roy, whose name means the king, is a knight—a New York Knight—who is attempting to restore prosperity to the land with the aid of his bat Wonderboy, an Excalibur-like weapon. Whether readers grasp all the novel's allusions or whether the mythic subtext enhances the novel, these allusions clearly elevate Roy Hobbs as a heroic figure.

Robert Coover's *The Universal Baseball Association—J. Henry Waugh, Prop.*, is the postmodern, metafictional baseball novel par excellence. Henry Waugh plays a fantasy baseball game, rolling dice and consulting various homemade charts to determine the outcome of each game. But Henry does not simply play the games; he compiles record books of the league's statistics, documents the political history of the league, and writes biographies of the league's stars. The novel shifts between Henry's lackluster life as an accountant and the imaginary baseball universe he has created. For Henry, the game he imagines is more real than real baseball: "Real baseball bored him—but rather the records, the statistics, the peculiar balances between individual and team, offense and defense, strategy and luck, accident and pattern, power and intelligence" (45). Enthralled by the inherent balance of baseball's box score, Henry's equanimity is shattered when Damon Rutherford, a future Ace who has just hurled a perfect game, is beaned and killed by an extraordinary occurrence, a dice roll of 1–1–1.

Following Damon's death, Henry's life falls apart, and he retreats from the real world into the imagined one. Presented with the opportunity to avenge Damon's death, Henry, the author–God of his Universal Baseball Association, wrestles with whether he should intervene, faking a dice roll to murder the pitcher responsible for Damon's death. In the end, Henry loses control, unable to separate the game from reality, and the Association takes on a life and mythology of its own.

Michael Oriard observes that baseball fiction typically relies upon "either a nostalgic remembrance of the past or a representation of the American innocent confronting complex reality" (7). While Oriard's statement applies to most baseball novels, it is most evident in realistic and quasi-realistic baseball fiction.

Situated somewhere between the magic of Malamud and Coover and the realism of Harris and Greenberg is Darryl Brock's *If I Never Get Back*. In Brock's novel, Samuel Clemens Fowler, a journalist from late 1980s San Francisco, travels back in time to 1869, where he plays professional baseball with the Cincinnati Red Stockings, carouses with the real Mark Twain, falls madly in love with a spirited Irish widow, and runs afoul of a violent political conspiracy. In 1869 Cincinnati, Fowler witnesses "the growing pains of a nation moving from its Anglo-centric and agrarian roots to expansionism, economic competition, and multicultural strife" (Carino 83). On the ball field, competition is fierce, and rules are exploited to gain an advantage rather than to promote fair play (Carino 85).

As Brock's Fowler chases get-rich-quick schemes with Mark Twain and crisscrosses the country with the Red Stockings, he escapes his modern-day troubles in the novel's nineteenth century, an artificial and "self-referential[ly] nostalgi[c]" pastoral setting (McGimpsey 67). Under the nostalgic spell of this boy's game, Fowler has no desire to awaken from his pastoral dream. Because of Brock's use of the time-travelling conceit, Fowler occupies a unique space; looking forward from 1869 and looking backward from the 1980s, he can be awed by the promise of Yankee ingenuity and the drive to succeed, as at the same time he laments the deleterious effects of such technological progress in his own time.

The most historically accurate of the realist baseball novels, Eric Rolfe Greenberg's *The Celebrant*, is told from the perspective of Jackie Kapp, a Jewish immigrant, who is fascinated by New York Giants pitcher Christy Mathewson. A narrative of innocence lost, the novel opens when Jackie witnesses Mathewson's 1901 no-hit game against St. Louis. Inspired by the pitcher's mastery of his craft, Jackie, a jewelry designer by trade, creates a commemorative ring to celebrate Mathewson's accomplishment. But when he is offered the opportunity to meet the baseball hero, Jackie defers, content to remain "a worshipper from afar" (82).

Later, Jackie's father-in-law surprises him by inviting Mathewson to join them for dinner at his club. When the older man insists that there is "nothing real" about baseball, Mathewson responds, "except the men who play it" (85). As Mathewson explains, "Baseball isn't anything like life. Baseball is clean lines and clear decisions. Wouldn't life be far easier if it consisted of a series of definitive calls: safe or out, fair or foul, strike or ball. Oh, for a life like that, where every day produces a clear winner and an equally clear loser, and back to it the next day with the slate wiped clean and the teams starting out equal" (86–7). As the messy reality of life intrudes into the diamond world of "clean lines and clear decisions" (86), the illusion of "a world without grays" (128) is lost, and the novel chronicles this disillusionment through three games that Jackie witnesses: Fred Merkle's base running "boner" in 1908, Fred Snodgrass's dropped fly ball in the 1912 World Series, and the Black Sox' 1919 deliberate loss of the World Series.

While most realistic baseball novels are set in the past, some parts of baseball's history have not received the same attention as others.[11] Remarkably, few literary baseball novels have been written about the Negro Leagues. Peter Rutkoff's *Shadow Ball: A Novel of Baseball and Chicago* (2001) focuses on the 1919 season, imagining a secret plot between Chicago White Sox owner Charles Comiskey and Negro National League pioneer Rube Foster to integrate the American League. William Brashler's *The Bingo Long Traveling All-Stars and Motor Kings* (1973) provides a realistic depiction of the trials and tribulations of an independent black barnstorming team in the pre–Jackie Robinson era. Mark Winegardner's *The Veracruz Blues* (1996) recounts Jorge Pasquel's 1946 Mexican League raid on the major leagues in a multifaceted novel told from the perspective of a journalist and his interviews with three ballplayers (one white, one African American, and one Mexican) and Pasquel's former lover.

As we have seen, many baseball novels explore complex issues of character and identity, of history and myth. To delve deeper into these themes, let's examine two groups of lesser-known baseball novels about Cuban and Native American ballplayers.

Baseball Fiction and the Cuban Prospect

Although Peter Bjarkman and other historians of Cuban baseball have thoroughly debunked myths about Fidel Castro's pitching prowess, such stories are a staple of contemporary baseball fiction set in Cuba. For example, framing the batter's duel with the pitcher as a conflict between "Big America vs. Little Cuba," the protagonists of Max Apple's "Understanding Alvarado" (1975) and Jim Shepard's "Batting Against Castro" (1996) both face Castro's curves with the game on the line. In "Understanding Alvarado," a retired player who travels to Cuba to bring former teammate Achilles Alvarado back to the American League wishes that "all political stuff could work out like baseball with everybody where they belong at the end of the season and only one champion of the world."

Four novels explore the Cuban prospect as a motif in contemporary baseball fiction: Bill Granger's *New York Yanquis* (1995), Tim Wendel's *Castro's Curveball* (1999), Darryl Brock's *Havana Heat* (2000), and Brian Shawver's *The Cuban Prospect* (2003). In *The New York Yanquis*, a disgruntled Yankees owner fires his entire team, paying Castro to replace them with Cuban players. Billy Bryan from *Castro's Curveball* is a former minor-league catcher, who played ball with the Habana Leones during the winter of 1947. Returning to the island over forty years later, Bryan recalls his discovery of Castro, a charismatic revolutionary with a devastating curveball, and his attempt to recruit the future dictator for the Washington Senators. Touring Cuba with McGraw's Giants in during the 1911 off-season, *Havana Heat's* Luther Taylor imagines he has found his own "ticket back to the bigs" with a highly touted pitcher some believe is better than Mendez or Mathewson (179). *The Cuban Prospect's* Dennis Birch is a retired journeyman catcher and a second-rate scout who travels to smuggle the island's hottest commodity, the stellar southpaw Ramon Sagasta, back to fame and fortune in the United States.

Wendel's Billy Bryan observes that Castro was "many things to many different people." He was "an exceptional pitching prospect ... a dangerous revolutionary ... a dash of excitement.... Castro was as heroic as someone out of an adventure tale—the chosen one who could lead any army to victory.... Castro was a hurricane unto himself" (189). But in his history of Cuban baseball, Bjarkman argues, "Fidel the ballplayer is even more of a marvelous propaganda creation than Fidel the lionized revolutionary hero" (299). Accounts vary, but the story always describes Castro as "a promising pitching talent" scouted by Joe Cambria and the Washington Senators, as well as the New York Giants, the New York Yankees, and the Pittsburgh Pirates. Tales of Castro's pitching prowess are "never more than the smoky essence of an unrelenting myth" (Bjarkman 312). While young Fidel might have been drawn to the island's national game and "its central position of pitcher ('the man always in control')," Bjarkman maintains that Castro's future in law and politics was "already assured" and that "his reported fascination with baseball could never have been more than the competitive showoff's momentary diversion..." (Bjarkman 305).

Jim Shepard's short story follows a couple of "banjo hitters" (1)—"Pinemaster[s] from the Phabulous Phillies"—sent down to the minors late in the season who decide that winter ball in Cuba is "the savvy move: a little seasoning, a little time in the sun, some senoritas, drinks with hats, maybe a curve-ball Charley *could* hit..." (4). Castro comes into an extra-inning game against a Cienfuegos club stocked with U.S. players and gets in trouble on the mound. The story ends in "pandemonium" when Castro makes an error, heaving the ball into right field and allowing at least two runs to scores. As the narrator rounds third, "there was Castro blocking the plate ... his face scared and full of hate like I was the entire North American continent bearing down on him" (16).

But while short stories present "this whole Cuba thing" as a stark battle between a pitcher and a hitter (or between opposing teams), the plots of base-ball novels set on the island focus on smuggling outstanding Cuban players—in one case, Castro himself—out of Cuba and into the fold of American baseball. In these novels, the U.S.–born narrators are often washed-up former players or scouts on the outside of the major leagues looking in. At least since Jack Keefe and Henry Wiggen, pitchers ("lefthanders in a right-handed world," as Wiggen says) have often been the protagonists in baseball novels, and three of these four novels are narrated by former pitchers. In *Castro's Curveball*, the exception, Billy Bryan is Castro's catcher and "personal pitching coach" (8).

The motif of the Cuban prospect is part of "a pervasive othering in base-ball fiction" (Morris 99), and the player is always a natural talent and always an other (in social, cultural, and linguistic terms). David McGimpsey observes, "In baseball fictions the subject of racial, ethnic, and gender tensions are con-tinually drawn out, not as a declaration that the game has been a sterling bul-wark of American equality, but because its real history as an all-white, all-male bastion makes it a dramatically imposing institution to challenge" (McGimp-sey 94). In *Playing America's Game*, Adrian Burgos examines "the image of Latinos as persistent foreigners in baseball and U.S. society" and considers how "in baseball, portrayals of Latino ballplayers as part of a recent wave divorce them from the history of Latino participation" (244). Despite the fact that the first professional Cuban baseball league started only two years after America's own National League, the Latino players in these novels are depicted as outsiders—outsiders to the game and outsiders to America.

In *Castro's Curveball*, when Bryan, a "thirty-one-year-old baseball lifer" (11), is sent to scout Castro in the late 1940s, he sees "the opportunity I had been waiting for my whole life" in his prospect (85), but Billy's success—and his contract for the coming season—are tied to Castro's success. Castro delays signing with the Senators, disappears for days at a time to train with his "com-rades-in-arms" (89), and appears more interested in politics than in pitching. Billy eschews politics—he follows baseball because the game provides him with a sense of certainty, where "an out was always an out" (11)—so he doesn't grasp how the young Castro views the game as a propaganda tool, imagining he will "pitch for the Washington Senators during the summer and return home a hero" (148). "Life isn't baseball," Bryan complains. "In baseball you can win. Sometimes" (194).

From 1900 to 1908, Luther "Dummy" Taylor pitched for nine major-league seasons with the New York Giants, accumulating 116 wins, 106 losses, and a 2.75 ERA. When Taylor accompanies McGraw's Giants on their Cuban barnstorming trip in the winter of 1911, the pitcher is trying to get back to the big leagues. As he begins to come to the realization that he may never get back, Taylor discovers Luis, a promising deaf pitcher, and McGraw promises Taylor a spot in spring training and a chance to rejoin the Giants if he can sign the Cuban kid. "If Luis was my ticket back to the bigs," Taylor says, "I'd go all the way to hell to land him" (179). Near the end of the novel, when a Taylor-coached squad of Cuban boys squares off against McGraw's club, Taylor understands, "I was pitching this game through Luis" (278).

The Cuban Prospect's Birch is a less-than-likeable narrator, a second-rate scout who describes himself as "a groundless man" (79). For Birch, as for Bryan and Taylor, the pitcher's defection offers a welcome opportunity to prove himself to the major league organization and to redeem his own failure as a player.

Before Birch meets Sagasta, he idealizes the young phenom. Throughout the novel, as he reflects on his mission to deliver Ramon Sagasta to the baseball world, Shawver's narrator meditates on the inscrutability of greatness. "The great are great all the time," Birch notices, "even in suffering, even in defeat" (209). For the scout, ordinary people, even ordinary major-league baseball players, cannot fathom that "the same forces that had blessed me with mediocrity bestowed greatness upon" the Cuban pitcher (205).

The Cuban ballplayer, Birch believes, represents his own "possible salvation or destruction," as well as his last shot to achieve baseball immortality as "the man who smuggled the man out of Cuba" (50): "To be the man who served the man who triumphed over this moment.... Vic Wertz, who hit the ball that Willie Mays caught and is remembered for. Dale Mitchell, who gave himself as the final out when Don Larsen threw the perfect World Series game. These names are trivia questions now, but it seemed to me that to be the answer to a trivia question could imply playing a great role in this game, to have given oneself to a great cause" (49–50).

David McGimpsey has shown how baseball novels featuring Latino players are, like baseball novels centered around African American players, "notable for how the spectacle of difference is used to make a point about the corruption of the once great game" (McGimpsey 126). For Bjarkman, "If modern-era professional baseball leaves a sour aftertaste for many North American fans fed up with out-of-control spendthrift owners and today's gold-digging (even steroid enhanced) big leaguers, Cuban League action as played under Castro's communist government has long provided an attractive alternative to baseball as a free-market enterprise" (Bjarkman 300).

In Bill Granger's *The New York Yanquis*, set shortly after the 1994-95 Major League Baseball strike, team owner George Bremenhaven laments paying "fifty million dollars ... to finish third," blustering that he needs "to reinvent baseball" (21) and "[seize] his team back from the bloodthirsty, bloodsucking, scum bag agents and players and unions" (8). Bremenhaven (and the State Department puppeteers pulling his strings) bring twenty-four Cuban ballplayers to New York "to break the union, demolish the agents, end arbitration ... in the name of international peace and brotherhood" (82), and he recruits Ryan Shawn, a washed-up relief pitcher and the only Spanish-speaking player on the Yankees, to lead the team.

This Cuban experiment hits a hitch when the new Yankees are too good, winning the American League East pennant and facing the Cincinnati Reds in the World Series. The Cubans' success at America's national pastime embarrasses U.S. officials, and as Castro celebrates, government officials force George to sell the Yankees to the game's first black owner.

Native American Ballplayers and Hybrid Baseball Novels

For American Indian ballplayers such as Louis Sockalexis, Charles Albert "Chief" Bender, John Tortes "Chief" Meyers, Jim Thorpe, Zack Wheat, and Mose YellowHorse, baseball served as "a tool for assimilation and for prestige and profit, but the players ... often found in the sport their own means of cultural resistance and source of pride" (Powers-Beck 30). We see this dynamic at work in Paul Metcalf's *Will West* (1956), Todd Fuller's *60 Feet Six Inches and Other Distances from Home: The (Baseball) Life of Mose Yellowhorse* (2002), and LeAnne Howe's *Miko Kings: An Indian Baseball Story* (2007). These three mixed-genre representations of Native American baseball narratives explore the poetics and politics of cultural resistance by weaving together original stories with documentary history, newspaper clippings, photographs, comics, letters, journal entries, and poetry.

In his introduction to *Narrative Change: Postmodern Discourse on Native American Indian Literatures*, novelist and critic Gerald Vizenor explains how mixed-genre assemblages like these "return to the past, to the traces, fragments, and debris of memory and history" to create vibrant counter-narratives that resist mainstream cultural narratives of the United States and its national pastime (6). As counter-narratives, it is interesting to consider the ways in which these stories—"intertextual weaves of many discourses, many voices"—exploit innovative narrative structures that "presuppose [multiple] consciousnesses that do not fuse; [these texts] are events whose essential and constitutive element is the relation of a consciousness to *another* consciousness, precisely because it is *other*" (Bakhtin, qtd. in Vizenor 9).

Metcalf's *Will West* follows the fortunes of a Cherokee pitcher who travels westward with the bush-league Rebels, his life story interspersed with firsthand accounts of the European "discovery" of the New World. Metcalf's writing juxtaposes an array of documentary materials to assemble textual artifacts "that are intertextual weaves of many discourses, many voices" (Hurlbert and Bocchi 31). Metcalf labels his collage-like compositions "narrative hieroglyphs," comparing them with the "unusual hybrid form" of the totem pole. Considering his creative process, Metcalf writes, "Each patch in the patchwork is a hieroglyph, but the narrative aspect gives it momentum" (Hurlbert and Bocchi 39).

Todd Fuller states, "The imagination is as viable a source of explanation of the past as is historical fact." Beginning with two brief lines from the *Baseball Encyclopedia* and unfolding from a deliberately "nonlinear chronology" (34–38), Fuller's *60 Feet Six Inches*, a biography of Mose YellowHorse (1898–1964) emerges as a collage of imagination and memory, "both a community collaboration and a kind of old-time Pawnee storytelling session" (29). According to legend, YellowHorse threw "a fastball with more gas than Texaco" and earned a reputation as "the only Indian in history to bean Ty Cobb." Contemporary observers thought "the Pulverizing Pawnee" might possess a magical right arm, until one day Mose's magic stopped. Fuller's account of YellowHorse extends beyond his baseball days; this is a deep narrative of "assimilation, identity, and survival," and, to his credit, Fuller refuses to solve the contradictions within his subject "as an Indian, a baseball pitcher, a troubled man, a respected tribal leader, and a celebrated figure" (28, 29). Whether YellowHorse "a) blew his arm out in a game versus Salt Lake in 1924 (by his own admission), or b) drank his arm to death (by one account), or c) slept his arm to death (by one account), or d) fell his arm to death (by one account)," Fuller insists that "any story that details stress to YellowHorse's right arm finally offers as good an explanation as any other" for the abrupt end to the pitcher's baseball career (116). The multiplicity of narratives underscores the inadequacy of relying upon a single dominant voice to represent disparate experience.

LeAnne Howe's *Miko Kings* chronicles the story of Henri Day's all–Indian ball team, battling the Seventh Cavalrymen for the 1907 Twin Territories Pennant. The prelude to Howe's novel opens with the filming of *His Last Game* (1907), according to the novel "the first moving picture about American baseball" (7).[12] Hope Little Leader, the Miko Kings' best pitcher, is cast as "an aging, stoic plains warrior," but the producer has woven his braids like a little girl's (7). In the film, Hope plays pitcher Bill Going; according to the script, "He's the hero of the story and embodies the feral native in his natural habitat—undomesticated, untamed, and uncorrupted" (8). In the film,

Hope's character resists the temptations of gamblers, who then attack him. After he shoots one of these dastardly villains, he's sentenced to face the firing squad. The pitcher—one of only two Indians in the film, the other decked out in a flowing headdress and buckskin—briefly escapes to pitch and win the ballgame against the local rivals—he pitches for a team of white players with "Choctaw" labels pinned to the front of their baseball uniforms. After winning the game, the honorable Indian returns to face the firing squad, and he is shot to death seconds before the sheriff receives his reprieve. Implicitly at least, Howe contrasts the simplistic racial narrative of the film—the only good Indian is a dead Indian—with the complexities of her novel, a nonsequential narrative that travels across a century of time, seamlessly blending fact and fiction before splitting into two different endings.

Howe's novel juxtaposes the tale of the Miko Kings and their championship game in 1907, the last days of Hope Little Leader, delirious and without hands, languishing in a nursing home in 1969, and present-day Ada, Oklahoma, where narrator Lena Coulter discovers an old U.S. Mail pouch stuffed with papers in a house she inherited from her Choctaw grandmother. A photograph of the 1907 Miko Kings sparks Lena's curiosity and motivates her to explore "the context of their lives" (16).

Unable to locate "individual stories" in her search of local newspaper archives, Lena is visited by the time-traveling spirit of Ezol Day, "Henri's oddball niece" (10) and philosopher of time. "That night, she unwrapped the team's stories as one might open birthday gifts. Out of order, but with a passion for celebration. Out came memories of glorious summer days and baseball diamonds blistered by blue skies and hot winds. Out came Ada's storefronts and boardwalks. Eye-catchers and newspapers. Fireflies and fastballs" (22). For Howe, stories and "Indian baseball [are games] of collaboration" (220), and the narrative that emerges as the novel represents the intermingling of Lena's research and Ezol's diary.

As Ada prepares for the Twin Territories series, a nine-game event that pits the Miko Kings, winners of Henri Day's Indian Territory League, against Fort Sill's Seventh Cavalry team, winners of the Oklahoma Territory League, "everyone watching the team warm up knows they're about to witness the greatest Indian ball club ever assembled, because once the season ends, the future of the Twin Territories League is uncertain. On November 16, 1907, in less than two months, Indian Territory is being legislated out of existence, along with Oklahoma Territory. A state is being sewn together from two parts. With the creation of Oklahoma, with the privatization of tribal lands, everything changes. Indians will be written out of Oklahoma's picture. And history" (22–23).

Lieutenant Richard Henry Pratt, an army officer stationed at Fort Sill,

Oklahoma, started a program for Indian youth at the Hampton Institute in Virginia in 1878 and opened the Indian school at Carlisle the next year. Pratt explains that the school's purpose was to erase the students' indigenous pasts, languages, and cultures, and to acculturate Indians to white ways:

> It is this nature in our red brother that is better dead than alive, and when we agree with the oft-repeated sentiment that the only good Indian is a dead one, we mean this characteristic of the Indian. Carlisle's mission is to kill THIS Indian, as we build up the better man. We give the rising Indian something nobler and higher to think about and do, and he comes out a young man with the ambitions and aspirations of his more favored white brother. We do not like to keep alive the stories of his past, hence deal more with his present and his future.[qtd. in Powers-Beck 7].

Ezol Day explains that "time is not the same for whites and Indians" (152). Maintaining that "Choctaw words are tools for moving back and forth in time" (164), she explores the interconnectedness of language, time, history, and identity in her 1905 article "Moving Bodies in Choctaw Space" (37–38). "The laws of physics do not distinguish between past and present," Ezol insists, and "neither does the Choctaw language..." (37). In *Will West*, Metcalf writes,

> It is those of us who cannot untangle ourselves from the past that are really dangerous in the present because we are only partly here our eyes are blind because our appetites are turned inward or backward chewing on the cold remnants of our inheritance of our facts of our history to try to find who we are what we are where we came from what is the ground we stand on to whom does it belong and did it belong [7].

As Ezol tries unsuccessfully to patent her paper and native knowledge "before the likes of Mr. Dorsey from the Field Museum come and steal it and claim it as theirs..." (152), Lena contemplates space and time and surprises readers with the blunt statement that "on October 5, 1907, Hope Little Leader will throw the last game of the Twin Territories Series" (186).

After his lover leaves him because he is broke and the team is on the verge of financial ruin, Hope decides throw the game, taking money from local gamblers to buy a house and plant a crop. With the series tied at four games apiece, Hope gives up a hit, plunks a batter, and walks the bases loaded, before lobbing "a big easy down the middle of the plate" (198). Eventually, it is revealed that non–Indian gambling interests undermine the outcome of the Miko Kings' game, having wagered heavily on the contest in order to wrest control of the team and the league from Indian hands. Hope Little Leader's teammates are furious about his obvious betrayal of the team and the community. Although he attempts to flee with the gamblers, his teammates track him down, and his punishment for throwing the game is to have his hands cut off.

Here, however, the novel's time splits. Watching the final game of the 1969 World Series on television, Hope is visited by the spirit of a Choctaw lacrosse (*toli*) player, and he returns to the prairie diamond, where he disappears inside the sun and redeems himself, "throw[ing] everything he's got at the Cavalry," winning the game and the pennant (218).

For the native American characters in these three hybrid texts, playing baseball becomes a political act, a complex assertion of individual and cultural identity. "This is where the twentieth-century Indian really begins," Miko Kings owner Henri Day claims, "not in the abstractions of Congressional Acts, but on the prairie diamond" (232).

This chapter has provided an overview of some important literary baseball novels and suggested some avenues for further discussion or critique. As an introduction, the chapter has focused on the literature itself, rather than secondary source material; however, there are several excellent scholarly studies of baseball fiction that students might want to consult: Cordelia Candelaria's *Seeking the Perfect Game: Baseball in American Literature*, John Lauricella's *Home Games: Essays on Baseball Fiction*, David McGimpsey's *Imagining Baseball: America's Pastime and Popular Culture*, Timothy Morris's *Making the Team: The Cultural Work of Baseball Fiction*, Michael Oriard's *Dreaming of Heroes: American Sports Fiction, 1868–1980*, and Deanne Westbrook's *Ground Rules: Baseball and Myth*.

Notes

1. In *The Great Gatsby*, Nick meets Meyer Wolfsheim (a fictionalized version of Arnold Rothstein), the gambler who fixed the 1919 World Series, while in *The Sound and the Fury*, Jason Compson rails at the 1927 Yankees' Murderers Row.

2. For example, the central character of Percival Everett's fine 1983 novel *Suder* plays third base for the Seattle Mariners, but Everett's novel revolves around jazz music and themes of memory and insanity much more than baseball.

3. Perhaps this is one explanation for the fact that none of the best baseball fiction is set during the era of multi-million-dollar free agents. Novels published during the free agency era are either set in a nostalgic past or, occasionally, in the minor leagues.

4. In "Horatio at the Bat, or Why Such a Lengthy Embryonic Period for the Serious Baseball Novel" (*Aethlon* 5.2: 1–11) novelist Mark Harris examines what we might call the baseball novel's inferiority complex: "For a long time we haven't wanted to say that a novel about baseball is a novel about baseball because we wanted to believe it was about something else—something more respectable, something more serious, something, for example, a serious, studious, scholarly person could talk about without losing caste among his peers" (1).

5. The most extensive bibliography of baseball fiction is Timothy Morris's "Guide to Baseball Fiction," http://www.uta.edu/english/tim/baseball/; see also Noel Schraufnagel, *The Baseball Novel: A History and Annotated Bibliography of Adult Fiction* (Jefferson, NC: McFarland, 2008).

6. *The Great Match* was published anonymously in 1877 and misattributed to John Townsend Trowbridge in 1881. Recently, Geri Strecker has discovered that the novel was

most likely written by Mary Prudence Wells Smith, a popular author of young adult and historical fiction. See Geri Strecker, "'And the public has been left to guess the secret': Questioning the Authorship of *The Great Match, and Other Matches* (1877)," *NINE: A Journal of Baseball History and Culture* 18.2 (Spring 2010): 11–37.

　　7.　The full text of many of these early novels has been digitized. Titles such as Frank Merriwell's *Baseball Victories, or, Fast Work on the Diamond* (1906) and *Baseball Joe on the School Nine, or, Pitching for the Blue Banner* (1912) are available through Google Books, books.google.com.

　　8.　Examples of magazine fiction by Van Loan, Lardner, Fullerton and others can be found in *Dead Balls and Double Curves: An Anthology of Early Baseball Fiction*, ed. Trey Strecker (Carbondale: Southern Illinois University Press, 2004) and Charles Van Loan's *The Collected Baseball Stories*, compiled by Trey Strecker (Jefferson, NC: McFarland, 2004).

　　9.　Harris continues the adventures of Henry Wiggen in *Bang the Drum Slowly* (1956), *A Ticket for Seamstitch* (1957), and *It Looked Like Forever* (1979). *Bang the Drum Slowly* is the most popular of these novels, due to the film version (1974) starring Michael Moriarty and Robert DeNiro.

　　10.　It should be noted that while Barry Levinson's film adaptation of *The Natural* (1984), starring Robert Redford, is an excellent movie, the filmmakers made significant alterations to Malamud's original story.

　　11.　For example, several baseball novels address the 1919 Black Sox scandal. In addition to *The Celebrant*, see Brendan Boyd's *Blue Ruin: A Novel of the 1919 World Series*, Peter Rutkoff's *Shadow Ball: A Novel of Baseball and Chicago*, and Harry Stein's *Hoopla*.

　　12.　*His Last Game* is available on *Reel Baseball: Baseball Films from the Silent Era, 1899–1926* (Prod. Jessica Rosner, Kino, 2007, DVD).

Bibliography

Apple, Max. "Understanding Alvarado." *Writing Baseball.* Ed. Jerome Klinkowitz. Urbana: University of Illinois Press, 1991. 147–158. Print.

Bjarkman, Peter C. *A History of Cuban Baseball, 1864–2006.* Jefferson, NC: McFarland, 2007. Print.

Brock, Darryl. *Havana Heat: A Novel.* New York: Plume, 2001.

_____. *If I Never Get Back: A Novel.* New York: Crown, 1990. Print.

Broun, Heywood. *The Sun Field.* New York: Putnam, 1923. Print.

Burgos, Adrian, Jr. *Playing America's Game: Baseball, Latinos, and the Color Line.* Berkeley: University of California Press, 2007. Print.

Candelaria, Cordelia. *Seeking the Perfect Game: Baseball in American Literature.* New York: Greenwod, 1989. Print.

Carino, Peter. "Mark Twain, Westward Expansion, Immigrant Unrest: Baseball and American Growing Pains in Darryl Brock's *If I Never Get Back.*" *NINE: A Journal of Baseball History and Culture* 9.1 (Fall 2000): 83–91. Print.

Coffin, Tristram Potter. *The Old Ball Game: Baseball in Folklore and Fiction.* New York: Herder and Herder, 1971. Print.

Coover, Robert. *The Universal Baseball Association—J. Henry Waugh, Prop.* New York: Plume, 1968. Print.

Fuller, Todd. *60 Feet Six Inches and Other Distances from Home.* Duluth, MN: Holy Cow Press, 2002. Print.

Graber, Ralph. "Baseball in American Fiction." *English Journal* 56 (Nov. 1967): 1107–14. Print.

Granger, Bill. *The New York Yanquis.* New York: Arcade, 1995. Print.

The Great Match *and* Our Base Ball Club*: Two Novels from the Early Days of Base Ball* [by Anonymous and Noah Brooks]. Eds. Trey Strecker and Geri Strecker. Jefferson, NC: McFarland, 2010. Print.

Greenberg, Eric Rolfe. *The Celebrant.* Lincoln, NE: Bison Books, 1993.

Harmon, William, and Hugh Holman. *A Handbook to Literature.* 9th ed. Upper Saddle River, NJ: Prentice-Hall, 2003.

Harris, Mark. "Horatio at the Bat, or Why Such a Lengthy Embryonic Period for the Serious Baseball Novel?" *Aethlon* 5.2 (Spring 1988): 1–11. Print.

_____. *The Southpaw.* Lincoln, NE: Bison Books, 1984. Print.

Howe, LeAnne. *Miko Kings: An Indian Baseball Story.* San Francisco: Aunt Lute Books, 2007. Print.

Hurlbert, Mark C., and Joseph Bocchi. "An Interview with Paul Metcalf." *Sagetrieb* 5.3 (Winter 1986): 31–46. Print.

Kennedy, Lucy. *The Sunlit Field.* New York: Crown, 1950. Print.

Lardner, Ring. *Ring around the Bases: The Complete Baseball Stories of Ring Lardner.* Ed. Matthew J, Bruccoli. New York: Scribner's, 1992. Print.

Malamud, Bernard. *The Natural.* New York: Avon, 1982. Print.

McGimpsey, David. *Imagining Baseball: America's Pastime and Popular Culture.* Bloomington: Indiana University Press, 2000. Print.

Metcalf, Paul. *Will West. Paul Metcalf: Collected Works, Volume I, 1956–1976.* Minneapolis, MN: Coffee House, 1996.

Morris, Timothy. *Making the Team: The Cultural Work of Baseball Fiction.* Urbana: University of Illinois Press, 1997. Print.

Oriard, Michael. *Dreaming of Heroes: American Sports Fiction, 1868–1980.* Chicago: Nelson-Hall, 1982. Print.

Partridge, Stephen, and Timothy Morris. "Baseball in Literature, Baseball as Literature." *The Cambridge Companion to Baseball.* Ed. Leonard Cassuto and Stephen Partridge. New York: Cambridge University Press, 2011. 21–32. Print.

Peterson, Richard. *Extra Innings: Writing on Baseball.* Urbana: University of Illinois Press, 2001. Print.

Powers-Beck, Jeffery. *The American Indian Integration of Baseball.* Lincoln: University of Nebraska Press, 2004. Print.

Shawver, Brian. *The Cuban Prospect: A Novel.* New York: Overlook, 2003. Print.

Shepard, Jim. "Batting against Castro." *Bottom of the Ninth: Great Contemporary Baseball Short Stories.* Ed. John McNally. Carbondale: Southern Illinois University Press, 2003. 1–16. Print.

Strecker, Geri. "'And the public has been left to guess the secret': Questioning the Authorship of *The Great Match, and Other Matches* (1877). *NINE: A Journal of Baseball History and Culture* 18.2 (Spring 2010): 11–37. Print.

Vizenor, Gerald. *Narrative Chance: Postmodern Discourse on Native American Indian Literatures.* Norman: University of Oklahoma Press, 1993. Print.

Windel, Tim. *Castro's Curveball.* New York: Ballantine Books, 1999. Print.

About the Authors

John A. **Fortunato** is a professor at Fordham University in the School of Business, where he teaches classes in communications and media management. He is the author of four books, including *Commissioner: The Legacy of Pete Rozelle* (2006) and *Sports Sponsorship: Principles & Practices* (2013). Among the journals his articles have appeared in are *Public Relations Review*, *Journal of Sports Media* and *Journal of Brand Strategy*.

Steven P. **Gietschier** is an associate professor of history at Lindenwood University, where he is also university curator at the Margaret Leggat Butler Library. As an archivist and managing editor with *The Sporting News*, he managed its research center from 1986 until 2008, wrote the annual "Year in Review" essay in *The Baseball Guide*, and edited *The Complete Baseball Record Book* for five years. His articles and reviews have appeared in *NINE: A Journal of Baseball History & Culture*, *The Baseball Research Journal* and the *Journal of Sport History*.

Mitchell **Nathanson** is a professor of legal writing at the Jeffrey S. Moorad Center for the Study of Sports Law at Villanova University School of Law. The author of *The Fall of the 1977 Phillies* (2008) and *A People's History of Baseball* (2013), he has twice won the McFarland-SABR Award for the best historical or biographical baseball articles of the year. He has been a scholarly advisor for two documentaries, including HBO's *The Curious Case of Curt Flood*, and he is at work on a biography of Dick Allen, to be published in 2015.

Trey **Strecker** teaches English and coordinates the interdepartmental minor in sports studies at Ball State University in Muncie, Indiana. He is the editor of *NINE: A Journal of Baseball History & Culture*, the editor or co-editor of three anthologies of baseball-related fiction, and his work has appeared in *Critique: Studies in Contemporary Fiction*, *The Review of Contemporary Fiction*, *Elysian Fields Quarterly*, *NINE*, *American Book Review* and *TLS: Times Literary Supplement*.

David George **Surdam** is an associate professor of economics at the University of Northern Iowa. His dissertation, on Northern naval superiority and the economics of the American Civil War, was supervised by Nobel laureate Robert W. Fogel. Surdam has published six books and has more forthcoming on the economics of professional team sports, leisure in 20th-century America, and the Civil War blockade.

Index

209